A Sorcerer's Book of Art

A SORCERER'S BOOK OF ART

BY
GREG CROWFOOT

TEMPLE ISLAND PRESS

© Copyright 2007, Greg Crowfoot. All Rights Reserved

No part of this book may be reproduced or transmitted in any form or by any means, electronic, or mechanical, including photocopying, recording, or by any information storage, and retrieval system without written permission from both the copyright owner and the publisher of this book.

Published by
Temple Island Press

ISBN-10: 1-59330-489-7
Greg Crowfoot

To my wife Linda for all of her help and support, and the Mistress of All Magick for Her inspiration and guidance.

Table Of Contents

Introduction	1
Chapter I: The Sight	7
Chapter II: The Inner Fire	25
Chapter III: Tools of Art	47
Chapter IV: Dreaming True and Faring Forth	63
Chapter V: Past, Present and Future Lives	79
Chapter VI: Familiars	93
Chapter VII: The Magick Mirror	111
Chapter VIII: Going into The Field	125
Chapter IX: The Elementals	129
Chapter X: Ghosts and Exorcism	141
Chapter XI: Magick, Initiation and The Great Work	173
Bibliography and Recommended Reading	189
About the Author	191
Endnotes	193

INTRODUCTION

Some people are born into the world with a unique destiny. Mine was Magick[1]. But I didn't know this until I was eight years old. Like any American child, my existence up to that point had been fairly typical. And then one night (as is the way with those who serve our Lady), I had a dream that set the course that my life was to follow.

It wasn't like any dream I had had before. The details were vivid and a Voice (that I now know of as the Little Voice), told me about a life I had lived before this one.

Then as the dream ended, I was told two final things by the Voice. The first was that there was magick in the world and second was that it was my destiny to learn all that I could about it. I remember waking up, filled with a complete certainty that what I had just experienced was wholly real and completely true. And, as the reader might guess, things were never the same for me after that event.

For years after the dream, I was haunted by encounters with things that I was taught by my teachers and my parents, did not exist. The home I lived in was old and haunted, and I saw my fair share of ghosts and other supernatural phenomena. And I also sensed that there were forces in the universe, just beyond my grasp, which once understood, would enable me to transcend the boundaries that supposedly circumscribed the world around me.

I remained convinced that the elusive thing called magick by the Voice was to be my vocation. I knew that it was only a matter of finding the right key to unlock its secrets and realize my future. That key came to me of its own accord, and like my dream, quite unexpectedly. By that time, I was 14 years old and living on a rural farm. The area around the farm was thickly wooded, and I was in the habit of taking long hikes into the forest using the logging roads that cut through its immensity.

Although I enjoyed these walks, each time I went into the woods, an eerie feeling would eventually overcome me. It was a sense that something that I couldn't identify was there among the trees, aware of my presence and watching me. And as sunset would approach, I could feel *it*, coming through the forest to find me. Having only a limited esoteric vocabulary, I saw it in my minds eye as a huge bear, and I would run out of the forest filled with terror of the creature.

But one day, the Lady guided my steps to a point of no return. That day, I had ventured deeper into the woods than ever before. And when sunset came along with the now-familiar feeling of dread, I turned as I always had, to run away. But this time I was too far from home to make it back before what I had feared found me at last.

Only it wasn't the bear I had imagined. Instead it was a luminous ball of white energy, hovering over the dirt road blocking my retreat. The same mental voice that had visited me years before in my dream spoke to me again at that moment.

In a calm, matter-of-fact tone, it confirmed that what was floating in front of me was the very thing I had been so afraid of. And it also informed me that the strange ball of light was there to test me. The stakes were straightforward: I would live or die depending on my response.

Of course, I was eager to find a way to pass this strange trial, and the Voice stated that the only way to survive the test was to remove 'myself from myself'. An image from the silent movies came to me; of a heroine tied to a railroad tracks with a huge train bearing down on her. There was also a hero in the vision, rushing in at the last second to untie the heroine and rescue her from the train.

As this metaphor played out in my mind, I realized that the heroine was none other than my conscious self and that the hero of the film was a part of me that I had only suspected to exist. It was that part of all of us that is beyond the conscious self, the silent observer of all that we experience (which I would later come to know of as the Iron Man). And in identifying what the hero truly was, I suddenly experienced the present from the same state of awareness. I became the Iron Man for just a moment.

At the instant this happened, the ball of light rushed forwards and passed straight through my body. The sensation that I felt was like a warm wind passing through my chest. Then, just as suddenly as it had appeared, the light was gone and along with it, all my feelings of terror. I had survived the test.

I walked back to the farm in the twilight, a changed person. From that moment onwards, the world was never the same. Where before I had only felt faint traces of the supernatural around me, I now began to perceive it clearly and sharply[2].

And more importantly, the same Voice that had saved my life now began to serve me in other ways. It began to help me learn about the magick I had been seeking since my dream and it guided me to find sources of knowledge that aided me in this endeavor.

Eventually, I became acquainted with Buddhism, Shamanism, Ceremonial Magick, Rune Magick and finally with the Greco-Roman tradition where I dedicated myself to the Goddess Hecate, the patroness of all Witches and Sorcerers[3] like myself. And as I learned, I also taught what I had learned both publicly and privately.

In all, my magickal path has spanned some 30 plus years of continuous study and exploration. This work is a compendium of much of what I learned, but is certainly not all. Some of what I came to call the Art cannot be conveyed by the written word, and other aspects are simply too dangerous to be made common knowledge.

And what is the Art? To quote from a prior work I authored, *"Crossroads: The Path of Hecate"*, the Art can be defined in this manner:

"...Historically, scholars have always divided magic and religion from one another. Although some religious acts are magical in nature (such as prayer being used to heal), the practice of magick per se is generally viewed in the 20th century as something outré –as an act of the individual pursuing individual goals, versus that of society at large. But this was not the case with the religion of the classical Greeks and especially among those who followed Hecate in classical times.

For the ancients, magick and religion, and the occult works of the individual and of the collective were all one in the same. There was no distinction that neatly separated the two spheres. Certainly, for those dedicated to Hecate in particular this was, and is the case. While there are many other modern traditions that embrace the Hellenic deities yet eschew occult practices, the study of the Art is intrinsically interwoven with Her path and the practice of the magickal arts are in and of themselves an act of religious devotion--regardless of whether they are performed as part of a group ritual, or as an individual act.

With that said, the Art itself and its relevance require examination. The Art is as old as mankind. It has been known by many names, to many peoples through the centuries: as magick, as spell casting, as witchcraft, the arcane arts and by many other terms beyond counting. But the Art is, in the end, both universal and transcendent to all times and places as a thing unto itself.

All people have the seeds of its growth within themselves; from the first moments they take a breath, to the very end of their days. But for most, a fleeting glimpse of the Hidden World, the world of the super-natural, is generally all they experience.

For the follower of the Queen of All Witches however, the Art is a living, breathing thing and the Hidden World, a visible, tangible experience. The components of the Art are not limited to one school nor one tradition, but should partake of whatever is proven to be of true value. As such, the Art is always growing and changing as Mankind itself strives for wisdom. The very essence of the Art is to embrace what works and to adapt it to ones own unique pathway towards Knowledge and Illumination..."

After a lifetime of study, I have come to compare mastery of the Art to that of learning the martial arts (which has also comprised some of my personal studies). Like a martial art, mastery is not a 'quick-fix' by any means. Instead, learning the Art is a slow process of continuous spiritual and magickal growth. It requires time, perseverance and above all else, courage and the deep desire for knowledge that transcends all other concerns.

To achieve this goal, certain magickal skills must be learned and perfected. There have been many schools and many teachers that have offered what they believe are the essentials, and I am certainly no exception. What I have found to be critical areas of learning comprise the lessons I have presented here. The reader might or might not agree with my choices, but they are based upon my own experiences as both a teacher and a student, and I believe from the results I have enjoyed with my students over the years, that their selection and arrangement is effective.

I have presented each area of knowledge in the same manner I have taught them; each subject is presented in three distinct components that work together to provide the lesson.

The first component is my discourses on a given subject. I have attempted to make these as complete and as clear as possible; a task that has proven to be no mean feat. Until this work was written, the bulk of my knowledge was presented orally and I have tried to present everything to the reader that I would have offered to a student on a one-on-one basis. Naturally, it is impossible to anticipate every possible question or issue that might arise, and I apologize in advance for any area that is not explained fully enough.

The second component is the hands-on exercises. These comprise a continuous process with each skill complimenting and dependent upon the one before it. While some readers might be tempted to take 'shortcuts' around certain exercises and focus only upon those that are of direct interest, I urge them instead to take all of the steps along the path—omitting none. To return to my analogy of the martial arts for a moment, learning only one basic move in a martial art is not mastery of that art. The same holds true here: the failure to properly learn all of the necessary skills will result in an incomplete and imperfect understanding of the Art and little, if any, competence in the long run.

The third and last component is the stories of noteworthy events that I have personally experienced. While they may not always relate specifically to the lesson that precedes them, I tell them here for the same reason I have told them to my students over the years. Far more than literary devices to 'spice up' my material, they offer knowledge of their own about the Art, and the Hidden World for those who listen—and read--carefully.

Some of these tales will seem quite unbelievable, but I assure the reader that they are true events that have been presented as fully and clearly as I can recollect. I can certainly understand any skepticism that might arise; given the plethora of hoaxes and misinformation in the world today, it is easy, even fashionable, to discount the incredible.

But despite this, I urge any potential critics to consider one question before dismissing my accounts completely: if they can point to even one event in their own life that defies rational explanation, is it not possible, or even probable, that more inexplicable things might exist that they have simply not yet encountered? Everyone has had some brush with the supernatural, however humble.

As I once said to a student, the only real difference between the average man and the sorcerer is that the sorcerer makes it their principle business to be at the right place and time to encounter the Hidden World, while for the average man that same meeting is largely accidental and haphazard. With all this said, I will now turn the reader's attention to our first subject, the Sight.

CHAPTER I: THE SIGHT

The universe is full of magical things patiently waiting for our wits to grow sharper. -- Eden Phillpotts

The Sight[4], or Seeing as I once called it, was one of the first skills in the Art that I developed. When I was 16, my father ran a commune in San Francisco and made his income by holding 'self-help' seminars that were based on the teachings of an EST-style group called 'Morehouse', combined with his own half-baked ideas. There were many seekers of truth in the Bay Area of the late 1970's, and he actually managed to support himself off of them.
   Always looking for new ways to attract student/customers, he decided to take advantage of the craze that was then surrounding the works of Carlos Castaneda. Knowing of my interest in the occult (although not really respecting nor understanding it), he gave me the task of creating a course based loosely on the shamanistic practices that Castaneda chronicled. The course was never intended by him to be more than a 'shill' to bring people in to take more courses from him and he had no idea what he had actually set in motion. Nor did I.
   The next great step in my spiritual journey was about to begin.
   I embarked on my task with great enthusiasm and read through every book I had by Castaneda. It quickly became clear to me that the material I was using as my reference was vastly superior to my father's 'pop psychology'. Castaneda's work detailed a sophisticated and complex shamanic system that centered (among other things) on the ability to visually perceive psychic phenomena through an exercise that he simply referred to as Seeing.

I quickly abandoned any idea of trying to fit Castaneda's material around my father's ideas and I focused my efforts instead on discovering exactly what the mysterious act of Seeing was. Castaneda was deliberately vague about how it was performed and many of the exercises that he did detail turned out to be dead ends (which I now know was a deliberate effort on his part to throw off anyone from attempting to follow in his footsteps).

But I was determined to 'crack the code', and I found valuable clues to accomplish this in two incidents that had happened to me. The first had occurred a year earlier. My father had flirted with a study of Zen Buddhism and I had had the opportunity to go on meditation retreats with him at a Zen Monastery in Northern California. During that time, I experienced what the Buddhists monks had called 'makyo', or supposedly illusionary effects. The most dramatic of these was the appearance one morning of a brilliant blue aura around a fellow student while we meditated together in the training hall.

While the monks had validated such phenomena as being real, they had urged us to ignore such things in favor of achieving a deeper meditative state. But I had gone away from the retreat sure that something significant had happened that required further examination.

The second clue came from an event that took place while I was in school, in gym class. The coach had brought us into the auditorium and was in the process of lecturing to us about the need to be competitive in sports. I was extremely tired at the time and began to 'tune out' his words. As I sat there, gazing at him with nothing in particular in my mind, a brilliant blue aura similar to the one I had seen in the Buddhist monastery suddenly surrounded his head and shoulders. It remained around him for at least a minute, then it went away.

I began to wonder if the 'makyo' I had experienced during these two events, were not in fact the same visual effects Castaneda was reporting as Seeing. So to test my hunch, I embarked on an experiment and proceeded to meditate, but with an eye towards the visual changes that took place. When I saw a faint aura appear over the molding of a wall in front of me, I became excited, and asked for the help of a fellow commune-dweller in conducting a further experiment.

I asked the person to sit in front of me and simply mediate on my face, while I did the same in return. In short order, both of us experienced bizarre visual distortions of the each other's features, accompanied by strange lighting effects.

I came away from this in an ecstatic mood—the basic act of meditation with attention placed on the phenomena—not away from it—seemed to be the very key to Seeing. By the time I held my class, I had duplicated the effects with other people and I unveiled the exercise with confidence to my audience. I had discovered or more correctly, re-discovered for myself, the ancient Art of the Sight.

Throughout mankind's existence there have always been individuals who were gifted with the ability to perceive things that others could not: people who could see things that were considered supernatural and mysterious. In some societies such people were elevated to the status of shamans and wisepeople, and they were consulted in all matters of importance. In others, their special power to see was feared and reviled--and its possessors were made into out-casts or worse.

The ability to see things such as the aura, or to perceive the presence of ghosts has never been solely limited to a select few. History abounds with countless incidents of otherwise normal people having brief glimpses of phenomena that were beyond their conventional level of experience--- and this continues up into our present age. Nor has this ability been limited strictly to human experience: dogs and cats, our partners in civilization, have long been known for their inexplicable ability to perceive things beyond the ken of their masters.

But the tendency in the West has by and large been to label the ability to see psychic phenomena as either something very special, or to discount it entirely. And either approach falls short of truly understanding this ability.

In the East, and among the peoples of Latin America, a different attitude has prevailed. There, in cultures with a less cynical or fearful approach to the unknown, this ability has been treated not only as something natural, but also as a skill that is in its essence, innate to all human beings.

I refer to this skill by one of its oldest names, the Sight. And it is my position that purposeful training to awaken the Sight is of major importance in properly mastering the Art as a whole. The Sight is without question one of the primary building blocks upon which all subsequent training in this program of learning depends. While there are many other occult disciplines that never touch upon this ability, nor focus on it as a specific talent, it is my stance that the inability to develop and use the Sight as a component of magick is similar to trying to paint a picture with a blindfold—and just as ludicrous.

The Sight is an ability that hearkens back to the very dawn of our existence as a species—an ability to perceive what is otherwise invisible yet present all around us. As such, it is not supernatural and *outré'*, but something that is in reality "super-natural". It is as much a part of us as our other more developed senses are.

For most people, the Sight only becomes active at times of stress, or great fatigue, or at seemingly random moments. However, it is like any other perceptive skill, and can not only be trained up to a level of usefulness, but also refined to respond to the users Will.

The Sight can best be described as a perceptive ability that ranges from purely visual perceptions to a deep intuitive 'knowing' often coupled with mental images that compliment and complete perception. As such, those who are either gifted with the Sight, or have deliberately developed it, can experience it in both ways, and in all variations in between. For the purposes of this Chapter however, the emphasis will be on developing the purely visual aspect of the Sight.

The Sight is both an easy skill to learn and an ability which can take years to fully master. Even so, with dedication and effort, a beginning student can learn enough to employ it usefully in their studies. The only barriers to training in the Sight are lack of belief, unwillingness to do put forth an effort, and fear of the unknown.

Materials: Before engaging in the following practical exercises, the student should obtain a journal to record their experiences, questions and observations. After each exercise, these details should be recorded for later review and examination.

STILLING THE WATERS

Most of what we perceive of the world around us stems from our personal interpretation of it. Not only is this perception the product of our normal sensory abilities, but also of our mental attitudes and beliefs, which are themselves the by-products of our culture's collective idea of reality.

In a sense, much of our perception of 'what is real' is more a matter of reinforcing a form of self-hypnotism that we learned as children to agree with and participate in (in much the same way that the people of the famous tale "The Emperors New Clothes" did). Employing the Sight is a way of stepping back from our collective illusions and see the world around us as it actually is, free of cultural preconceptions and beliefs.

The reader is invited to think back for a moment, to the time when they were children. Back then, the world was a marvelous and magickal place, and for many of us, a time when we actively perceived 'psychic' phenomena. But then, with the reinforcement of society, this innocent view of the world gradually changed, and adapted itself to fit in with the beliefs (and disbeliefs) of those around us. Most of us discarded our early perceptions as being 'silly' or 'childish' and eventually learned to ignore and then forget them. The monster in the closet was forgotten in favor of more adult demons.

And while we did gain membership in the 'grown-up' world, and a certain level of freedom, we also simultaneously sacrificed something special in ourselves. And that 'something' was in part, our ability to use the Sight and to interact with the magickal side of reality. Reawakening the Sight is a way of recovering and reclaiming our original connection with the world as a magickal place, filled with energies and things that we knew as children to be true, and that our pre-technological ancestors also knew and interacted with on a daily basis. The first step in achieving this is the act of stilling the internal waters of our mind and taking the time to fully observe our surroundings as they truly are.

Exercise One: Stilling the Waters

Begin by sitting in a comfortable position, either on the floor, or in a chair. The surrounding environment should be as free as possible from distractions or interruption. Place your hands in your lap with one of them resting in the palm of the other and with the thumbs lightly touching one another[5].

Then, close your eyes and take three, deep calming breaths. When a feeling of calm pervades you, continue to sit there without engaging in any internal conversation about any subject.

This action is actually much harder than it might sound. Like the waters of a pond that are disturbed by movement, human beings live with a constant state of internal mental chatter that generally only ceases when they are asleep, unconscious, or dead. This 'internal dialogue' as Castaneda called it is an ongoing descriptive process where everything that is experienced is classified, evaluated, judged and reacted to generally to the extremes of emotion. And it is difficult for most people to disengage from this internal cacophony and to Still their Inner Waters.

And even when they manage to do so, the mind can play its tricks to reengage them. It is not uncommon for example, for people to put aside all concerns about their daily affairs and still become caught up in a discussion about the very act of doing this! I remember a moment in my own training in meditation when, after weeks of trying, I achieved a moment of complete stillness only to mentally shout out in surprise, "Gee, its quiet in here!"

But if one can manage to achieve even a few seconds of mental stillness, then a very great thing has been accomplished. It was once said by one of my teachers in Zen that 'he who could still his mind completely for only one full minute could rule the world'. This statement underscores just how difficult it can be to silence the mind's chatter. It can take many years, and sometimes even a lifetime to achieve complete silence for any appreciable length of time, and any victory that one wins in this arena is significant indeed.

This exercise should be performed daily and as you go about your daily affairs, it should be augmented with what we can call a 'moving' version (or as it is referred to in Buddhism as *Kinen*). As you perform whatever tasks the day calls for, you should endeavor to engage in only that amount of mental dialogue that is *absolutely necessary to perform the task at hand, and nothing more*. Value judgments concerning the activity, plans for future activities and other thoughts should not be engaged in. Instead your focus should be solely on the work at hand, and the present moment.

Like sitting meditation, this is also harder than it seems and may take some time to perfect. But it will not only extend the act of Stilling the Inner Waters into the realm of daily activities, but also provide a platform from which you can interact with the world from a 'centered' point of view where among other things, you are in complete control. The fact is that our modern society manipulates most of us by using the ploy of distraction and plays upon our uncontrolled passions that are fueled by our unrestrained internal reactions. In a sense, the act of Stilling the Waters is not only a magickal act, but also the most radical act of revolution that one can undertake. It can be quite literally the process of stepping out of 'the machine' itself and seeing the world for what it is, rather than what others selfishly want us to believe it to be.

THE IRON MAN

One thing that may become evident during the act of meditating is the presence within oneself of what Rev. Roshi Jiyu-Kennett, the abbot of the Zen Monastery I studied at, called the Iron Man (which the reader will recall my mentioning at the beginning of this book). The fact is, our perception of who and what we think we are is largely the result of our ongoing internal description of ourselves. In reality, beneath that part of us that has passions and reacts (or over-reacts) to external stimuli, there is another component of our being that most people rarely acknowledge. This is that element of our being that is purely an observer, the component that remains unmoved like a seasoned warrior by the turmoil of daily life around us. Instead it takes existence as it comes, free of the encumbrance of uncontrolled emotional responses, a pure observer.

In the process of learning to Still the Waters, it is this same immovable self that one should strive to discover and emulate. We have all heard its voice—the one that is calm in all adversity, the voice that tells us that we are tired or happy or hungry, but is in itself none of these things. It is the inner observer of all things we perceive.

Stilling the Waters and becoming a participating observer of what is around us unites us with this state of mind. And as we become the Iron Man, this state of being allows us to respond to the world's challenges with our full faculties, free of emotional distractions that would otherwise rob us of our innate inner strength and true reason.

THE PENTAGRAM OF THE SENSES

After working with Stilling the Waters for at least a week, the next step is to heighten your external awareness and regain the high levels of sensory perception that our ancestors enjoyed (and that peoples in less materialistic cultures still do[6]). This can be readily accomplished through a series of exercises that I collectively call the Pentagram of the Senses[7].

The Pentagram of the Senses has been taught in many formats by many different schools. It is composed of exercises that involve the normal physical abilities to see, touch, smell, hear and intuitively *know*. Exploration of component of the Pentagram should be undertaken for a single day, with the results kept in your journal.

Exercise 1: To See

In this exercise, you are to simply pay complete attention to all visual stimuli that occurs throughout the day. You should take the time to stop and observe colors, textures and strive to perceive the appearance of things in your environment without making any value judgments about them, seeing them as a pure observer.

For example, if you are in an environment with other people observe them carefully: how are they dressed? How do they move? Do they appear calm, agitated etc? Use this opportunity to determine as much as you can about the other person from simple observation alone. You will be surprised at how much you can learn about others simply by observing them.

Another excellent way of exploring the sense of sight is to visit an art exhibit. Once there, silence any preconceived prejudices you might have and take the time to sit and truly observe the works on exhibit. Carefully note how they affect you.

Art, like music speaks directly to our inner self, and its message is often lost or obscured when our biases are allowed to intrude. Ask yourself; does a certain piece provoke a strong reaction for you? Or a certain color? Notice how different visual stimulus affects your mood and energy level. You may be surprised at what attracts you and what does not.

The reverse of this, the absence of visual input, should also be experienced without letting preconceptions or fears take center stage. Take a few minutes to explore a darkened environment. Let your eyes adjust, and then take note of what you can, and cannot see, and notice how differently things seem to you with the absence of light.

Exercise 2: To Hear

As its title suggests, this exercise involves the act of hearing. Use the day to closely listen to your world, taking moments to stop and close your eyes, hearing all of the sounds around you. Not only may the level of noise surprise you, but also what you can and cannot hear, along with the vast amount of information you gather from this sense without realizing it. Take note of how sound affects you and your mood.

A very pleasant and important component of this exercise is the effect that music has on you. Music was considered by the Pythagorean School to be not only the gateway to understanding the true nature of the world around us, but the purest expression of the Universe itself. It is definitely not an experience to be missed. Take some time during the day to carefully listen to several pieces of music. Try a variety of selections; works that you know and love, and others that you are less familiar with, or have never tried listening to. With each piece, allow yourself to let the sound of it completely fill you and notice the change in mood each one provokes within you.

Exercise 3: To Smell (or Taste)

In this exercise, focus on the sense of smell, and by extension the sense of taste (which is related). The emphasis here should be placed on noticing the smells of your surroundings, both overt and subtle.

When you eat or drink, close your eyes and truly experience the taste of your food. As a compliment to this, you should not only eat what you normally would, but also try something new, or even something that you would otherwise not care for, without applying a pre-judgment to the experience itself. Let the experience of the taste speak for itself.

And if you are in public during the day, make note of the smells around you, both pleasant and unpleasant. Carefully observe the difference between natural and artificial scents and examine how each scent alters your emotional state.

Exercise 4: To Touch

The next point in our Pentagram is to explore your sense of touch. Take the opportunity to carefully feel the textures of the world around you. As with taste, textures that are considered both pleasant and unpleasant should be investigated, free of prior bias.

To help facilitate this exercise, items around you should be touched both with and without the aid of sight. As you explore, notice the smoothness or roughness of an item, the specific difference between one kind of texture versus another etc. and how texture and touch affects you.

Exercise 5: To Know (The Little Voice)

One by-product of Stilling the Waters is a greater ability at precognition, or as it is sometimes referred to, the ability to hear the Little Voice. Like the Iron Man, this Voice is that part of us that is beyond our surface passions. It is this same Voice that often speaks with foreknowledge of the future and offers a perception to us of the world as it truly is.

The Voice speaks to us when we get a feeling of impending disaster, which turns out to be true. It is what makes us think of someone before they call us on the phone, or to think of them only to learn that they were thinking of us at the same time. It is the voice of our intuition that rises beyond societies efforts to suppress it. It represents the primal part of ourselves that 'knows' what is logically impossible for us to know.

You are urged take note of the Voice whenever it speaks to you, and to further develop this instinctive sense, *act* upon its council whenever possible (or at the very least acknowledge it when it turns out to be correct). The very act of listening for and to the Little Voice will in turn heighten this ability, and sharpen it.

For our exercise, you should go through your day, and remain aware of any intuitive feeling that comes over you. When it does, take note of what it is telling you and watch for anything in your environment that validates that information. If you are in public, try to *feel* your environment and the people around you.

Ask yourself: are you completely comfortable, or is there any sense of tension from those around you? Do the people near you feel as if they are happy, or sad, and is this at variance with how they appear visually? And most importantly, what impression do you get from them—what do you *know* about other people—and the world around you on an intuitive level? You may be surprised by just how much information is routinely ignored and blocked out by our assumptions and distracting inner chatter.

DEVELOPING THE SIGHT

After several weeks of practice Stilling the Waters and exploring the Pentagram of the Senses, it will be time to engage in specifically developing the Sight itself. The following exercises are to be performed at least once a day, and should be documented in your journal.

Exercise 1: Primary Exploration of the Sight

This first exercise stems from our previous experiments with Stilling the Waters, but focuses on visual experiences. The environment for this endeavor should be quiet, semi-dark[8] and free from any distraction or interruptions.

As before, you should sit in a comfortable position, with your hands folded lightly in your lap. Your eyes should rest on a spot in space in front of you that is comfortable for you to look at without eyestrain. Preferably, a blank area of a wall or a location with few visual distractions should be chosen for this purpose and your eyes are to be kept open during the exercise. If you notice that your eyes begin to feel dry, feel free to blink to relive them, but avoid the tendency to do so overmuch. The goal here is to keep them open as much as possible[9].

Once seated and staring at a spot, you should still your mind, bringing yourself to a state of mental calmness. At the same time, you should allow your vision to go in and out of focus as it will and let your gaze naturally rest on the spot in front of you. After taking several initial calming breaths, your respiration should be kept even and normal.

Your task in this exercise is to maintain inner calm, while at the same time passively observing any and all visual phenomena that occur, without directly influencing your vision, engaging in inner-dialogue about what you might or might not see, or interrupting the process in any way. A good method to use to help maintain ones detachment and be able to keep track of all that occurs visually is to tell oneself that everything one might see is nothing more than effects on a television screen. This self-suggestion can help greatly in some cases.

A total of five to ten minutes should be allotted to this exercise. At the end of this period, you should record everything that you observed, however trivial it might initially seem to you. Typical effects that are witnessed during this exercise can be apparent changes in the brightness of the room, flashes of light or sparks, shifts in the color of the scene in front of you, or luminous clouds. A feeling of the body floating has also been reported by some students, and in many cases, there might also be the perception of small points or balls of light or energy passing through your visual field at high speed. These can be transparent, or light or dark in appearance and sometimes seem to change directions rapidly.

While there is the culturally taught tendency to discount such phenomena, or to ascribe it to eye fatigue, much of these phenomena are in fact the result of successfully enabling the Sight for the first time. It is a first glimpse into the otherwise Hidden World.

Exercise 2: A Partnered Exercise

If you are fortunate enough to have a training partner, the same exercise detailed above is to be repeated, but with your partner assisting you.

Sit opposite one another with each person assuming a comfortable position. Your gazes should be specifically focused either on the tip of the other person's nose, or upon the area commonly referred to as the 'third eye', which is above the two physical eyes. Both of you are to let your vision go in and out of focus without making any effort to correct it, and your main endeavor is the same as in the single person version: to passively observe any and all visual effects that might occur.

Although this exercise seems easy enough, it can prove difficult for some students. Many individuals experience nervousness while staring directly at another person's features (which is the result a natural survival instinct, coupled with cultural mores) and it is not uncommon for one or both parties to break out in nervous laughter. However, there is in fact nothing humorous about the exercise, and you and your partner are urged to maintain a serious frame of mind.

A helpful visualization, which can counter any problems in this area, is for the participants to pretend that they are looking not at another person, but instead at an image in a mirror, or to borrow from our first exercise, a modern television screen. With this imagery employed, the tendency towards laughter will shortly cease.

The exercise itself is to last a minimum of five minutes and a maximum of ten. During this time, both parties are to note all effects that they experience. Additionally, both persons are to keep their gaze on their partner's nose or third eye region and resist any temptation to let their eyes wander to any other part of the other person's features or to look away. No matter what does or does not occur visually, both parties should continue the exercise until the full time period has elapsed.

Once this has occurred, you and your partner should immediately share with one another all effects that you each witnessed. Again, nothing should be omitted, no matter how 'silly' or trivial it might initially seem.

Commonly, the effects that both parties may witness can range from those experienced in the first exercise, to more dramatic ones such as changes in the other persons features (aging, elongation, changes in hair and eye color and structural distortions etc). In addition many students report the appearance of animal-like forms superimposing or replacing human features, and even instances of partial or total invisibility.

Other effects that have been routinely reported include the appearance of luminous areas (particularly around the eyes) or the face assuming a scull-like appearance. It is also not uncommon for both parties to witness the same visual phenomena, sometimes simultaneously.

Each of the effects that I have mentioned has specific causes or theories concerning their appearance. Rather than distract the reader at this early stage with this information, I will only state as I had before, that their perception represents significant steps towards developing the Sight and leave things at that. As the reader moves onwards in this book, and experiments on their own, many of these effects will be explained to their satisfaction as a result of their own efforts, while others are better suited for more advanced levels of study. However, I will share some of what I learned through experimentation concerning the phenomena of partial and total invisibility:

As I experimented with the Sight with the help of friends and students, there were naturally many questions about 'what' we were seeing. There were many theories about the causes of different effects, but the debate concerning one visual effect in particular was quickly settled. This was that of invisibility.

In this case, the Seer sees part or all the other person simply vanish. This can occur for extremely brief moments or last for several minutes. I distinctly remember the first time that I experienced this.

I was working with a close friend and student, and we had been engaging in a partnered experiment for at least ten minutes. Towards the end of the session, I suddenly saw his head and neck disappear completely and I found myself looking at the inside collar of his shirt. I could even read the label!

This event shocked and intrigued us both. Subsequent experiments revealed that this was actually a rather common event, and took place when the person being observed reached a deep state of profound meditation. I also later learned that, like the Sight, this was also nothing new. In various mystical disciplines in India, certain yogis have been known to produce the same effect, and also as the result of deep meditative practices.

Exercise 3: Primary Work with the Magick Mirror

The third exercise for developing the Sight is a solitary one. In this case, you are to seat yourself in front of a common mirror. The mirror should be in a room that is gently lit.

Sit comfortably. Your point of gaze should be the reflected image of the tip of your own nose or third eye area. The exercise itself should last from five to twenty minutes, **but is not to exceed 20 minutes. In addition you are strongly cautioned against being tempted to perform this exercise in a fully darkened room**[10].

Once the exercise time has elapsed, record your experiences in your notebook, making sure to detail all of the effects you witnessed no matter how inconsequential they might seem.

In the past, some students have been reluctant to perform this exercise and the reader might feel the same way at this stage. It should be pointed out however that this reluctance generally arises from an instinctive sense that certain dangers may be present while working with a mirror. And certainly, work with mirrors *is* potentially hazardous. However if the exercise is limited strictly to the steps as they have been outlined here, without changes or additions and the environmental conditions and time limit are both abided by, then the exercise, while potentially startling at points, will nevertheless be a safe and educational one.

Like the partnered exercise, there will be numerous visual effects. However, they tend be far more pronounced and dramatic in nature as the reader will see for themselves.

For me, the mirror was a source of great wonder from my earliest days as a student of the Art. Not only did I experience fascinating visual effects in my early work with it, but also some surprises that led in turn to more advanced practices. Like many, I was aware of the stories surrounding mirrors, including the childhood tale of "Bloody Mary". I knew that the mirror offered possibilities that went far beyond simply developing my Sight. One afternoon, an event came to pass that confirmed this conclusively for me.

I had been practicing my Sight in front of a wall-sized mirror in my bathroom. After many minutes of gazing, the scene in front of me suddenly cleared. But instead of seeing my own reflection and that of the room behind me, I found myself looking at the very clear image of another person.

She was lounging on a gilded couch, propping her head up with one arm. Her dark-skinned body was well proportioned and her jet colored hair hung in tight ringlets that framed a high-boned face and eyes so dark that they seemed black. She had the air of a noblewoman and she was adorned with gold and jewels that I instantly associated with Egyptian artifacts that I had seen in museums. Behind her, heavy curtains obscured the rest of the room.

*I gasped in shock and she smiled back at me, as if she were amused at my reaction. If anything, **she** did not seem surprised at all!*
Then the vision ended.

I immediately realized that somehow in a process I did not understand at the time, that my mirror had shown me a vision of another reality, and another time. It was the first step in my experiencing what incredible potential the Magickal Mirror actually had. In later years, I had the opportunity to speak with a Witch from the Gypsy tradition and she told me a similar story of unexpectedly viewing a scene from her childhood while performing the same exercise. We both had a good laugh over the surprise each of us had felt.

Exercise 4: Seeing the World

Once some experience has been gained with the Sight, a useful aid in its development is the regular employment of this skill during one's daily routine. Like the *Kinen* I mentioned in the section on Stilling the Waters, this is an act of moving meditation, but with an eye towards observing visual phenomena.

During your day, take a few minutes to practice the Sight. In the beginning you can use something uncomplicated as your 'target', such as a still scene with few elements in it.

However, as you progress, you should try using the Sight while observing other people and things. While bright lighting might tend to interfere with seeing certain effects, one work-around for this is the practice of viewing the edges around things instead of gazing at them directly.

Careful observation will reveal that a discernable energy field exists around all things, and especially living beings. We will examine more about the nature of this energy field in the next Chapter: The Inner Fire.

TALES FROM THE HIDDEN WORLD: LANDING ON THE MOON

As I promised in my introduction, in addition to exercises to help develop skill in the Art, I will also relate some of the more interesting tales from my own experiences with the Hidden World.

The stories I present are completely true, and accurate to the extent that time and memory will allow. But I certainly do not take the reader's belief for granted. Rather, I *expect* disbelief and skepticism. We do not live in an age of belief. Instead our time is one of doubt. Those we had placed our trust in have told too many lies to us and too many hoaxes have been perpetrated for anyone today to believe *anything* without questioning.

And frankly, I would have it no other way: I have told my students over the years that there is nothing wrong with being a healthy skeptic. Skepticism is only unhealthy when it is carried to the point where there is no room whatsoever for the revision of ones beliefs in the face of new information.

I urge the reader therefore to retain a certain amount of their doubt and to believe only in what they themselves learn is real. I am completely confident that with first-hand experience, that what I claim will first become possible, then entirely plausible. All I ask in the meantime is that the reader merely allow for the possibility that not all the facts may be known about any subject---even this one. I contend that the wisest policy when dealing with the unknown is to always be ready to ask the question, "What if?" and then see what comes to pass.

After six months of continuous practice, my Sight had developed greatly. In addition to Dreaming True, I had learned some of the Art of Faring Forth. But beyond these basic skills I knew very little else except that I had only scratched the proverbial surface of things.

Once again, Castaneda's writings about his own adventures pointed to greater possibilities and because of them, I eventually I decided to take my ability with the Sight as he had, 'into the field'. I was certain that I would experience events similar to his—it was simply a matter of putting myself in a natural environment and letting things take their course.

When I broached the idea to my students, no one wanted to try the experiment with me, except for one fellow named Joel. When he heard what I had in mind, he and I agreed that we would go out the following weekend to Bolinas Bay, an area that had a reputation for strange events, and try out our abilities with the Sight. We had no real idea of what we would encounter, or even if we would encounter anything at all, but we were willing to at least give it a try.

When the weekend came, we boarded a series of busses and made our way to the tiny beach community. For the first few hours we wandered around the small town and then decided to go to the beach. As we walked onto the sand, a strange old woman passed us. As she did so, she suddenly looked me directly in the eye and said, "Darkness will overcome you." Then she laughed cryptically and walked on.

I had no idea what she meant or that her words would prove to be prophetic, not only for the course of the evening ahead of us, but also for my path as a whole. Instead, I brushed off her statement as one made by a lunatic.

Finally when nightfall came, we made our way up onto some nearby cliffs and began to practice our Sight. Initially, nothing happened, but then as we continued, I began to notice things occurring around us. At first they were just random flashes of light and perceptions of movement in the air around me, but then as I looked out over the waters towards the Golden Gate Bridge, I saw a ship sailing towards it.

It took me a moment to realize that the ship was an old sailing schooner, and another to understand that it was glowing all over with a soft green phosphorescence and that its sails, were ragged and tattered. It was the classic ghost ship straight out of an old Hollywood movie. Amazed, I watched it for a few seconds. Then it vanished into nothingness just short of the Bridge.

I was very excited by what I had just witnessed, but when I mentioned it to Joel, I learned that he had not seen it at all. I began to wonder if my experiment was really working.

Joel seemed wholly unimpressed to that point, having experienced little himself. And frankly I still can't blame him for feeling as he did at that point in our venture.

As it was, it was getting late and neither of us had made any provision for staying the night. We reluctantly decided to try and make our way back to San Francisco. Of course, the busses had long since stopped running into Bolinas, and we were forced to walk out of town and over to the main highway, Marin Route 1, hoping to thumb a ride. Fortunately it was a warm summer night and a full moon lit the way for us.

But there proved to be no traffic on the highway. And not having a better plan, we continued walking towards the last place we remembered there had been a bus stop with the vague notion of staying the night in what shelter it might offer and catching a bus in the morning. We traveled in silence, but as we made our way down the roadway, we both began to hear something up on the bluffs to our left moving with us.

At first I wasn't sure that we were being followed, but every once in a while a loose piece of gravel would come rolling down the slope and once I heard what sounded like a wet cough. Joel had also heard the noise, and as we moved on, we both started to feel a little nervous about our situation. It seemed that someone was definitely up there.

Then as we came to an open area, something moved out from behind a bush ahead of us. For a moment I expected to see a human being, but as it came out into the moonlight, I saw that what had been trailing our steps was anything but human.

The creature was perhaps 4 feet tall at the most, with a black, leathery skin. Its arms hung all the way to the ground and I saw that it had only three clawed fingers on each hand. Its head was pointed and featureless and what passed for eyes were two bright yellow points of light. The thing stopped on the median line and faced us. I had the distinct impression that it grinned at us with a certain predatory amusement although it had no mouth I could detect.

Joel and I saw why a second later. A second creature, identical to the first, came out from behind us. We now had the steep hillside to our left, and the waters of Bolinas bay to our right. There was no way for us to leave.

At this stage, most people would have been frightened out of their wits, but I wasn't. As strange as the event was, I had half expected something like it to happen if our experiment proved successful. I know now that my experience in the woods years before had prepared me for this, and I simply accepted what I was seeing.

And searched for a solution. I knew that we were in some kind of danger.

But the only thing either of us had in the way of a weapon was my flashlight. With no better idea in mind, I took it out from my pack and shined it at the creature in front of me. But instead of frightening it, or even illuminating it, the beam actually passed through its body. As the light shined onto the pavement, I heard or rather felt, the equivalent of laughter at me for employing such a useless tactic. Looking back now, I have to admit that it was a rather feeble move on my part.

But then, just a suddenly as they had come out onto the roadway, the two creatures turned and shambled back into the bushes. For a moment, neither of us understood why they had retreated, but then, we heard something behind us and glancing over our shoulders, saw the headlights of an approaching car.

When the vehicle drew near, Joel and I put out our thumbs, desperate for a ride. The driver pulled over for us and we got in to the car, eager to leave the area behind as quickly as possible. As it turned out, the driver and his passenger were professional gamblers, on their way to game in the City and they dropped us off close to my home. Joel and I parted company there, and I walked the few remaining blocks.

By the time I reached the three-story Victorian my father was using for his commune, the full impact of what I had been through had hit me. Joel and I had managed to use our Sight and had experienced something that had been undeniably supernatural. And more importantly, we had both seen the same creatures at the same time. It was, for me at least, the occult equivalent of landing on the moon. I knew then that an incredible world of potential and adventure had just opened up.

I came upstairs, and found my father and my fellow commune members still awake, and I told them my tale. But their reaction was even more amazing and less expected than what I had seen.

Instead of being as excited and astounded as I was, I watched as each person's eyes became glassy with distraction and disinterest. No one cared about the implications[11] at all and I went away to my room profoundly disappointed.

But I shouldn't have been surprised. I had never told anyone about my experience in the woods with the ball of light out of fear of being ridiculed, but I had naively expected to be better received on this occasion than I was.

What had been begun in the forest had come to full fruition in Bolinas; I had unwittingly reached a spiritual point of no return. Castaneda had warned about this in his book "A Journey to Ixtlan", stating plainly that one could never go home after truly becoming a magician, but in my haste to get on with my experiment I had overlooked this important truth. When one has enough exposure to the Hidden World of Magick, old paradynes of seeing the world drop away, along with common points of reference, separating an individual inextricably from their fellow men and their mundane concerns. I had come home only to find that it no longer existed for me. From this point onwards, I would be forced to live two lives: one that I could share with anyone, and another that I could only tell about to a select few.

It was a bitter lesson to be sure.

But thankfully, the response I received the following week in my class was markedly different. When Joel and I related our adventure, the other students were thrilled by it and eager to try out a trip into the field for themselves. By the following week, we had organized another expedition and this time, Joel and I had the rest of the class for company[12]. It was the beginning of many years of such 'field trips'. I had no idea what lay ahead, but there was certainly no turning back.

CHAPTER II: THE INNER FIRE

Magic is the sole science not accepted by scientists, because they can't understand it.---*Harry Houdini*

Another basic component of the Art is understanding and manipulation of the Inner Fire. Work in this area will not only help to develop the Sight further, but also trains the important ability to manipulate psychic energy.

For untold centuries, it has been known that an energetic field or 'aura' both interpenetrates and surrounds the human body. This energy or the Inner Fire[13], as I refer to it, is not only a subtler part of the body proper, but is composed of the very essence that animates our body and imparts us with life. Whole schools of thought exist on the specific composition of the aura and the nature of its various layers, but our focus here is to examine and explore the Fire in basic introductory terms.

Using the Sight, the Inner Fire is relatively easy to observe[14]. Consciously directing this Fire is accomplished by a combination of proper mental visualization and correct breathing technique. **This is an essential principle of personal magick that will be revisited again and again in this book: that the body's inherent psychic energy naturally responds to what the mind visualizes for it, in conjunction with the breath.**

The following exercises are intended to help develop the manipulation of the Inner Fire using these components properly.

Exercise 1: Exploring the Inner Fire

One easy way to view the Inner Fire is in a semi-darkened setting. After Stilling the Waters and using your Sight, hold out a hand and slowly move it across a neutral background in front of you. As you do so, note the area in the air around your hand, specifically one to two inches in space (and with your fingertips specifically, anywhere from one to six inches out in space from them). What you will notice as you move your hand is what could be compared visually to a conventional heat wave—a transparent to semi transparent disturbance of the air space around the extremity. This is your Inner Fire itself, surrounding your physical body.

As a compliment to this exercise, you should also revisit your mirror. As with our previous exercises, the setting should be semi-dark and free of distractions. In this case, instead of fixing your gaze on your reflected features, you should look at the edges of your body and take careful note of the space around it. It may be possible at this stage to not only perceive the Fire, but to view it under this state of heightened awareness displaying colors or flashes of luminosity. The meaning and actions of these colors *is* important, but for this level of development they have little bearing and I leave it to other works to explain their significance. The act of seeing these colors is what is significant.

Exercise 2: Further Observation of the Fire

Once you have had the opportunity to examine your Inner Fire in a controlled semi-dark surrounding, the next step is to observe at it in natural sunlight, and to examine the energies surrounding other things.

Among the practitioners of Voudou (or Voodoo), the Fire is sometimes referred to as the Little Good Angel (the *ti-bon-ange*) and the Big Good Angel (the *gros-bon-ange*), and a very simple exercise was developed to view the densest part of the Outer Fire in natural light. In this case, observe your body's shadow on the ground.

Even without the Sight, it should become immediately apparent that a thin transparent field surrounds your body, through which sunlight refracts. In some circumstances, the subtler parts of the Fire can also be seen extending quite some distance away from this dense field (which itself tends to measure anywhere from 1/8th to an inch or more out from the physical body)[15].

Another area to explore is the same Fire as it surrounds other people and things. This involves looking not at the person directly, but like our previous exercises at the space around them. Movement of any kind on the subject's part, when viewed against a neutral backdrop will quickly display the disturbance caused by the layers of their Outer Fire as it interacts with the environment around them. It will tend to appear in much the same manner as the energy around your hand; as a heat wave-like disturbance or distortion, extending out from the person into space.

In addition, you are urged to take a few moments to observe the space around plants and trees (especially at sunset or dawn when lighting and energetic conditions are at their best). This can prove quite educational.

One characteristic of plants especially, is that their Fire is grossly extended at these times to take full advantage of the energetic rays from the sun, which, like water and nutrients, acts to nourish them and invigorate their growth. If nothing else, after trying this, you will never look at a garden or a tree the same way.

CONTROLLING THE FIRE

The Inner and Outer Fires are components of the pure life energy we have within us. Learning to manipulate this energy is important not only to develop the Sight, but also to enable you to interact with your environment on a magickal level. Like the Sight, this basic ability is integral to the Art, for without the ability to manipulate the basic energy within us and extend it properly, one is left with no coherent means to influence the surrounding environment.

Exercise 1: The Breath and Gathering the Fire

Centuries of experimentation have shown that the Inner Fire is controlled and moved through a combination of controlled breathing and proper visualization. Therefore, our primary exploration begins with this act.

As always, you should sit comfortably in a quiet place and close your eyes. Then, after taking three deep, calming breaths, put attention on feeling your body around you. Take note of any sensations in your limbs, of the feeling of your heart beating in your chest and the like.

After a few minutes, begin to picture your entire body filled with a soft white light. When this has been achieved, take in several more breaths, visualizing this energy coalescing together into the area of your solar plexus as you breathe inwards. This area is called the 'Hara' in the Orient and it is considered to be the center of the body's life energy.

Once the energy has been gathered in this location, picture it forming itself into a round luminous ball about the size of a conventional basketball. When you have held this imagery in your mind for several more minutes, visualize the ball slowly dissipating back into your body and its energy redistributing itself there as you gently breath out.[16] This exercise should be repeated several times over the next week.

Exercise 2: Extending the Fire

The next step in working with the Fire involves all the elements of the first exercise, but with a distinct change. This time, after visualizing your Fire gathering into a ball in your solar plexus, mentally direct it to flow from there up through your trunk and down your arm, and from there out through your fingertips into space, breathing out as you do so.

Your hand should also be extended in front of you and you are to observe for any activity that occurs in the space around it (in much the same manner as you did during the earlier exercises involving the Sight). Careful note should be taken to perceive exactly how far into space the energy extends, and you should visualize your Fire moving further and further out from you with each breath. With work, you will note that your energy field extends greater and greater distances away from you.

If you have a training partner, there is also another exercise to help explore the manipulation of the Fire. In this variation, one person, the receiver, sits while the other, the sender, extends their energy out through their hand.

When the sender is ready, they are to move their hand slowly towards the receiver while projecting their Fire outwards from themselves, stopping when they, or the other person feel a change in sensation or temperature.

Generally this will occur one to three inches away from the surface of the receiver's physical body and it can be experienced as anything from a tickling sensation, a feeling of heaviness, or a rise or drop in the perception of temperature. The precise distance where this change is first sensed is the outside limit of one of the denser layers of the receiver's Inner Fire.

To aid in the process, a 'brushing' motion should then be made by the sender, approaching the receiver from a distance and slowly sweeping across and over the area where contact was felt (while avoiding actual physical contact as they do so). Both parties should take note of what they experience while this is being done.

For solitary practitioners, the same exercise can be accomplished employing a slight variation. Take one hand and after extending energy through it, bring it in and towards your opposite arm, stopping when a change is noted. The process is then repeated, using the brushing technique mentioned above.

In addition to these exercises, certain energy centers of the body can also be easily stimulated[17] and allow you to experience the limits of your aura and the effects energy has upon it.

One of these centers is the famed 'third eye'. In this case, project your Fire out of your index and middle fingers, and while continuing to project it, move towards this area making a gentle circular motion as you approach. As soon as a spot is reached where a change in sensation is noted you should stop and withdraw your hand. The sensation this action produces can be quite pronounced. The process should be repeated several more times, or until the sensation becomes uncomfortable[18].

This particular exercise should be repeated daily, even after you have moved on to more advanced subjects. Not only does it allow you to experience this particular energy center, but through repetition, stimulates this center and heightens its sensitivity, an action which in turn lends itself to greater abilities with the Sight.

Exercise 3: Breathing Solar and Lunar Fire and the Basic Grounding Maneuver

Just as the Fire can be moved through the body with the action of the breath, energy can also be taken into the body from external sources. The most basic exercise in this area works with sunlight.

Sunlight not only provides all living things with the nutrients and radiation that are important for biological processes, but also imparts what could be termed a spiritual essence that feeds the Inner Fires of our being. Normally this occurs as part of a passive process, but in this exercise, a deliberate effort will be made to tap directly into this source of healthful energy.

The exercise is to be performed in a sunny area outdoors. After Stilling yourself, face the sun and spread your arms wide[19]. As you do so, take in deep breaths, visualizing the sunlight coming down through space and into your solar plexus as a rich golden light that radiates out from there into the rest of your body. As soon as this has occurred, immediately cup your hands over your solar plexus, and as you hold your breath, visualize the energy you have just received circulating throughout your body. Then release your hands and breathe out.

By now, the reader has undoubtedly recognized this maneuver as an expansion and a variant from earlier sections. It is a basic grounding maneuver which will be revisited many more times in this book from here on out and its mastery is important. This particular exercise represents an excellent opportunity to do so in a safe and healthful manner.

When it is properly performed, many students note immediate sensations of intense warmth coming over them, coupled with feelings of euphoria and raised levels of energy. This exercise should be performed several times, and you should also feel free to repeat it as often as you desire.

In addition, the reader is invited to try a variation and perform this same exercise with the full moon. If this is undertaken, careful note should be made of the difference and qualities of the two energies. Rather than comment any further, I will leave the matter to the reader to experience this for themselves.

Exercise 4: Vril Wasser

One adjunct to working with Solar Fire is the creation of an energized beverage that can be used not only to refresh but also to re-energize a person. It comes from the magickal schools of the 19th and 20th century in Germany, and is called Vril-Wasser ('*Vril*' being a term that describes the Life-Energy).

To create Vril-Wasser, a clean clear glass bottle should be filled with distilled water. A small amount of honey should then be added to this and the mixture is then set out in the sunlight. After several hours, you can remove the bottle from the sun and set it to cool.

The final step in the preparation then involves breathing some of your own energy into the water. This is done in the same manner that you projected your Fire outwards to observe it, through a combination of gathering it, then breathing outwards from you along with complimentary visualization.

In this case, your energy should be projected outwards and into the water itself. One effective method for doing this is to simply hold the bottle in your hands, and push the Fire out through them, through the glass, and into the water, visualizing it penetrating and mixing with the water.

With this step performed, the water can then be stored for future consumption, or drunk on the spot. *Note: because of the absence of preservatives, this mixture can easily spoil and extended storage is not recommended.*

Exercise 5: Breathing Color

Materials: Several pieces of colored cardboard or poster board, representing the primary and secondary colors should be obtained for this exercise, along with a stand or chair to display them.

Color is the expression of light in different wavelengths. Just as different colors have different visual qualities, they also emanate different energies that not only affect our moods, but according to some, our health and even the surrounding qualities of reality itself. In this exercise, you are invited to explore the nature of color for yourself, and experience color on more than a visual level. At the same time, work with colors will also lend itself to the ability to discern the differences between different vibrations or types of psychic energy.

To do this, a colored piece of paper or cardboard should be set up on a stand or chair. Still the Waters, and as you had with sunlight, visualize yourself breathing the color on the cardboard into yourself as an energy. See the color in your mind's eye coming into you as an energetic cloud and filing you with its unique energetic qualities.

After working with one color, the cardboard should be removed and another color put in its place, with the exercise repeated.

As you breath in each color, observe the different sensations that come over you with different colors and make note of this in your journal. You may find that some colors are quite pleasant, while others are less so, and you may notice that certain colors provoke different emotional and even physical responses within you as you breathe them in. As for the details concerning different colors and their energetic qualities, I defer to experts in this area and the reader's own findings.

Exercise 6: Scrying Objects

The ability to scry or 'psycometrize' an object is part of the process of learning to breathe energy and utilizes the same skill to accomplish this feat. All objects carry an energetic 'record' of the events that they were present at. This is especially true of those that enjoy a great deal of use, are kept close to a person, or are used while their owner is in a state of heightened emotions.

This is possible due to the fact that inanimate objects, while not living in the sense of plants or animals, do possess an energetic field or rudimentary Fire because they exist as material things[20]. This same Fire can be influenced by other energies around it and can carry with it impressions of the forces that caused that change to occur. The Art of Reading an Object is the ability to sensing the nature of these energetic impressions and interpreting them correctly.

For the first exercise, you should use something with a known history. As you hold the object[21], breathe in the energy of the object itself in the same manner that you did with the sun and moon; picturing the energy contained within the object coming into you and as it does so, let whatever sensation and mental images arise in your consciousness.

Commonly, sensations such as smells and emotions are experienced along with mental images of colors or even specific times or scenes. Of course, knowing the history of the object will make interpreting these images, or 'reading it', quite easy and the purpose here is only to become acquainted with the procedure.

The next exercise should be performed with an object whose history is only partly known. If a partner is available, their job should be to provide the item and to answer any questions that the 'reader' has--confirming whether anything that the reader senses is correct or incorrect. With practice one can achieve a surprising number of successful 'hits' in a fairly short amount of time.

Another exercise that should definitely be experienced is work with historical objects. For this, a trip to a museum is called for. Naturally, such items are protected behind displays and most people are correctly discouraged from handling what are often priceless items of historical and scientific value.

However, these items can still be Read. Using the same exercise for breathing solar and lunar fire, the energy, and the imbedded imagery, contained within these objects can be discerned without ever having to make physical contact. Of course, being a public setting, the 'arms-wide gesture' employed in our work with sunlight would be somewhat conspicuous, and quite unnecessary[22].

Instead, simply gather your Fire, move it outwards from you, and to and through the object. Then breathe it back in, letting the images come to you as you do so. This can be done without any obvious gestures (with the exception of the final maneuver of putting the hands over the abdomen as an aid to retaining the energy momentarily).

You will quickly find that a museum is quite different than what you might have been used to. The objects contained within most museums have amazing and wonderful stories to tell us and their energies vary widely[23]. Some students who attempt this type of reading soon become regular visitors, especially to certain sections and specific items.

One word of warning should be voiced however. Not all of the contents of a museum are 'friendly'. Artifacts from the past can contain either positive or negative imprints and while some can provide truly ecstatic glimpses into the past, others can hold equal amounts of horror[24]. In exploring them in such an intimate manner, you should always be cautious. Any indication of negative energies, especially at this relatively early stage of the development of the Art, should be avoided.

Exercise 7: Simple Fiery Constructs

The next stage of working with the Fire involves the creation of basic energy constructs. The most basic is an energy ball.

In this case, hold your hands out in front of your body, at the level of your solar plexus, cupping them as if you were holding a large ball. As you breath out your Fire, visualize it forming itself into a large sphere that fills the space between your hands and your trunk. This work should continue until the energy construct is visually perceptible.

Once a basic ball has been created, the next level is to create another sphere. This time however, cup your hands closely together and breathing your energy down and into the cupped area, picture the energy coming together into small but extremely dense ball of light. When you feel ready, slowly and gently open and pull your hands away from the area and step back.

The Sight will reveal a disturbed area in space the same size as the energy ball you have created. If you slowly approach the area with your hand extended, you may notice a perceptible rise or drop in air temperature in this same area, and possibly a tingling sensation.

After observing the sphere, you should dissolve it by waving your hand through it until it is no longer perceptible. The purpose of this action is to instill the habit of being thorough in your Work (making sure to banish what you create), and also ensure that this loose and otherwise uncontrolled energy does not undergo any undesirable changes at a later stage.

Exercise 8: A Partnered Exercise: The Energy Ball Game

A cornerstone of many schools to help train students to work with Fiery Constructs is the Energy Ball Game. Those readers with prior occult experience may recognize it immediately.

In this exercise, one person creates a small energy ball while their partner stands several feet away. Once the ball has been visualized, the student who created it then sends it at their partner. This is accomplished by releasing the ball, and then as they are breathing energy out from their flattened palm, pushing outwards at the ball while simultaneously *Willing* it to move. A gentle touch is required here, and initial efforts may result in the immediate disintegration of the ball, but with a small amount of practice, the ball will remain intact and travel outwards towards the other person.

The 'receivers' main job is to observe the progress of the ball and when it comes close enough, to attempt to catch it by gently cupping their hands around it. Then, after adding more of their own energy to the ball, they are to return it to the original sender, who repeats the process, and so on.

The purpose of this game of psychic 'catch' is to help to develop the ability to create and manipulate energy forms through conscious Will and to learn how to make them respond and move to that same Will. Regular practice can rapidly improve skill in this area and lend itself to much more advanced operations.

Exercise 9: Seeking with the Fire

Up to this stage, we have been working with extending the Inner Fire over relatively short distances. The next step in our learning process is to increase your psychic 'reach' and the first exercises require a partner.

The receiver stands some six to ten feet from the sender. The sender then holds their hand palm out towards a spot to one side of the receiver's body. The sender then pushes their Fire out from their hand as far out in space as possible, visualizing it lengthening and growing way from them as they do so.

At the same time this is occurring, the receiver gathers up and extends their own energy throughout their body and outwards in all directions in order to increase their energetic 'signature' for the sender to perceive.

The sender then slowly sweeps their arm towards the receiver, moving across the other person, and completing their arc at a point in space somewhere on their opposite side. The maneuver is then repeated by reversing and sweeping in the opposite direction[25]. For the receiver, the result should be a feeling of something making contact or brushing over them, and for the sender, a sensation of contact against their palm, or a feeling of pressure as they pass across their receiver.

Any and all changes in sensation experienced by either party are to be noted, and when they feel ready, the roles should then be reversed. Naturally, as proficiency with this maneuver is gained, the distance between the two parties should also be increased. This not only strengthens the ability to project over greater spans but also aids in increasing perception of energy over greater distances.

In a variation of this, a game of hide-and-seek can also be played where the receiver conceals himself or herself from the sender and it becomes the sender's task to Seek for their location, using the Fire in the manner described above to accomplish this. The only variation is that having no immediate reference on the location of the receiver, the sender must sweep across a general area where they suppose the receiver to be, observing for any changes that might give away their presence.

For solitary practitioners, who do not have the benefit of a partner, this exercise can still be explored, albeit with some modification. The sweeping maneuver is the same, but in this case the target can be either another person nearby them who was chosen by the sender as opportunity presented them, or a pet. Even houseplants, having a Fire of their own, can be used as a practice target in this case[26].

One point that is important regardless of whether one has a partner, or does not, is that beyond the ability to feel and locate a target, that there is the greater skill of being able to perceive the basic qualities and nature of what is being Sought.

As you (or you and your partner) experiment with Seeking, you should make sure to take careful note of how contact with another beings Inner Fire feels and what responses and impressions that contact provokes within you.

As you discovered during our experiments with reading and Object, it is not only possible to feel general energy, but also derive very specific information (either in the form of emotions or mental images, or both) from that same energy.

Every living being has a unique energy vibration that is just as distinct as one fingerprint is from another. This unique individualized energy can also change its qualities based on the person's health or emotional state. Strong emotions for example, are particularly easy to perceive. In fact, the ability to 'read' another person's energy and their emotional intent is normal to most people, but seldom noticed for what it is. While facial expressions and body language certainly play a role in our interaction with others, there are many situations where the 'feeling' one gets from another person is quite different (and generally more accurate) than what they are allowing others to see[27].

Exercise 10: Simple Healing

Energetic healing is a very complex subject, but at this stage, having mastered some of the basics of working with the Fire, a certain rudimentary skill can be obtained immediately.

The operation here is an elementary one. As always, Still yourself and visualize your Inner Fire. But this time, instead of circulating it through the body (which certainly generates its own healthful effects by stimulating the bodies energy centers), envision the Fire moving to and through the site of your problem.

For example, in the case of a sore muscle, the Fire is to be moved through the painful area. It is also helpful to picture the affected area in one color and the healing energy coming into it in another, such as red for the problem zone and blue for the healing energy.

As your Fire is moved through the affected area, you should also visualize the color of the healing energy replacing that of the pain and picture the area becoming less inflamed and more and more healthful as this occurs.

This basic maneuver can have remarkable results, as I myself can attest. In one case I had been training with a partner in the Japanese art of the sword, and my partner's bamboo *shinai* had struck me on the arm. A bruise immediately appeared, and my partner (who was skilled in the art of moving the Fire, or 'Chi' as he referred to it) immediately channeled energy through the area.

In literally seconds, the bruise vanished completely and the area no longer afflicted me. Of course, my friend was a very seasoned practitioner, and the results you might enjoy might be somewhat less dramatic and take a bit longer to achieve. The ability to move the Inner Fire with a healthful intent has far–reaching benefits for those who master it, and the student should welcome the opportunity to learn this skill however painful the initial reason to employ it might be.

Exercise 11: Basic Energy Exchange

An expansion on working with solar and lunar energies involves a partner. In this first exercise, both parties should join hands. One person should be designated as the 'sender' and the other as the 'receiver'. The sender breathes their Fire out through their hands, while the receiver visualizes breathing the senders's energy directly into themselves, then ending the maneuver using the energy grounding technique we learned in working with solar and lunar energies.

The roles should then be reversed. Once both parties have tried sending and receiving, the next step is for both persons to send out their Fire with one hand while drawing in the other parties Fire with the other hand. The idea here is to create a traveling loop of energy passing between both persons.

When this has been accomplished, the two people should also try a variation where they face their palms towards each other, but do not touch. Once again, energy is to be sent out and taken in, creating the loop. The distance between their hands should gradually be increased until the exchange of energy is taking place from across a room, or a distance of roughly ten or more feet.

As an addition to all of this, both parties are also encouraged to experiment with projecting energy while raising their emotions. Self-guided imagery, such as revisiting happy moments or reliving events that cause anger in the sender will help in bringing up the desired emotions. The receiver's job in this case is to report what they feel and if they are sensitive enough, identify the specific mood that is being projected by the sender.

Exercise 12: Sexual Energy Exchange

Energy exchange happens naturally during sex between partners. However, a concerted effort to focus this exchange can have dramatic results and if the student and their partner are on intimate terms, this exercise exchange should definitely be attempted.

In this case, as intercourse is proceeding, the sender is to visualize their Fire being projected out through their solar plexus into that of their partner. The receiver breathes this energy inwards at the same time, and then returns it back to the sender, once again creating our loop of continuous energy. This exercise may produce a variety of effects, which can range from increased sexual stimulation to an actual transference of thoughts and emotions.

VAMPIRISM OR INVOLUNTARY ENERGY EXCHANGE

Vampires do in fact exist. While some writers such as Stephen Kaplan have stated the controversial idea that 'true' vampires (in the Hollywood sense) are a reality, the practice of energetic vampirism is a very real and established phenomena. There are essentially two kinds of vampire: those who derive nourishment from blood and those who gain it from energy (with variations in between).

Individuals who consume blood and claim to derive energy from it is something medical science has acknowledged for a long time, and while this was once considered a relatively rare practice, it is becoming increasingly common[28]. Whether or not they actually do obtain nourishment is a matter of scientific debate. However, from a metaphysical point of view, blood, like any other component of the body, certainly does contain its own Fire, and as the reader has seen, it is certainly theoretically possible for nourishing energy to be derived from it. Therefore such persons who engage in this practice should rightly be considered vampires, although the claim that some have made that this custom also increases life spans or grants special powers is another matter entirely, and open to debate.

The second type of vampire, the 'energy vampire' is quite common. This can occur either as the result of a deliberate practice or as a natural trait. Certainly, everyone has encountered individuals who seem to thrive on negative energy, or become energized while others around them appear to become drained of their own[29].

One of the things I learned in my studies was that the ability to pull energy from another person is in fact the natural offshoot of basic energy work. As our prior exercises illustrate, the act itself is a simple one, which can be undertaken face-to-face (or even through intermediary communication mediums such as a telephone). In the Orient, this ability, when deliberately employed, is referred to as 'stealing *Chi*'.

Many modern 'vampyre' groups take the official position that stealing energy from an unknowing, or unwilling partner is unethical and frown upon the practice. However, while this certainly might be the case, there are definitely energy vampires among us who have no such scruples and do as they please, taking as they will from those around them, using modified versions of the techniques we have already explored in this chapter.

Vampirism without prior consent also occurs as part of basic human interaction and generally employs no special training or experience. For example, simply shaking hands often involves an unacknowledged exchange of energy between the parties (this being the unconscious act of 'tasting' the other person to gauge their character).

Involuntary drainage of energy also takes place during the sex act as a normal by-product of the act itself. As Kaplan pointed out in his book *"Vampires Are"*, and as I have personally observed working in the medical field, the elderly are another good example: they become invigorated by exposure to the very young (with Kaplan stating that this socially accepted form of energy drainage is brought about by the natural and unconscious attraction that the elderly have towards the vibrant life-force children possess).

As I see it, the issue is not whether nonconsensual energy-vampirism is 'right' or 'wrong'. Rather it is how a student who does not desire to be drained by an act of vampirism can potentially prevent this from occurring[30].

There are many fine books on the subject of psychic self defense, including and especially Jason Miller's *"Protection Magick & Reversal: A Witches Defense Manual"*. Vampirism is only one of many hazards that exist for the novice in the Hidden World and I recommend that the aspiring student study such material in earnest. To compliment these excellent works, and help counter this specific problem I also offer the following additional tactics.

The first of these is the awareness that such an act is occurring, and removing oneself from the source of the drainage. This may sound painfully obvious, but all too often, the tendency of victims of energy vampirism is to deny that it is occurring, or to simply fail to recognize the event. As Patricia Briggs aptly stated in her work of fiction, *"Bloodbound"*, "The devout belief that the world is explainable is both a terrible vulnerability and a stout shield. Evil prefers it when people don't believe." Certainly this is the case with aggressive energy vampires, and as a novice myself, I suffered from this very shortcoming, discovering the truth of the matter the proverbial 'hard way";

When I was still fairly 'green', I fell victim to an act of vampirism without realizing that it had occurred until it was over. I had been invited to speak at a friend's home on the subject of magick. One of the members of the audience proceeded to engage me in what shortly became a heated debate on the 'rightness' of magick as regarded by Christianity.

As the conversation became more and more unfriendly, her partner pulled out a pair of crystals and holding them in his hand like antennae, sat through the entire conversation with his eyes closed and a serene expression on his face. I was so involved in the argument that I barely noticed him, but I did soon become aware of feeling physically drained, coupled with a severe headache. The conversation ended and the pair departed together.

Only when they were gone, did my host and I realize that the effects we had both felt (for she had felt the same symptoms) had left with them. When I remarked at how rude the first person had been, my host expressed shock at her attitude, which apparently had never been exhibited before then. As we compared notes on the event, it dawned on both of us that a trap had been laid for me, and I had walked into it without knowing. Not surprisingly, I refused all further contact with the pair and urged that my host follow suit.

But assuming that removing or isolating oneself from the problem is not practical, there are other methods available to deal with the problem. One of these is what I call the Warriors Defense. Carlos Castaneda describes this method in his pivotal writings on sorcery, the *"Don Jaun"* series of books.

In this case, when a negative or draining energy is perceived, the practitioner assumes what can be called a 'guarding position', which is done by covering their solar plexus with their hands. This action helps to block the influx or egress of energy through an otherwise vulnerable area in the body's natural energy field. In effect, one is cutting off access to their life-energy. Like any defense, it is not by foolproof, but can certainly be effective in many situations.

Another defensive maneuver, also borrowed from shamanism, is for the party being drained to actually **allow** the drainage to occur, but visualize any and all negative energy[31] they have within them being breathed out and released **into** the attacking party. Shamans throughout history have always known that disease has an energetic component and that it could be removed from an afflicted party using a method of breathing the malignant energy out. This variation not only removes negative energies from the targeted person, but also transfers them to the attacking party, along with whatever physical maladies that accompany it.

Certainly, an experienced energy vampire can assimilate and convert this, and many such persons actually thrive on negative energy, but in other cases it can be a far different matter. The maneuver itself is fairly elementary and easy to master[32]. The following exercise is offered to the reader to understand and master its mechanics:

Exercise 13: Breathing Out Negative Energy

After Stilling the Waters, take several deep breaths. Then, visualize any negative, unhealthful energy in your body appearing as a dark black mass or shadow. Gather this same dark energy up inside you and as you exhale, see it leaving your body and dissipate in the air[33]. If you are conducting this activity in conjunction with any work with solar or lunar forces, see their healthful energy entering you with your next inhalation, gathering in your solar plexus and then distributing itself throughout your body.

As an adjunct to this, if you are experiencing a headache, or a similar issue, try to see the malady in your mind's eye as an energy-form, and as you breathe outwards, visualize that same negative energy leaving you---and with it all pain and discomfort. Naturally, this is not intended as substitute for medical treatment, but should instead be complimentary to such scientific measures.

TALES FROM THE HIDDEN WORLD: THE NIGHT OF THE WOLF

A year and a half after my trip to Bolinas Bay, I had left San Francisco and moved to Los Angeles. My classes in shamanism were a thing of the past and I had only two private students, Dennis R. and Louis G. While Dennis had joined me while I had still lived in the Bay area, and had gone on a few 'field trips' already, Louis was a newcomer to Magick. After having spent a year completing the basics, it had finally been decided to take him out for his first field experience.

Up to that point, the destination of choice had been Death Valley National Monument, but I was eager to explore different locations and we all agreed on a trip to the Yosemite Valley instead. Dennis drove down from the Bay Area and met us in Modesto and together we drove up to the park arriving there late in the afternoon. It was summertime and naturally at such a popular destination, no camping reservations were to be had, so when our first day ended, we wound up sleeping, as many do, in our car in one of the larger parking lots.

I awoke just before dawn the following morning, feeling that something special was about to happen. Overcome with this sensation, I let myself out of the car and walked into a nearby patch of woods.

It was still quite dark in among the trees and I stopped a short ways in and sat down to have a cigarette. As I did so, I noticed some movement about 100 yards away from me through the trees. I watched as what I first thought was a coyote walked into view, moving down a nearby access road. But I had seen coyotes before and this animal was much, much larger. I realized that I was seeing a wolf instead[34].

And there was something else accompanying the wolf; a small luminous ball that hovered in the air above it with a dull glow. Then as the light from a car began to grow behind it, the wolf stopped and looked straight through the forest in my direction. It knew that I was there, watching it and it seemed to be making up its mind what to do next.

It glanced back over its shoulder at the oncoming car, and made its choice, walking off the roadway and into the trees. As it did this, the strange ball of light disappeared. The creature walked up to within a dozen feet of me.

I stayed absolutely still, not knowing what would happen next. But the wolf didn't seem to consider me a threat and moved right by.

Once it was gone, I got up and left the grove, crossing the same access road into another, smaller stand of trees. By now, the sun was starting to illuminate the eastern sky, and I sat down again to marvel at a spectacular view of the valley coming to life with the dawn. But movement caught my eye, this time to my left.

I looked over to what was the main highway that runs through the Valley and saw a young woman walk into view. She appeared to be about 20 years old, with long wavy blond hair that reached the small of her back and she was wearing a dark colored top and a long, multi-colored skirt.

As she stepped fully into view, the woman glanced over her shoulder back down the roadway. Then she continued to walk forwards.

As she reached a point that was almost directly in front of me, the air immediately around her body began to shimmer. Then suddenly, her body flattened into a thin bar of luminosity that then compressed immediately into a small glowing sphere.

This ball of light glided over the pavement for a few more feet before it changed, expanding itself outwards and filling out into the shape of a wolf. The animal paused at the edge of some bushes and regarded me for second, before walking into the concealment of the foliage. I was still in open-mouthed shock as a car passed by, crossing over the same spot where the woman had been just seconds before.

It was dawn. I got up from my seat and walked for several minutes around the area before I returned to the car. My companions were just waking.

I quickly told them what had happened and both of them wanted to go out into the woods right away and see this for themselves. But by this time the campgrounds were coming to life, and they knew as well as I that there was little chance of seeing much more than summer tourists. They became angry with me for not waking them, but I pointed out that I had had no idea that anything was going to happen when I left the car and that I certainly would not have had time to leave what I had been encountering to come back for them.

While Dennis and Louis agreed that I was right, I was given a stern warning to wake them the next time I had the urge to get up in the middle of the night for any kind of adventure.

Our day after that was spent sightseeing, but our real interests lay in what the park might have to offer us after dark. We were all highly encouraged by my experiences and hopeful that we would see more as a group later on.

When sunset came, we were ready. We had already scouted out a road into the forest that had seemed promising. It lead off of the main highway and deep into the woods, well away from the main campgrounds, but close enough for us to walk to from our parking spot. Dinner, as the reader might imagine, was a hurried affair, and as soon as we had finished with it and packed up the few things we thought we would need, we set off.

Perhaps one of the more memorable parts of our trip in was the hoards of people going the other way--and the looks we got from them. Everyone, except ourselves was headed back to the supposed safety and comfort of the lights of the campgrounds and they clearly thought there was something odd about us. Of course, they were completely correct.

Eventually, we reached a point where we were alone. The sun had set by this time, and the woods were dark, but from a combination of our Sight and our eyes adjusting to the setting, we were able to see our way quite well.

The first thing we all noticed was the movement of energy among the trees. Some of it was dark and smoky colored, and other parts seemed to be quite luminous in comparison. I surmised from this that in a living forest that a natural energy exchange occurs between the trees and assumed that this was exactly what we were witnessing in the dim light (I would come to know differently years later, but that is another tale).

When full darkness came, we had reached a small bridge that spanned a tiny creek. Dennis, a heavyset man and not in the best physical shape, was tired of walking by this time, and we agreed to let him take a break on the bridge to catch his breath.

But as we walked up towards it, we saw a wolf standing in the middle of the span. It did not retreat as we moved towards it. Instead, it snarled at us and we stopped in our tracks.

It was obvious to everyone that we were not going to get past the animal, and we all very carefully turned around to go back the way we had come. There was another surprise waiting for us. Standing in the roadway in the opposite direction were two men.

For a moment, they seemed normal enough, but we quickly realized that they were not affected by the wolf's presence in the least. In fact, they seemed to be intent on blocking our path just as the wolf had done, or at the very least wanted to force us to squeeze past them. At that point, I made a quick decision and told my friends to follow me as I ran towards the men yelling.

The men dove out of our way, and the wolf, which had stood his ground up until now, started to run after us, nipping at Dennis's heels. I immediately realized that we could not outrun the creature and decided on another course of action instead. I yelled for my friends to stop, and as they did so, the wolf ceased to chase us. Instead, it backed off and followed us from several feet behind.

I looked around for the two men, but they were gone. However, others had replaced them. In addition to the wolf, several people had appeared from among the trees and joined us as we walked along.

They all looked normal enough; in fact were it not for the setting, I would have thought them to be fellow campers, but they ignored the animal behind us and walked through the trees to either side of us with an ease and an assuredness that definitely did not match the mood of the people we had seen earlier on our way into the forest.

Then out of the corner of my eye, I saw someone immediately to my right and hazarded a glance. It was a young woman. She seemed to be about 15 years old with stringy brown hair and a faded green dress that reminded me of images I had seen of the poor living in Appalachia. We moved along together for a minute or so more, with the girl saying nothing to me and looking straight ahead.

Then, without warning, she suddenly ran in front of me and started to fall towards the pavement face first. But her body never hit the ground.

At the last possible second before impact, her body shimmered like the woman I had seen that morning. Then it immediately compressed into an amorphous lozenge-shaped haze that moved rapidly over the roadway to the opposite shoulder. The cloud righted itself there and expanded into the shape of another woman. She was still as young as the first, but now she was a blond, with her hair carefully feathered, and her clothing looked new and expensive. She looked every bit like any of the classic "Valley Girls" of the time.

Louis and Dennis had both seen this transformation as well, but other than a nervous glance in my direction, they said nothing. Whatever jealousy they had felt about my earlier experiences was certainly gone by now, replaced by deep concern over what would happen to us next. We continued on, completely unharmed by our escort, which by now was approximately 15-20 individuals walking to either side of us.

Then, as we saw the first lights of the campgrounds shining through the trees, they began to drop back into the shadows until only one figure remained with us. He was an old man, with silver hair, wearing a plain-checkered shirt and faded jeans, but he carried himself with a definite aura of command. He *stayed with us until we reached a stop for the local tram. Then, he too turned back into the darkness.*

The tram came by a few minutes later and we boarded it. As soon as we reached our parking lot, we decided to leave the Valley immediately. We had no idea what would happen next, and although our escort out of the woods had been benign enough, we were uncertain if things would remain friendly. An hour later, we were out of the mountains.

Louis and I headed to Los Angeles and Dennis to the Bay Area. Collectively, we were exhausted, and Louis and I agreed to spell one another with the driving. I tried to stay awake to keep him company, but eventually, I surrendered to my weariness and fell asleep.

Louis awoke me some time later in a panic. He told me that somehow, there was a wolf in the car with us, sitting in the back seat. I looked up in the mirror and met the gaze of two eyes staring back at me and saw the unmistakable silhouette of the animal. Perhaps it was sheer tiredness, mixed with being overwhelmed by what we had encountered, but my reaction was to simply agree that yes, one did seem to be there, and that I was going back to sleep and that Louis should try ignore it.

Louis wasn't certainly comforted by this recommendation, but kept driving. He told me later that the apparition stayed with us for several hours after this, but eventually, vanished as mysteriously as it had appeared[35].

Time passed and eventually I returned to Yosemite and encountered the shapeshifters again. On one such trip, deep in the middle of winter, Dennis and I had traveled into the forest. We had decided to each try out 'soloing' along the same road we had been on on our first trip there.

Dennis went well ahead of me and found a spot for himself to sit down at on the banks of a stream that bordered the road, while I searched for my own place to work. I had just stopped on the bridge where we had encountered the wolf on our first trip to take a break, when a man and a young girl came walking towards me. I was instantly on my guard without knowing fully why.

The man came up to me and asked me how to get back to the campgrounds. I said nothing, but simply pointed down the road. The man thanked me with a pleasant smile and he and his companion walked in the direction I had indicated.

It was only when they had gone that I realized what it was about him and the girl that had bothered me so much. For one, it was extremely cold, and neither he nor the girl were wearing jackets of any kind (in fact, the girl was wearing a short skirt that was entirely impractical for the weather). And then there had been a detail that I had somehow not noticed until they had walked away from me, this being that the girl's feet had never touched the ground. Instead she had floated beside the older man[36].

Dennis and I met up a few minutes later, and any remaining doubts I had about the strangeness of our encounter were completely erased when he told me about his own meeting with the pair. According to Dennis, he had been sitting beside the stream, practicing his Sight when the two had walked up to him and the man had sternly asked him "Where's your friend?"

Dennis had been surprised by this, but before he could fully cognate this odd question, the man had smiled and asked him for directions instead.

On another occasion, I encountered shapeshifters of a different sort. By this time, I was working as a patrolman for a private patrol company in Los Angeles. My patrol area was in Malibu, which is mainly a rural area dotted with the mansions of the very rich. In my roll calls, I had been told to pay special attention to a market located along Pacific Coast highway. Numerous burglaries had happened there and the perpetrators had been gaining access to the building by prying open the air conditioning system vents on the roof.

One night, as I drove my patrol car into the lot, and swept the roof with a spotlight, I spotted two men up on the roof. I quickly called in my location, and got out of my car, and ordered the men to come down.

Instead, the men ran to the edge of the roof, and jumped off it onto a nearby dumpster and from there to the ground. Then they ran down into a gully that bordered the market's parking lot.

I drew my gun and went after them. As I ran over to the gully, two coyotes crested the opposite side. They looked over their shoulders at me for a moment, and then ran off into the underbrush.

Intent on catching the burglars, I ignored them and shined my flashlight down into the dry creek bed thinking that they were still down there somewhere hiding from me. But even without the flashlight, I could see everything in the barren gully and there was no sign of the men—and no places for them to have hidden themselves.

That's when I made the connection with the coyotes I had seen. I fruitlessly checked the gully for a few minutes more, and then accepting the fact that they had escaped, went back to my car to make my report (omitting mention of the coyotes).

A year passed. By that time, I had left the patrol company, and had gone to college full time. There I had the opportunity to make friends with a man who was a long-time resident of Malibu, and more importantly, was friendly with the migrant Latino workers who camped in the area.

Eventually he told me that the workers were deeply concerned about several men who had come into the area, illegal immigrants like themselves— but with a difference. The migrants, largely from rural areas of Latin America, and strong believers in the Hidden World, knew that these men were sorcerers, and skilled at shape shifting[37]*. They were known to assume the guise of coyotes.*

CHAPTER III: TOOLS OF ART

Iron is full of impurities that weaken it. Through forging, it becomes steel and is transformed into a razor-sharp sword. Human beings develop in the same fashion.
---Morihei Ueshiba

In the last Chapter, the reader was introduced to the concept that physical objects have an energetic field that can be impressed by events around them. In addition, the idea that a physical object can be 'read' by a process of breathing energy through it was also presented. In this chapter we will explore the nature of magickal objects, their purpose and their construction.

A magickal object is any item that is used for the specific purpose of aiding the magician in performing an act of magick. Such objects are generally only employed for that purpose and exist in a class that is entirely separate from normal everyday tools. Typically, most magicians have at least one such item, while many possess several.

Magickal objects have, like conventional ones, a Fire of their own. However, through concentrated development and specific use by the magician, they have much greater amounts of energy within them than mundane objects do. This energy is comprised of their own naturally occurring energetic field and that which is imparted to them by their user[38]. As such, they act as devices that help to focus the magicians personal Fire and to accentuate and add to it in much the same manner as a capacitor stores up and discharges an electrical charge.

Magickal objects tend to be of special construction for two reasons: the first is that by being constructed in a more exotic manner, they tend to help the magician to consciously separate their magickal operation from mundane acts, and in so doing help to create a complimentary psychological environment for their work to be undertaken. The second reason is that different materials have in and of themselves, different types of vibratory energy (just as different colors have different energies), with some being more conducive than others to the specific act of magick. In short, the Tool of Art is both a 'prop' to aid in a magickal operation and a necessary element in that operation at the same time.

Because of their nature and the fact that they can be so intimately a part of the magician's own energy, physical/energetic contact with them is normally limited to the magician and those that they trust. This tends limit the type and amount of energetic impressions the object receives and simultaneously ensures that it remains clear of anything that might be extraneous to the magician's purposes. For this reason, magickal Tools are also often initially cleaned using specific processes prior to their initial ritual use[39].

TYPES OF TOOLS

For most magicians the most common general magickal Tool of Art is either the wand or the dagger. These two items are often chosen for reasons of tradition, their appearance and for the physical materials that tend to comprise them. While there are certainly many other kinds of magickal Tools, these two are the most representative and versatile for most workings.

It is the dagger in particular that will be used as a reference for our study of Tools of Art from here on out. For followers of Hecate, the dagger or *machiaria*, represents one of Her sacred symbols and is considered the most basic Tool for the novice magician to create and wield.

Exercise 1: Cleansing the Tool of Art

Materials: For the sake of the following exercises, the student should procure a dagger for magickal use. This dagger is not to be used for any other function, save personal self-defense. Ideally, it should be double edged and come with a sheath for protecting it from the elements. In addition, it should be new if at all possible.

For cleaning the Tool, the student should also have clear, clean water, salt and some conventional stick-style incense. For scribing their Tool, a wood burner, or an etcher, along with red paint and a brush is recommended.

Before we can even begin to work with the Tool of Art, we must learn to properly clean it of any prior energetic impressions[40]. This is why the requirement was made to purchase a new item: the newer the item, the fewer energetic 'memories' it will have and the smaller the chore.

You should begin by wiping the item down with a conventional cloth, cleaning off any oils, dirt or fingerprints. Once this is done, the Tool-to-be should be set aside.

The next step is to prepare the ingredients for cleaning the energy of the Tool. The first ingredient for this is salt water.

To prepare this properly, you should first pour out a measure of salt onto a plain dish. Then, hold your hand over the dish and breath your Fire out and into the salt, visualizing it interpenetrating the salt and imparting it with a strong, cleansing energy.

Next, the water the salt will be mixed with should be infused with your energy using the same visualization. When you have finished doing this, mix the two ingredients together.

The charged saltwater should then be held in both hands, and once more, you should breathe your Fire into and through the mixture, again charging it with energy. Once this step has been completed, the salt water should be set aside.

The next component is stick incense. This should be lit and as it is held, it should be imparted with your Fire in the same manner as the previous two ingredients. Make sure to visualize your energy going up through the stick, through the burning end and out through the smoke.

You are now ready to clean your Tool of Art.

Grasping the Tool in one hand, sprinkle a tiny bit of the charged saltwater over the dagger (making especially sure to get some of this onto the blade). Visualize the energy of the Tool itself being cleansed as you do so. Then, take the incense and pass the dagger through it, envisioning the smoke taking away any impurities with it as it wafts up and over the blade.

Exercise 2: The Magickal Name and Personalizing the Tool of Art

The Tool is now ready for the next step, which is personalizing it. While some practitioners do not mark their Tools with their Magickal Name, many do and the student should either use a Name they already have, or formulate one. For those readers who are not familiar with what a Magickal name is, I will briefly explain.

A magickal, or 'craft name' as it is sometimes called, is a name used by the magician for purely occult purposes. On one level, it represents the magician's personality as a magick-user.

On a deeper level, the magickal name is literally an invocation of the inner personal power of the magician. When it is employed, it not only helps to bring the user into a magickal frame of mind, but also vibrates out into the universe as an expression of energy that is completely unique to them.

Magickal names are usually derived from names that are part of the culture that the magicians practice is based upon, or from terms in the language of that same tradition. However, magickal names can also be based on other sources, such as historical or fantasy literature. Whatever is the source, the magickal name that one chooses should be both intimate and empowering.

Numerological values can figure prominently in the selection and adoption of a magickal name, and some practitioners invest a great deal of time and research in this area, verifying that their chosen name has the right numerical balance. For those who agree with this idea, a numerology chart has been included in the Appendices along with some basic number meanings.

When the magickal name is scribed onto a Tool of Art using a magickal alphabet, the alphabet not only acts to conceal the magicians name from mundane eyes[41], but also helps to impart into the object's own energy the vibratory essence of that name, modifying this energy and personalizing the object. This is because magickal alphabets are by their nature and shapes, graphic designs that channel the primal energies extant in the Universe and with proper application, manifest them in a specific and focused manner in the same way that a set of components act to create a modern circuit board.

Like the Name, magickal alphabets are generally congruent with the tradition of the practitioner. For adherents of Northern magick for example, the Runes are used. Among European Witchcraft traditions the Theban alphabet is often employed. For followers of Hecate, there are two magickal alphabets that are the most appropriate to the time and culture when Her worship was at its zenith; Greek and Phoenician[42]. Both are presented in the Appendices for use in inscribing the Tool of Art and other purposes.

Depending on the type of material the Tool handle is made of, the letters of the Name can be carved, or wood-burned into the surface of the handle. Alternately, the letters can also be engraved onto the blade itself if the user has such skill and the tools to do this.

In keeping with my experiences with the Northern Tradition, the letters should also be painted. In Runic magick, this generally involves the use of red paint (with enamel being the most practical and durable for the task). Some practitioners also add a drop of their own blood into the paint[43]. This is a practice that I myself follow.

With the object carved, and in the parlance of the Northern Traditions, 'reddened' with our paint, the next step is the act of 'singing' or chanting over the letters themselves. This involves intoning the sound of the individual characters, while tracing their shape with a free finger (while simultaneously projecting Fire into the carvings of those characters). This action of chanting over each letterform acts to energize the carvings and invoke the specific powers inherent in the individual characters[44].

With these steps completed, the Tool of Art is now both literally and figuratively a part of the student. It is ready for the next stage, which is Training it.

Exercise 3: Training the Tool of Art

Training the Tool of Art, involves not only 'charging' the Tool with the student's Inner Fire, but also increasing its overall energy and focusing that same energy to a usable degree. This begins with the act of breathing Fire into the object.

You should begin by visualizing your Fire gathering within yourself. Once this has been done, take the object into your dominant hand. Then as you grasp the object breathe your Fire down through your arm, through your hand, and into and along the body of the dagger. As this is being done, you should observe the dagger with your Sight, noticing any changes in the space around the blade. A slight movement of the blade to the left or right may help in observing the energy field around the metal in the same manner that you observed your own Fire in our earlier exercises.

As a compliment to this exercise, you (or your partner) should explore this energy field together. There are several methods to do this.

In the first, you (or your partner) approaches the blade's tip with the flat of the palm of a free hand as you simultaneously breathe Fire through and down the blade. You or your partner should stop moving your hand towards it when you notice any effects.

Generally, these consist of a feeling of sudden warmth or coldness, or a 'tickling' sensation in the palm. This is the result of the energy field of the free hand coming into direct contact with the extended energy coming out of the blade.

A second method for exploration involves the use of a copper penny. Grasp the penny in your free hand, holding it lightly between your thumb and first two fingers (so that there is just enough of a grip on the penny to retain it, but so that it is also loose enough to wiggle freely).

Next, approach the dagger[45] and move the penny in the space around the dagger's tip and blade-edge with a gentle brushing motion (without making any physical contact with the blade itself). The reaction of the penny that you may experience has often been described as being similar to that of a magnet encountering another magnetic field of equal polarity (which in a sense, it is). There should be a sensation of resistance moving against the penny as it approaches the field around the blade.

Another exercise that should be investigated is a variant of one I mentioned in the chapter concerning the Inner Fire. As the reader will recall in the section on Seeking, the sender projects their fire outwards and attempts to make contact with the energy of the receiver and then 'feels' the receiver's presence with that extended energy.

In this case however, instead of using your naked palm, the Tool of Art is employed for the act of Seeking. Begin by having your partner extend their bare hand, facing it outwards towards the blade. Then, project your Fire into and through the blade into space and at your partner.

Use the same sweeping motion I described in Seeking; moving from outside the area of your partner's palm, across it and over to the opposite side (without making physical contact at any point). Repeat your sweep in the opposite direction. A distance of anywhere from a few inches to several feet of separation between you and your partner's hand is recommended.

During this exercise, both you and your partner should be aware of any sensations that are experienced as you move across their hand with the Tool. For the person wielding the Tool, this is often described as a sensation that is felt in the palm of the hand holding the tool that varies from what has been described as a 'tickle' or tingle, to a pronounced feeling of having brushed against something solid.

For the receiver, this can be the feeling of being touched by something as the blade moves across their hand, or sensations of coldness, heat or tingling that may or may not linger for some time after the experiment[46].

When you feel that you have had enough practice with this exercise, a variation worth attempting is to have your partner stand in front of you, but without holding out their palm. In this case, sweep across their entire body. As always, note any sensations that are experienced.

In addition to these basic explorations, you also should work with your Tool regularly. Practice breathing Fire through it, and more importantly, use your Sight to observe the behavior and shape of the energy field around it. Ideally, the blade's Fire should surround the blade itself to a distance of approximately two to five inches, with the energy at the very tip of the blade extending out into space anywhere from several inches to a foot (or more). The tip of this energy should be coherent and terminate in a distinctive pointed shape. If for some reason this is not the case, then you should focus your efforts on visualizing it doing so until it conforms to your Will.

Exercise 4: Dreaming with the Tool of Art

This next exercise in Training our Tool is a product of Latin-American techniques involving *Power Objects*, the shamanic equivalent of the Tool of Art. It has proven highly effective in helping to Train a Tool properly.

After a week of basic work and exploration with the Tool, you are ready to add this exercise to your other activities. Very simply, the Tool is to be taken at the end of the day by you to your bed. There you are to sleep with the Tool, preferably maintaining body contact with it through the night[47].

At this early stage, this exercise is to go on for no more or less than a period of two-weeks at which time it is to cease. Practice has shown that this amount of time is ideal for charging a Tool of Art and that longer periods can be detrimental to the process, and to the student's sleep-patterns[48].

Exercise 5: More Fiery Constructs

After you have completed a fortnight of sleeping with your dagger, the Tool is ready for the next level of Work. This involves the creation of Fiery glyphs with the Tool of Art, a step which itself leads to much more advanced magickal operations.

Drawing a Fiery Construct involves the same principles as the creation of an energy ball. To begin, gather your Fire and project it down your arm and out through the blade of your dagger.

However, instead of simply projecting it out into space, describe a circle in the air as you push your Fire outwards, visualizing the energy leaving the blade and being deposited in the air. The act of projecting the Fire and drawing the circle should be one continuous act with no break in your concentration or movement. It is generally best for to draw the circle slowly and center your efforts on making sure that it is complete and unbroken.

Once the circle is finished, you should withdraw the dagger from the area it was created in and take a moment to walk around the area. Note the disturbance in the air where it was created, and if you so desire, reach gently into the area with your free hand, feeling for any temperature changes or sensations of any kind as you do so. Properly done, you should note a definite presence in the area, along with marked changes in sensation as you touch it.

The next step is to destroy the construct. To do this, project energy through your Tool and wave the energized blade through the area several times. A variant of this operation is to hold out either your free hand or the dagger, and breathing in, visualize the energy of the construct being pulled back into you through the blade or your open palm and from there back into your body. This action is concluded using our basic grounding maneuver, making sure to visualize the energy you have just taken back into yourself being dissipated through your body.

After you are satisfied with the results of this exercise, the next step upwards involves creating a circle again, but this time adding a five pointed star, or pentagram, to the design. Again, you should observe your completed design[49].

You may note that the effects it exhibits are more pronounced than the circle by itself. This is due to the fact that the pentagram is by its nature a powerful magickal sigil and when encircled, radiates outwards with much more force than an empty circle would. Once again, when the exercise is complete, you are to destroy the construct in the same manner as described above.

A SIMPLE TATVIC IMAGE

One technique, borrowed from Ceremonial Magick, which may aid immensely in creating a Pentagram of Fire, involves daily meditation on its form using a Tatvic image'. The word *Tatva* is Sanskrit and means 'thatness', or 'principle' and a Tatva itself represents an aspect of reality.

As I came to understand them, Tatvic images, are both the graphic representation of a force (or diety) and because they symbolically express that same force, are simultaneously aspects of it[50]. In effect, the principle we are speaking of here is the ancient idea that the symbol of a powerful thing *is* the thing itself and as such, the symbol can be used to invoke the force it represents.

To understand and appreciate the use of Tatvic images, the reader is urged to try the following exercise: using a piece of cardboard, draw a pentagram inside of a circle. After creating this image, meditate on it daily. During the day, stop and take a few moments to concentrate on visualizing the energy form appearing in the air in front of you in precisely the same way as it was drawn on the cardboard image.

With a little practice, the energetic image will appear to you at will and you will have only to project your Fire into the energy form to activate it fully. Eventually, its image will become quite substantial, and you will be able to call up the energy construct almost as fast as you can think of it. More importantly, the force it represents will also manifest along with it, making it an energetic magical tool that you will have ready to serve you at a moments notice.

Exercise 6: A Basic Circle of Art

One of the most basic Fiery constructs that is employed in magickal work is the Circle of Art. Quite simply, it is both a protective enclosure and a focus-point for the magician's Will when Working magick (in much the same way that a camera lens focuses light). While we will discuss Magick Circles at greater length later, the student who has completed working with their

Tool to this point should know how to create a Circle in its most elementary form.

Begin by selecting a spot to stand and Work in. Preferably, this should be a level area that is free of debris and affords you a view of your immediate surroundings. Next, take your Tool of Art, and in the same manner as you created the earlier Circle and Pentagram, in the air, project your Fire outwards and describe a Circle around yourself on the ground. The Circle should be drawn clockwise and end at the same spot at which it was begun. Also, the process of drawing it must be a continuous act and you should visualize it rising up and around you as it is completed, surrounding the area around you with a luminous light and terminating at a place somewhere above your head into a cone shape.

Once the Circle has been completed, you should stand within this space for a few minutes, taking note of how different the spot now might feel to you. Not only do some students observe a feeling of greater focus and calm, but many also report a heightened sense of awareness about their surroundings, along with temperature changes and other phenomena. When you are satisfied that you have experienced enough, the Circle is to be destroyed in the same manner as our earlier constructs.

One important habit that should be developed at this early stage is that you should avoid leaving the confines of your Circle for any reason until your Work, whatever it might be, is completed. Walking out of a Circle is not only poor form, but disrupts the construct and in later operations can potentially open you to assault by negative energies that an intact Circle would have otherwise have protected your from.

Only if it is **absolutely** necessary to leave, you can 'cut' yourself out by pointing your blade at a point in the Circle and making a parting motion with the blade and your free hand (just as one would when opening a pair of curtains to pass through them), visualizing the circle opening up in that location. Once you step through, it is imperative that you repeat this maneuver and 'close it behind you, making it whole again. The reverse operation is used to enter an already extant Circle.

DOWSING AND PENDULUMS

Two other Tools that are part of the Magician's traditional toolbox also deserve examination. These are the humble dowsing rod and the pendulum. While they are by no means as versatile as the dagger or wand, or as romantic, they are well worth your time to learn about and master. We shall examine the dowsing rod first.

The art of Dowsing, sometimes referred to as 'water witching' has been with us for literally thousands of years. Classically, the dowsing rod is either a "Y" shaped piece of wood, a metal rod, or pair of rods. This tool is effective at finding things such as water and minerals, psychic energy spots and even answering questions. It is an easy tool to create, and I invite the reader do so and to try out the experiments that follow.

Exercise 1: Creating a Dowsing Rod

I personally prefer working with a pair of metal rods. While these rods can be made of many types of metal, my own experience is that copper is the best to work with, and the most easily available material. Brass is another popular metal, and there are many commercially made rods available in either.

To construct a pair of rods for yourself, two lengths of stiff, straight copper or brass wire stock are needed (either of which are easily available at any hardware store). For proper weight and length, I have found that they should measure from the tip of the users fingers to the elbow. Both rods are to be bent at a 90-degree angle approximately 4-6 inches down their length, creating a pair of "L" shaped objects (with the 'short' section acting as the handle or grip). As a useful added feature, the long ends can be tipped with glow in the dark paint or tape, making their movement more visible in low, or no light situations.

Some practitioners, including one I am a personally acquainted with, also prefer to encase the handle of their rods inside wooden dowels. This is done so that any motion that does occur happens strictly as the result of the rods action and not from anything inadvertently contributed to them by changes in the operators grip. I myself do not use this system, but I leave it to the reader to determine which arrangement is best and employ that.

Exercise 2: Working with the Rods

The newly constructed rods should be held loosely by the short end and perpendicular with your body. They should be grasped freely enough so that they are able to swing freely in your palms, yet not be dropped. The rods should also be kept as level as possible to help guarantee free movement on a horizontal plane.

Holding the rods outwards, formulate a desire to find something that is within your vision. The target can be a particular piece of furniture, a household pet or something else just as basic. Just as we had with the act of Seeking with a bare hand, start from an area outside the target, and sweep slowly towards it, maintaining the desire to find the object with the rods. As you do so, note any motion or reaction from the Rods.

Properly done, the rods will react as they pass in front of the object, either by vibrating, or more commonly, crossing together (in the case of a pair of rods), or by swinging around to point directly at the target. Students experimenting with the rods will also note that the rods will tend to cross more tightly as they pass directly in front of the target, and loosen up as they move away from it.

Exercise 3: Working With A Hidden Target

Once you have had enough opportunities to work with obvious targets, the next level is to work on finding a hidden one. The easiest way to arrange this experiment is to work in one room and attempt to locate something in another one (such as a family pet or a fellow resident). The rods are held level and you are to sweep them together in front of you in a slow arc, starting from the presumed outside area of the target, and moving across this target area until the rods cross.

Once the target has been 'found', you should then go and visually confirm its actual location. With practice, this can prove quite accurate and you are encouraged to try and locate targets at greater and greater distances.

Perfecting the Art of Dowsing with rods opens up many possibilities. Of course there is the traditional act of finding water and other resources. But beyond that, the rods can be used to locate other persons, determine the best location for events and in the case of modern mediums working with parapsychologists, to locate spirits. The only limitation of this humble, yet effective tool is the users imagination and innovation. It is for this reason, and their ease of use, that they have enjoyed great popularity through the centuries as a Tool of Art.

PENDULUMS

Another Tool that is related to the dowsing rod is the pendulum. The Art of hanging a weight on a string and divining answers goes back beyond recorded time. The ancient Egyptians for example, reportedly used a ring, suspended from a string over a bowl that was inscribed with symbols to divine answers to their questions. When the ring struck the symbols, the answer was spelled out for them in much the same way as today's "Ouija" board. In modern times, the pendulum enjoys use both as an oracle and like the rods, to locate things.

Exercise 1: Basic Work with a Pendulum

Perhaps the most elementary work with a pendulum involves divining 'yes' and 'no' answers to a question. To begin this experiment, you should procure a pendulum for yourself. The pendulum can be a simple weight suspended from a string, or a more elaborate device made from metal or crystal. Whatever the choice, the item should be comfortable to hold and have a long enough cord or chain to swing freely.

Grasping the end of the string, formulate a question in a meditative state of mind. As you do so, let the pendulum hang freely, and visualize a desire that the device answer your question by swinging in one direction for 'yes' and the other for 'no'. As you do so, you may note that the pendulum does in fact begin to move in a given direction. As a variant, some practitioners will perform this same exercise by initially twirling the pendulum slowly, then as they are formulating their question, observe which direction it tends to settle in. Either method is valid, and it is up to the reader to determine which is the most efficacious for them.

Exercise 2: Using a Pendulum as an Oracle

While 'yes' and 'no' answers will certainly suffice in many cases, it is also helpful to increase the versatility of the pendulum by employing a chart. There are many forms such a chart can take, ranging from diagrams with letters or numbers ranged in a circle or semi-circle (again being similar to the "Ouija" layout), to more complicated ones with specific answers for the pendulum to swing to. One such chart has been provided for the reader in the Appendices to copy and use, as they will. Alternately a personalized chart can also be created which will also serve just as well.

Whatever the layout, the exercise here involves using the pendulum to seek an answer, while suspending it over the chart. The movement of the pendulum and the sections it swings to should then to be noted. With only brief practice, the reader will find that such a chart can be a great aid in Working with a pendulum for divination.

Exercise 3: Working with a Map

A higher level of working with the pendulum involves the use of a map. In this case, a local map is spread out on a table, and the pendulum is held over it. The user then formulates a question that involves finding something on the map, with the map representing in the users mind a true representation of real space.

As you perform this experiment, slowly twirl the pendulum over the map area, being careful to note when and where on the map the pendulums revolutions appear to increase or decrease. Properly done, these areas can indicate where your target is—and is not. Once this has been done, you are then urged to go to the actual location and confirm whether or not your work was accurate.

This may sound difficult to a beginner, and there certainly will be a fair share of 'hits' and 'misses', but with practice, one's level of accuracy can and will increase. There are many practitioners who are incredibly accurate using this method, and if the accounts are to be believed, the pendulum and map combination has been effectively employed in the past to locate enemy forces during wartime, find lost pilots and hikers in the wilderness and even divine the location of hidden treasure or archeological artifacts. Given its successes, it is certainly a method worth exploring.

TALES FROM THE HIDDEN WORLD: THE PHANTOM OF IREDELL LANE

After spending some time as a security officer, I decided to 'move up' in the security profession and went to work for one of Los Angeles' many private armed patrols. These are overseen and licensed by the Police Commission and their main role is to provide mobile, armed security to businesses, neighborhoods, and individual homes on a subscription basis.

I had been patrolling in my marked car most of the night when I received a call to respond to home just a few minutes away. The panic-stricken caller had reported that someone had been in her backyard, trying to get into her home.

I raced to the location, and was met by the woman. She quickly showed me to a pair of wood and glass doors that opened out onto a small backyard. She told me that a man had been trying to get into the house through those doors. She described him vividly to me as a male Caucasian, with a long scruffy beard, and an overcoat.

As she gave me these details, I heard what sounded like boot-steps on wooden planking outside in the yard. I asked the woman if she had a deck outside or a Jacuzzi with a wooden platform, but to my surprise, she responded negatively. Then as I listened further, the boot steps seemed to change their location from the yard to somewhere above our heads.

Hearing the same thing, the terrified woman told me that she had an attic and led me to a small pull-down ladder. I loosened the snap on my holster and made my way up the ladder, shining my flashlight into the tiny space, certain I would find the intruder up there. But there was no one in the attic.

As I came back down, there was a knock on the door, and the woman opened it to admit two officers from the Los Angeles Police Department. I told the senior officer what had transpired so far. The officer could hear the footsteps as well, and at his orders, the three of us went outside into the yard, our guns drawn.

The steps were louder in the small yard, and clearly occurring somewhere above our heads. The three of us swung our flashlights up to the exposed roof, searching for the intruder, but although we could clearly hear the sounds on the roof, we saw nothing. Then as we continued to search, the footsteps changed in tone, assuming a hollow quality that then became a loud booming noise that suddenly was no longer on the roof, but inexplicably, up in the air above the roof. We continued to try to find the source of the noise, but the sounds rose up and away from us and into the sky.

The lead officer didn't say a word. Instead he holstered his weapon, turned off his flashlight and started back towards the house. At a loss for what to do next, I asked him what we should tell the woman. The officer turned, and asked me sternly. "About what?" I nodded, understanding his meaning instantly. Officially at least, nothing at all had happened in the yard.

When we came back inside, the woman asked me what we had seen, and I told her exactly what I was expected to say.

The two policemen then went back out to their car, and I used the woman's phone to call my dispatcher. The dispatcher was in a panic; while we had been in the yard he'd received dozens of calls from all over the area reporting that there were 'explosions' going off somewhere. He ordered me to seek out their source and I took leave of the bewildered woman and ran down to the police cruiser. I told the officers what the dispatcher had just reported, and we left together to scour the area. But although we could still hear low-pitched booming sounds in the air, the police and I found nothing and eventually parted company to resume our respective patrols.

That following week, the woman called for the patrol again. This time, it was daytime and two other officers from my private service were in the area. What they encountered shook them deeply.

According to one of the officers, (who I was friend enough with for her to take me into her confidence), they had responded to the residence just as I had. And like before, there had been the strange boot-steps. And, like me, they had gone into the yard to find the source.

But this time, they saw something. The officer told me that they had encountered a strange transparent apparition, shaped like a man that had vanished before their eyes. Unable to explain the event, they had done as I had, and told the poor homeowner that they had seen nothing.

As if all this was not enough, I encountered something a few nights after this. I was on a street below the same house, spotlighting a vacant home that was up for sale. Places like this were a breeding ground for trouble, attracting teens and vagrants, and I was alert for any sign that someone might be trespassing.

As I played the spot over the front, I saw someone dart into the walkway along the side of the home. I immediately radioed in my situation and got out to investigate. I was just in time to see the figure turn the corner and go into the back yard. I ran after him, identifying myself and yelling for the intruder to stop. But the figure ignored me and as I rounded the corner, ran into a small metal gardening shed. I drew my weapon and ordered the person to come out of the shed. But no one exited.

Finally, I threw open the door, expecting to see the suspect inside—but the shed was not only empty, there was no exit of any kind except the door I had just opened, nor was there any place to hide in. I realized then that I had been following the same phantom from the home above, or something very much like it. I briefly searched the area, and finding nothing, returned to my patrol car to report, once again, that 'nothing' had happened.

CHAPTER IV: DREAMING TRUE AND FARING FORTH

Our truest life is when we are in our dreams awake.---Henry David Thoreau (1817 - 1862)

For most people, dreams are little more than a psychological re-examination of recent events, or a symbol-laden glimpse into the workings of their subconscious. And while most dreams certainly *do* fit into this category, another type of dream, the True Dream, represents something far more profound.

Since ancient times, dreams have been considered an integral component of the Art. In classical Greece and ancient Rome, people often sought oracles from the dead through special rituals specifically designed to promote dreams. The ancient Egyptians were famous for their ability to not only interpret dreams, but also to send dream visions to others. And among the followers of Hecate, dreams have always had special importance, for Hecate is known in particular as the Sender of Dreams and the Giver of Visions.

The Art of Dreaming True is the ability to use dreams as a platform not only for receiving omens of the future, but also to use them as a window into this, and other realities--and to effect change in those realities. Like the Sight, it can be a natural gift, or a talent that can be developed. And even if a certain natural ability does exist, it can certainly be improved to a greater level of proficiency.

However, before we can explore this Art and the related skill of Faring Forth, one important matter needs to be addressed. This is the matter of proof.

Perhaps one of the greatest stumbling blocks to the successful development of this area of the Art (and perhaps to any of the skills associated with the Art as a whole) is doubt of an experience's accuracy. Over the many years I have taught students, perhaps the most common issue raised is the question whether what they were experiencing was 'real' or 'imaginary'.

Certainly, some of what occurs in a dream or in an act of Faring Forth is limited only to the individual's experience—but not all of it. One of the first things that I noticed when I was still developing this skill myself were examples where I either learned something that I could not have prior knowledge of[51], or experienced something while working with a partner that both of us collectively saw and which we had not agreed would be part of our joint experience prior to the event itself.

Generally such things can seem trivial at the time, and are often forgotten. But I urge the student to be alert for these small moments when they arise. Taking them into stock not only confirms the reality of a particular vision, but also goes a long way towards combating doubts that would otherwise completely impede any chance at progress in the Art of Dreaming and Faring Forth. To put it plainly, **a spontaneous, unplanned event that takes place for two people, regardless of the context they experienced it in, at the very least hints at, if not confirms, that a 'real' event has in fact occurred. In the same light, a phenomenon that occurs for one person that has also occurred for others performing the same maneuvers points to the same potential conclusion.** With this said, we will now examine the Art of Dreaming True in detail.

Exercise 1: Journaling Your Dreams

Because dreams work on and from the subconscious level, the most important primary step is to establish a method of focusing this otherwise involuntary activity and making it responsive to conscious desire. This is largely a matter of acknowledgement and reinforcement.

Such a task is best accomplished by the use of your journal, which up to now has been mainly used to record experiments in the Sight and other areas. For a period of one week or more, simply record every dream you have. This should be done in the morning when you awaken, and all of the details of your dreams should be included, no matter how inconsequential they might seem. If it is feasible, you should also arrange for a time during the night to get up and log your dream-experiences and if you awaken spontaneously (and especially because of a dream), make sure to jot down its details immediately upon doing so.[52]

DREAM INTERPRETATION

As for the content of dreams, the reader is encouraged to examine the symbolism within them for specific meanings. Dreams often have message for us about our future and understanding their symbolic language is an important key in deciphering this message.

However, it is not the purpose of this work to expound on the literally thousands of dream symbols there are, or their meanings—this job is better left to other sources. There are many fine books and internet pages available that will help anyone to construe the meaning behind anything that they encounter and the reader is encouraged to find a source for themselves that 'feels' the most accurate to them and to use that for their interpretations. Suffice it to say that any dream symbols that the reader interprets for himself or herself should be chronicled, and any waking life results compared with them.

Exercise 2: Willing the Dream-Self Awake

In the following weeks, you are encouraged to continue your journaling. However, in addition to this activity, as you are falling asleep, also mentally declare your desire to yourself to become **fully awake** and **fully aware** in your dreams. An affirmative statement such as the one James Donahoe proposed in his book *"Dream Reality"*, will more than suffice: *"I choose to have a conscious, controlled dream, and I choose to awaken in my dream and remember all of it in the morning."*

The purpose of this declaration is two-fold; the first is that it helps to ensure that the dream experience is fresh in your mind, and the second reason is that it will aid in the practice of programming your subconscious mind to respond to your conscious desires. It is in fact, an act of self-hypnotism, which once perfected, also offers great potential in many areas of self-improvement beyond dreaming itself.

There are two points where this statement can be effectively made. The first is during the normal course of the day as a repetitive affirmation. By repeating the statement over and over, you are implanting your desire for it in your subconscious, which will respond in kind.

The second opportunity is during the special stage between waking and sleeping states. This state occurs when the body has fully relaxed, but before actual unconsciousness has overcome the observer. It can be easily recognized by the series of rapid fire random images called "hypnogogic imagery" that occur in the mind as this true unconsciousness approaches the sleeper. It is here, while this is taking place that you must express your intentions[53].

Either or both of these methods can be used and you will find at some point in the process that you will in fact 'awaken' inside the context of your dreams. Once this has been attained, the next task will be to immediately acknowledge while in the dream-state that you *are* awake and then deliberately act within the dream in some manner, such as interacting with an element of the dream, or by changing some event. By doing so, you will not only intensify your level of awareness in the dream, but also the clarity of the dream around you. Castaneda suggested the tactic of gazing at an item in a dream, and then as it changes, switch ones focus to another object, a maneuver that acts to solidify awareness.

Learning to be conscious in a dream can be a difficult task. Like many students, I struggled in the very beginning with developing a waking state within my dreams. And for many weeks I tried to use suggestions to make this occur with no apparent success.

But then, one night, I found myself in a dream realizing that I was having a dream. The moment itself was a fleeting one, and when I awoke, I could only recall the portion when I had been aware of the act of dreaming. But it was enough to give me encouragement, and I continued with my efforts—and continued to have memory problems.

Eventually, I realized what I was doing wrong and added the suggestion to myself as I was drifting off, that I should not only be awake and aware, but be able to *remember* the dreams content. This ploy worked, and eventually I was able not only to be awake in my dream, but also able to choose whether I wished to remember the dream or not (based on whether I thought it was important enough to recall), all while still within the dream state.

Exercise 3: Controlling Dream Content

In the same manner that one can Will themselves awake in a dream, they can also influence its overall content. Just as in Exercise 2, an affirmative statement must be made to the subconscious. In this case however, the statement must be more detailed than simply wanting to be conscious or to recall the event. A statement such as *"I choose to have a conscious, controlled dream about a meadow in the forest tonight and to be awake in that dream and remember it when I awake"* is an example of a more detailed self-suggestion that one might use.

It is important to emphasize here that images and emotions play a large role in achieving a successful result at this stage. The subconscious is, more than anything else, a symbol-based level of awareness, and while words certainly help to convey an idea to it, the actual content and meaning of those words is what it truly understands.

Therefore, the 'feeling' and the visual image of the meadow are as significant as the words describing it (if not more so). Once you have managed to produce even a dream where only part of it coincides with your stated desires, you will have achieved a significant step in mastering your dreams. Like many other skills in the Art, practice is the key, and you should journal all of your results as you explore this area of knowledge.

Exercise 4: Dreaming with a Companion

As I stated in the introduction to this section, the ability to Dream True is more than just a process of being aware in a dream, or controlling its content. Dreams are in fact a reality of their own. The ancients knew that dreams were a bridge between the material world of waking consciousness and other realms of existence. Nowhere is this more sharply experienced than with partnered dreaming.

In this exercise, you are to coordinate the content of a dream with a partner, with both parties agreeing to have a dream with the same content. After dreaming, you and they are to compare your findings. If you have both done your work properly, you should find that you both achieve dreams that are either partially, or entirely the same in content as one another.

Once this step is achieved, the next phase involves a dream where the two parties agree not only to dream the same content, but also to meet one another in that dream and then compare what occurred afterwards. One example would be a dream where both parties agree to meet at a common location and interact there.

If both parties are lucid enough, and have enough control over their individual dreams, it is then possible for them to share this common theme, but also, and far more importantly, experience spontaneous events together at the shared location that were not pre-planned. In short, both dreamers can, with practice, experience not a 'dream' in the sense of a fantasy, but an actual event, taking place in another state of consciousness. The possibilities once this is achieved are as the reader might appreciate, potentially limitless.

One interesting side effect of concentrated work in lucid dreaming is what sometimes occurs as what we can call the daytime, or dream ghost. If a person becomes skilled enough consciously dreaming, they can sometimes appear to others who are awake, such as in the case of Tibetan 'tulpas'. I recall one incident where this occurred to me that serves as a good example.

It was late in the afternoon, and I was painting my bedroom in the commune my father ran. Then I felt as if I was being watched and I looked up and across from me at the windows of a house across the alley. Standing in the window was a student and a friend of mine named Judy (who, like myself, was exploring conscious dreaming).

Seeing her there surprised me because I knew that the apartment was vacant and that there was little likelihood that Judy could have entered it (or would have had any reason to have done so). And I also knew that at that time of day that Judy was supposedly napping in a room just down the hallway from mine.

I looked away for just a moment, and when I looked back, she was gone. Curious, and sensing that something strange was happening, I immediately left my room and went down the hall to confirm that she was not in the building with me.

But right then Judy came out of her bedroom. She was dressed in exactly the same clothes I had seen her in, and it was obvious that she had just awakened from sleep. Realizing that it would have been physically impossible for her to get from the third floor of the apartment next door and all the way across to her room in our building in such a short length of time, I asked if she had had a dream about watching me paint.

Judy looked quite surprised and told me that she had had such a dream, and that the dream had been strange because she had seen me through the window next door. Then I told her what I had just witnessed.

FARING FORTH

Faring Forth, or the ability to travel out of body, or to project the minds eye to see another place or time, is closely related to the Art of Dreaming. Both employ essentially the same level of consciousness and occur on the same level of reality. Not surprisingly, a talented Dreamer can project himself or herself into the vision of someone who is Faring Forth and vice versa fairly easily.

Even if the reader has managed to master their ability to Dream True, these next exercises should definitely be undertaken. Faring Forth affords a level of control and versatility that may not always exist in the dream state. And for those students who are still struggling with lucid dreaming, this skill might offer an easier pathway to accomplishing some of the same objectives.

Some might feel that the initial steps in this section are tantamount to mere daydreaming. And in a sense they are. The act of visualizing is, like the basic dream, the foundation from which the experience of something truly real can arise. What might begin as a simple picture in the minds eye can transform into a reality that can be experienced by others and effect them just as surely as something conventionally created. It is, as with all things in the Art, a matter of degree and proper focus.

Exercise 1: An Inner Retreat and Other Visualizations

Our first exercise involves visualization, coupled with meditation. You begin, as always by Stilling the Waters. When you have achieved a level of calmness, relax your body as much as possible.

When you feel that you are fully relaxed, you should visualize yourself sitting in a calm, quiet place. The scene itself should be one that inspires peace and tranquility for you. Each element of the scene should be pictured as clearly as possible; every texture, every smell and even the feeling of warmth or coolness should be described until the setting is sharp and clear in your mind.

This vision, or Inner Retreat serves two purposes: the first is that it is good exercise for practicing the process of visualizing a specific scene, and given its nature, can also provide an inner haven for its creator to visit at any time and place, providing them with a calm safe place to center themselves in. This elementary work should be repeated until the imagery comes easily and clearly to the mind's eye with little effort.

Simultaneous with this, you should also explore visualizations of other locations and settings, such as different terrains and environments (and even other planets). And if a partner is available, you and your partner should also take the opportunity to practice visualizing a common location together.

Initially, this should be done with an eye only towards the detail of each person's visualization. However, as practice continues, there should also be an awareness of anything that occurs spontaneously for either party (addressing not only the issue of proof, but also honing the skill of both persons to see common events together accurately).

As a compliment to this, one member should on occasion visualize something that they do not tell their partner about (starting with a primary element and working upwards in complexity). And, at the end of such an exercise, both people should mutually examine their experiences and if the spontaneous element was experienced, taken note of. While this might sound a bit daunting at this stage, with practice, it is actually rather common for an uninformed partner to see either exactly what the other person created, or something similar to it.

Exercise 2: Creating an Astral Self and Arming the Sprit

With a scene visualized clearly, the next step is the creation of a 'dream self.' Essentially this is the conscious act of describing oneself in an idealized form that is powerful and self-assured, and is fully equipped for anything that might lie ahead. There are no set criteria for this image: you can choose any age, race or sex with the only provision being that the form that you see for yourself embodies power, and inspires confidence and ability.

One method for doing this is to visualize your earlier retreat spot and then have a mirror or a reflective body of water appear within this space. See your idealized reflection in either surface. And, as with the scene itself, every aspect of that reflection should be described with care and attention to detail.

In addition to your overall appearance, you must also see yourself wearing your Tool of Art and any other items that your feel are personally significant and powerful. From this point on, whenever you Fare Forth, this new self-image should be the one you see yourself as being. And in referring to this image with yourself, you should also use your magickal name.

Far more than a basic exercise in visualization, these actions provide several important benefits for the aspiring Magician. Not only do they create a positive self-image to act from as an inner base, but with continued affirmation, construct a literal presence in the reality generally referred to as the Astral Plane. At the same time, these visualizations also help to establish a direct link between the Magickal Self, the Name and the Tool of Art within this same realm (making each more effective there).

Exercise 3: The Astral Temple

The next exercise involves the creation of what is called the Astral Temple. The Astral Temple is essentially the idealized image of a place of power for the student; a place where they feel both security and power.

The setting itself can be anywhere that expresses power and magick for the individual, such as a castle, an ancient temple, a mountaintop or the like. Just as you did with your Inner Retreat, every aspect of the Temple should be carefully visualized from the most basic stones in the walls to any items of furniture. Once it has been thoroughly visualized, the Temple, like our earlier Tatvic images, will tend to come sharply to mind from that point onwards, and with less and less effort.

At this point the reader might ask what the purpose of this particular exercise is. One is to help assist with inner development. In one school I trained with, a version of the Astral Temple was used as a backdrop for the student to visualize themselves overcoming personal obstacles, through a process of re-framing their self image within it. And in another, the Temple was used as a platform for rehearsing and learning martial arts techniques.

But the other use of the Temple is for learning knowledge that would otherwise be inaccessible to the student's conscious mind through what are called the Akashic Records. This can be accomplished when the Temple image includes a library of some kind. As an astral archetype, the library allows for the visitor to access information from their subconscious (and the greater universe that it is connected to) using the friendly and understandable interface of a special book[54] (or alternately from an item like a crystal ball, special mirror, or even a wise 'guide figure'). The reader is strongly urged to add such a feature to their own Temple and explore the virtually limitless benefits that this can offer them[55].

Exercise 5: The Cord and Torch

The Art of entering a deep trance state is one of the oldest aspects of the Art, and its use spans many cultures through the millennia. Shamans, witches, priests and magicians have all employed a wide variety of techniques over the centuries to help them achieve this specialized state of consciousness. The Egyptian priesthood for example, employed trance in their ritual work with the famous false door, or "Door of the Sky" to project their Ka. The Classical Greeks used trance for achieving oracular visions and in Pre-Columbian Mesoamerica, this same state was used in conjunction with specialized rituals and hallucinogenic drugs to help their priest/rulers communicate directly with the Gods.

Today, many of these ancient practices are still accessible, along with others that are the product of more modern times. And they are still used for the same purposes, although the names of the operations might have changed. Trance is used today for everything from astral projection, to hypnotherapy, to what is now called Pathworking.

The methods used to achieve it vary in imagery, complexity and effectiveness. One such method, which I became acquainted with early in my personal studies, was Brian Jameison's "Light Switch" method, which he presented in his book, *"Exploring Your Past Lives"* to help facilitate past-life regression. It employs the visualization of a modern light switch on various parts of the body that are 'turned off' to induce relaxation and 'turned on' again to reenergize the subject's body.

While I found it to be one of the most effective of the techniques available to the public at the time[56], and used it for many years, it still had certain disadvantages. The most glaring problem I and my students encountered was that the process of 'turning off' the body, and then 'turning it back on' tended to be a bit jarring for those who used it.

Eventually, I came to realize that the utilization of different imagery and energetic maneuvers could potentially produce a more profound trance state with less stress experienced by the subject. The issue became to find the right combination of imagery and maneuvers to achieve these improvements.

My answer came to me during a meditation and straight from the Lady Herself. I was told to use two ancient, sacred symbols of Hers: the cord (or rope) and the torch. Up to that point, I had associated these two items strictly from a religious standpoint; with the cord representing both the things we are bound to and bind us, and the torch as the light of wisdom and illumination. But as I considered Her suggestion, I began to appreciate their use from a purely metaphysical standpoint and realized that they in fact offered profound possibilities. This lead in turn to direct experimentation and their effect together was nothing less than dramatic. I not only reached a deeper state of relaxation, but also came out of the trance state more fully, and with more energy. Her method, which I came to call the Cord and Torch, is presented here for students to evaluate for themselves.[57]

Materials: If you have a partner, have them read the following italicized section to you. If not, employ a tape recorder and read the material into it, then play it back as you perform this exercise.

As always, the room that you are working in should be darkened, or dimly lit. Begin by loosening any clothing or belts that would otherwise distract you and remove any jewelry or footwear. Turn on the tape recorder, or have your partner begin reading the following:

First, close your eyes and take three deep calming breaths. Relax your body.
When you are ready, feel your feet as they lie on the floor. Notice if they seem tense in any way. Then visualize a silver cord with a large knot, wrapped around your right ankle. See the knot loosen and watch the cord fall away.
As it does so, feel the tension draining out of your foot like water and completely relax. If this does not happen right away, repeat the process until it is fully at rest. Then do the same for your left foot.
(When you are ready, raise your right index finger to signal me that we are ready to proceed.)
Next, feel your calves, and picture a knotted cord around each one. Loosen the knots and as the cords fall away let the tension release from the muscles there.
(When you are ready, raise your right index finger to signal me that we are ready to proceed.)
Move on to your thighs and repeat the process.
(When you are ready, raise your right index finger to signal me that we are ready to proceed.)

A SORCERER'S BOOK OF ART 73

Now see a cord wrapped around your waist like a belt. Unite it in your mind and feel the stress and tension leave your hips, lower back and abdomen.

(When you are ready, raise your right index finger to signal me that we are ready to proceed.)

By this point, the lower portion of your body should be completely at rest.

Now move upwards to your chest and see a cord tied around it. Untie this knot and as the cord falls away, feel the muscles of your chest and upper back relax.

(When you are ready, raise your right index finger to signal me that we are ready to proceed.)

Next, visualize knotted cords wrapped around your wrists. Loosen the knots and feel your hands relax completely.

(When you are ready, raise your right index finger to signal me that we are ready to proceed.)

Now see a pair of cords around you upper arms and perform the same action.

(When you are ready, raise your right index finger to signal me that we are ready to proceed.)

When your upper torso and arms are at rest, picture a cord wrapped around your throat. Untie the knot there and feel the muscles of your neck relax.

(When you are ready, raise your right index finger to signal me that we are ready to proceed.)

Finally, see a cord encircling your head at the level of your third eye. Untie this last cord and feel the muscles of your face and head relax completely. Let any remaining tension drain completely out of you.

(When you are ready, raise your right index finger to signal me that we are ready to proceed.)

With your body completely relaxed, see yourself floating in a safe, comforting darkness. Then see the darkness brighten around you, and open onto the scene you desire.

[The narrator should go on to describe the scene in detail for the subject at this stage. If the subject is working alone with a tape recorder to provide the narration, the description of the scene can either be made on tape prior to the journey, or this section can be left blank for the subject to visualize].

Fare into this place.

[The journey is then undertaken, with the subject's partner recording what is experienced and helping the subject with guided imagery where needed].

When you have completed your business, see yourself returning to the darkness. See it surround you. Then feel yourself back into your body.
It is time to reawaken.
Visualize a glowing ball of energy in your solar plexus—your Inner Fire coming to life within you like a torch in the darkness. See this energy gather itself up into a ball of pure luminescence. Watch as it grows in size and gains in brightness.
Now see the energy from your Fire flowing outwards through your body, down through your trunk, through your thighs and down and out through your feet. As it does so, feel life and healthful energy returning to these areas.
Flex your toes and tighten the muscles of your calves.
When the lower half of your body feels awakened, see the energy from this ball of light flowing upwards from your solar plexus, up through your chest, down your arms to your fingertips and up through your neck and out the top of your head. Repeat this process until each of these areas feels completely reawakened.
Flex your fingers and shoulder blades. Then take in three deep breaths.
Slowly open you eyes.
When you feel you are ready, roll to one side and sit up. **But avoid the temptation to do so abruptly as it may cause extreme light-headedness, dizziness or nausea.**

As always, at the end of this exercise, record your experience in your journal, or relate it to your partner so that they can document the event. You will note, that with practice, that this exercise will become easier, and that you will be able to not only relax your body more rapidly, but also enjoy a more and more profound trance state.

Exercise 6: Projecting the Spirit-Body

Our next level of our Work involves deepening our skills significantly through the projection of the Spirit-Body. The Spirit-Body (or Fetch as it is sometimes called) is the projected essence of the Magician that they travel within on their astral journey. With enough practice, not only will the practitioner experience their travels more vividly, but be able to project an energy form that is both tangible and visible to others.

The first step in the deployment of this Spirit-Body begins with the Cord and Torch method that we have already explored. Loosen all the cords around your body, and when you are completely relaxed, visualize yourself as you are, lying on the floor.

Then, see yourself rising up from your position, moving a few feet away in space, and then returning to your body. A short journey out through a door, down a hallway and back is ideal. As always, every detail of this brief trip is to be visualized as clearly as possible.

This set of maneuvers should be repeated and the distances traveled gradually increased. If you have a partner, their task will be to observe for any phenomena that occurs (including any visual evidence of the other person's spirit form, temperature changes in the room, etc.) Eventually, you should undertake to venture outside of your residence for short distances, being careful to observe your environment for anything that could help verify the accuracy of your experience (for example; the activities of other people, the movement of traffic and the like). Once these journeys have concluded, you are urged to re-visit the environment that you traveled through and check it against your astral perceptions for accuracy.

A higher level of this same Work involves projecting out of your body in the manner I have described, but with the added intention of appearing to your partner (or to other observers) in a specific shape. This ability, once fully cultivated, is the true root of many tales concerning spectral animals and apparitions that are in fact the projected astral forms of human practitioners. The central idea here is to envision not only faring forth, but also as doing so in a highly specific form. Experimentation and continuous practice are the keys to success in this advanced area.

FAMILIARS AND FARING FORTH

Almost everyone is familiar with the tales from medieval and Renaissance Europe of Witches who had special relationships with their animals, and reportedly traveled out into the world inside their animal's bodies. As fantastic as this may sound to some, the ability to do this is actually rather simple once the basics of Faring Forth have been learned. However, it also requires two things that cannot be either be taught nor artificially created: trust and cooperation.

For someone to work magick with an animal familiar, there must be not only a bond between the two parties, but also a 'comfort level' when it comes to magickal workings. However loving they might be, many animals are not at ease with magick and it is only with those that are, that this method of Faring Forth is truly possible. While an animal can certainly be encouraged in this direction by bringing it into the magickal environment (such as allowing it to be present during an exercise), the final choice truly rests with the animal itself and this cannot, and should not, be forced.

Assuming that the student is fortunate enough to live with an animal that they share a bond with, and the animal is one who is also inclined towards magick, the exercise itself is relatively easy. As many pet-owners[58] will attest, a natural communication normally exists between human and animal--provided that the human is attuned enough to their animal partner to understand it. Simply put, the act of Faring Forth in an animal is essentially a matter of communicating the desire to do so to the animal, and if permission is perceived, following through with the act.

Assuming that the animal partner is agreeable to the idea (and a surprising number are), you are then to perform the same basic actions involved in sending forth the Spirit-Body. However, instead of projecting out and down a hallway, you must picture yourself appearing inside the animal's consciousness—while perceiving the world from the animal's perspective as you do so.

The first time that this is attempted, it can be rather disorienting, especially with regard to visual input. We humans are used to seeing in color for example, and many animals see in black and white, or only in limited colors. In addition, there may be a change in the area of one's visual field. In my own experiments for example, I noted that the area I could perceive through my cat's eyes seemed wider and flatter than what I was used to perceiving with my human eyes.

Your first trip together should be a short one, with the act of being inside the animal partner's body being more than sufficient. Then, as you and your pet become more and more relaxed with the sensation, you should try staying with your animal partner as they move about, remaining within them for longer and longer periods and over greater distances. If nothing else, this process will provide deeper insights into the nature of your animal partner's existence and how it perceives the world (not to mention the opportunity to potentially share in some rather unique adventures).

Eventually, and with enough communication, a point can be reached where the animal partner will be willing to travel to specific locations with 'their human' riding within them[59]. This then is the classic fable, made real.

It should also be noted (although if a real bond exists between human and animal this statement is quite unneeded) that **the safety and well being of the animal must be of primary importance at all times** in this work. Unwarranted risks should not be taken with your animal familiar under any circumstances!

FARING FORTH WITH OTHER BEINGS AND GHOST RIDING

The ability to ride an animal familiar astrally is itself a basic skill in the Art and embodies the basic esoteric principle that consciousness can be projected and experienced from within **any** physical housing. Once mastered, this same skill also offers many possibilities beyond this initial level.

For example, not only is it feasible to Fare Forth within a willing host, but it is also possible to do so with beings that are not on intimate terms with the magician, nor necessarily consenting. A good exercise that can illustrate this, (and which can also lend itself to refining the basic skill of Faring Forth within another entity) involves riding an insect (or some other small life form).

In the classic version of this, the magician chooses a nearby insect and visualizes their conscious occurring within the being while viewing the world through its eyes. Once this connection has been made, the next step is to direct the insect to move in a given direction, or perform a specific action. Accuracy and success are then gauged by the simplest of standards: whether or not the being responds as it was commanded to.

Even though the Art of Faring Forth is certainly no longer new to me, I for one, still spend many a pleasant afternoon Faring Forth within a bee or a similar creature for the valuable practice that this affords. Naturally, my actions are performed with the same concern for the welfare of the insect as with an animal familiar and I urge the student to keep to the same standard. Life, no matter how different it might be from ours, is to be respected and cherished for the precious gift that it truly is.

Another variant of Faring Forth involves riding beings that are no longer alive. This is the Art of Ghost Riding. Unlike their living counterparts, ghosts are composed purely of energy, or spirit, and not only is general contact and work with them made easier for this reason, but also the act of Faring Forth within their 'skin'. And like an animal that possesses abilities different from our own, a true ghost or an echo ghost (please see Chapter 10, Ghosts and Exorcism for definitions on these two types) can perform feats that are not possible with a flesh and blood body, such as the talent they have for passing through walls and the like.

I encountered this Art myself quite by accident, and as the result of an incident which occurred my early childhood. It began with a haunting. Like a lot of practitioners of the Art (and parapsychologists for that matter) I grew up in house that was haunted, and the incident, like many others that occurred in that same home certainly had a great deal to do with forming my adult interests. This event was certainly no exception:

While I was in the kitchen getting some juice, I felt as if I was being watched. I turned around to see the semi-transparent form of a disembodied head floating about a foot over the floor, coming towards me. Terrified at this sight, I retreated from the kitchen and out the back door.

The following day, I went to school and told my friends about the event. One of them was particularly affected by my account and told me a tale of his own. It turned out that the same time that I had seen the head coming into my kitchen, he had had a vision of my kitchen from floor level, and had seen me run from him without understanding why.

While some could ascribe the apparition I saw as being a type of astral projection on his part, both he and I had a different sense of it altogether. We were both certain that he had somehow spontaneously 'hitched a ride' with the entity that I had encountered, and this startling idea stayed with me for many years.

It was not until I was well into my thirties that I confirmed for myself that this was in fact the case. My corroboration came to me in the form of a lucid dream. In the dream, I encountered a 'true' ghost that was making its nightly rounds of the area it haunted. But, as I realized what it was, I suddenly found myself looking out at the world around me through the ghost's eyes. Together, the two of us went through a wall, up through a garden and into a nearby home. Then the dream ended, but certainly not my curiosity.

Eventually, I experimented with this process in a waking state, and having a more than ample supply of spirits to deal with, found that this skill was actually rather easy to perform, being in a sense, a type of reverse possession.

As for the specifics of my experiments in this area, I decline to elaborate further. However, I will state that the only impediment to successfully Riding a Ghost is where the entity in question is a strong one and is unwilling to share its form for this purpose. Should the aspiring magician have the chance to do so, I invite them to try Ghost Riding out for themselves.

CHAPTER V: PAST, PRESENT AND FUTURE LIVES

Finding myself to exist in the world, I believe I shall, in some shape or other always exist.--*Benjamin Franklin*

The question of whether we survive death has obsessed Mankind since our species was evolved enough to ponder the universe. Countless thinkers and mystics through the ages have speculated about this subject, and their answers have spawned many religions that all claim to possess the ultimate answer to this profound riddle.

As for myself, I *know*, rather than simply *believe*, that I have lived before. I didn't start out wanting to know anything about life after death—instead, as I stated at the beginning of this book, the knowledge came to me at a very young age, and with it, an absolute certainty about the matter. I described the event itself in my book, *"Crossroads: The Path of Hecate"* and I reproduce it here, begging the reader's indulgence for any repetitiveness:

... I found myself on a grassy plain and a voice told me that I was in Montana in the year 1880. The dream then showed me the life that I had lived there, which I experienced on a vivid, first person basis, up to and including my own death.

Then the dream ended, and I sat bolt upright in bed knowing two things with absolute certainty; first, that I had lived before and secondly, that magick existed in the world and it was my destiny to find and master it.

Years went by and I had occasion to visit the ruins of Palenqué in the Mexican state of Yucatan. I knew from the moment that I arrived that I had also lived there in a former life, as a priest. As soon as I saw an opportunity, I snuck away from the other tourists and sought out a specific building that had called to me since my arrival. It was off to the side, and half covered by the jungle.

Somehow, I knew the place, and I walked straight inside it without hesitation. The inside back wall was covered with the grime of centuries of jungle growth, but I saw it with other eyes. Inexplicably, I knew there was a specific mural behind it, carved in the stone and I could see its details of it clearly in my mind. I reached out and brushed away some of the dirt. There, under my hands was the very mural, exactly as I had pictured it. I had come home once again...

At the time of these two events, I didn't have a name for what I had experienced. It was only much later, when I was exposed to the beliefs of Buddhism, Hinduism and other Eastern systems, that I was able put a label on what I already knew to be true.

The question that eventually arose for me was not so much 'who'[60] I had been—but why. And I believe that *this* issue is the most important aspect of this phenomenon (and the one which is most often missed by today's "New Ager's" who tend to get lost in the 'glamour' of it all).

But before I go any further, for those who are unfamiliar with the physics of reincarnation, a brief introduction is in order. To start with, the soul, being energy, is indestructible. As is the way with all energy in the Universe, rather than being annihilated at death, the soul simply changes form, and residence.

This is not a haphazard process: instead the lives that we live follow a pattern that is established by the nature of our most basic inner essence, and by what we learn from each life as we live it—or what we fail to learn.

This pattern is called Karma in the Orient. For many Eastern schools, the most basic purpose of this life is to resolve the issues in it that have been a part of our other lives, and in doing so, move onwards into more favorable existences that ultimately unite us with the Divine Essence that spawned us in the first place.

And where does all this fit in with the process of mastering the Art? **The answer is that it is nothing less than one of its most important foundations and the very dividing line between those who would truly master the Art, and those who would only learn a few occult 'tricks'.**

Many magicians have sought immortality, thinking that it was the ultimate quest. But in reality, immortality is *not* the summit of the mountain. In fact, if one believes in reincarnation, immortality it is a *given*—and a mere foothill at the base of the true climb. That spiritual ascent is the process of understanding of the true nature of former lives and mastering the lessons of those same lives, thereby ensuring that all future existences from here onwards are changed positively.

If as I believe, reincarnation is a fact, then the question of what we are doing in our present life about the Karma we have accrued from past lives becomes the most critical issue we can ever face. Given the agreement of countless Eastern masters of the Art, I think this is a safe assertion and certainly worthy of the reader's consideration.

As I have experienced it, the path up our mountain begins with an expansion on the Cord and Torch exercise we explored in the preceding Chapter.

Exercise 1: Exploring Your Past Lives: A Preliminary Exercise

Here we will employ a variation of Jamison's imagery and the Cord and Torch method of inducing a trance. There are of course, many alternative methods that have been used to explore past lives, but I have found that the following approach is the friendliest and easiest to work with. Once again, the use of a tape recorder, or your partner acting as your reader, is recommended:

After using the Cord and Torch method to completely relax, let yourself drift for a few minutes in a safe, restful darkness. When you are ready, visualize the darkness around you slowly brightening until you see yourself standing in a long hallway.

It made of white marble with a red carpet running down its length. To either side are closed doors made of a dark wood adorned with heavy brass knobs and hinges.

Look at each of the doors, and then tell yourself to go towards the door that leads to the last life that you lived before the present one.

See the door open and as it does, walk through it. And as you go in, see yourself in the body that you inhabited before your present one.

Look down at it and notice any details. Is it young? Is it old? Is it male or female? What color is its skin?

As you will, bring up one of your hands and look at it—see if it is rough or fine. And if you are dressed, determine what kind of clothing you are wearing.

Then look around you and notice if it is day or night.

Now look at the features of your surroundings. If you are in a building, ask yourself what kind of structure it is and note how it is furnished. If you are outside, what kind of environment is it?
*Your next step is to ask the question of **when** you are, and what country you are in. Let whatever answers come as they will.*
Next, try to determine your name. If you cannot discern your entire name, then endeavor to at least learn what your first name was[61].
Lastly, see what is happening around you. This is the first in a series of events that represent significant points in this former life.
When you have seen enough of this first event, see yourself moving forwards to the next significant moment that occurred in that life.
Once again, look around you for every detail of the event.
Then move forwards again to the next moment.
If there are other people in any of these scenes, note which of them seem to be the most prevalent. Try to determine who they are, and if possible, who these people are now in your present existence. Let whatever answers come as they will.
When you are done, see yourself going back into the darkness, and from there returning back into your body.

You may be surprised by what aspects of the past are still being expressed in your present existence, and equally so by who might still be playing a role in it. It is not uncommon for example, for someone who was a wife or a lover in a former life to be a sibling today, or for someone who was a tormentor or a competitor to still be acting in that role now, in another guise. As always, record your experiences at the end of the exercise.

THE BENEFITS OF EXPLORING YOUR PAST LIVES

One immediate advantage that comes from exploring past lives is that they can help us to identify present life patterns and both open the door for making important personal changes and enable us to move in greater harmony with our true selves. For example, if you keep having conflicts with a certain kind of person in this life, the root causes of that friction may become apparent as the legacy of a former life. Understanding such a situation can lead to a greater comprehension of the issue, and also reveal potential solutions to reverse such problem areas, or address otherwise unconscious life-patterns.

As another example, you may find your self drawn to a certain kind of activity, and there might well be a reason that has its origins before your were born into your present life. Realizing this may afford you the opportunity to view that same activity more clinically—and thence allow for either re-patterning your habits, or affirm for you that it is an element that you truly need in your life. Certainly, knowledge of the self, in any form is valuable and knowing about the details of your past lives gives you a much broader view of your existence than what is afforded by only studying the present one.

The exploration of former lives also leads, like the act of affirming conscious dreaming, to a wider expansion of the ability itself. Many people, who begin with basic exercises like the one I have presented, find that after time, that the memories of other lives begin to come to them either with much less effort, or completely spontaneously.

This was certainly my case. Half or more of the lives that I was eventually able to remember came of their own accord, or were reawakened in me by something like a particular scene, the time of day, or through vivid dreams. These additional memories were in a sense, a chain reaction that was initiated by my initial explorations, and many of my students have experienced the same door opening up for themselves, and for the same reasons.

FUTURE LIVES AND THE NATURE OF TIME

There is another significant benefit from working with past lives that is generally overlooked by those who explore the subject. This is the ability, with practice, *not only to view prior existences, but also to learn about the next life that comes after this present one. And with this, not only do we have the opportunity to merely 'preview' the next life, but also to actively ensure that what we have learned in this life is sent forwards for us to benefit from again.* This highly important Work is a combination of past-life regression, coupled with conscious manipulation of the time-stream. But before we can successfully manage this feat, we must understand the nature of time itself.

As most average people understand it, time is a linear affair, with the past coming into the present and from there, into the future. It is generally believed by the masses that once the past is behind us, it is gone forever, that the present consists of only our reality and that the future is both unknowable and unchangeable. In fact, this is as ridiculous and restricted a notion as the idea we all once held that the world was flat.

Time is far from linear, or limited to one stream. Time actually occurs on multiple planes of existence--and simultaneously. There is in fact no 'one' past, present or future. Instead there are many pasts that are still occurring, many presents that span multiple realities, and many futures. Or, to make the statement even plainer than this: there is no past, present or future, there simply *is* existence. Such terms are only convenient reference points that we use to describe reality, but are, in and of themselves, complete fictions.

But rather than let the matter go with this statement, let us examine each so-called component of time in more detail, starting with the past. A good example of the true nature of the past can be seen with many ghost stories one hears from Gettysburg National Battlefield.

Every year, visitors to the battlefield report seeing visions of the battle, apparently re-playing itself. Some conventional experts in the paranormal respond to these accounts by asserting that these scenes are 'echoes' of this Civil War event. But in the same breath they also often state that the spirits of the men in these scenes are somehow 'trapped' in these moments.

And yet, if we pull back and truly examine this assertion, its flaws become obvious. If as we normally believe, the past is truly gone, then a moment of it could not logically re-play itself. And it is also equally impossible for the participants of a past moment to be somehow trapped, because by definition these individuals no longer exist, and therefore cannot 'be' anything. But despite all this, visitors to the monument continue to experience moments from a battle thought to be long over.

However, if we apply the idea that there is no linear time, then these visions can be explained with fewer 'holes'. If the past as such does not exist, then these scenes are not re-runs at all, but are moments of an alternate 'present' that has opened up for the observer like a cosmic window. And by extension, the soldiers in such a scene are not 'trapped' at all, but are instead experiencing what is for them the present: for the soldiers, the Civil War is not over by any means, but is still occurring. Certainly, this interpretation begs the reader's attention as another hypothesis to explain some of the 'ghost stories' that we hear of.

An event that I personally experienced falls into this category or near enough to it to merit examination. It occurred on August 9, 1985:

I had taken a group of students up to Pt. Reyes National Seashore on what was one of many trips into the field. On this occasion, we hiked into the park near dusk and made our way up to an open meadow. At one point, after my students had concluded their various experiments, I felt the urge to go out into the middle of the meadow and simply feel all around me for any strong magickal currents (using the Seeking method I have described earlier in this book).

At first, I did not perceive anything unexpected. There were the usual currents of energy coming from San Francisco and its surrounding communities which were produced by it's large population of occultists, and occasional 'spikes' of activity elsewhere. But the real surprise came from the west, far out to sea and somewhere in Asia.

There, I received the strong impression that something truly terrible had happened. The most immediate analogy that came to my mind was that the

sky itself was bleeding—caused by some act of man. Almost as soon as this imagery came to me, I knew that a nuclear weapon had been—or would be--detonated.
A profound depression came over me. Filled with dread, I decided that it was time to leave the meadow. As we descended back down to the main trail, the trees in the area, which were largely devoid of leaves, only served to heighten my sense that great devastation was imminent.
The next day, still overcome with gloom, I made a point to read the newspaper (a thing I normally did not do at that time in my life), certain that I would read the news of an atomic weapon being used, or that I would learn of a nuclear disaster at some overseas reactor.
As it turned out, I was right about the disaster—but not the date. The articles in the paper informed me of just such a detonation, but one that had occurred in 1945. I had not known it, but our trip to the park had coincided with the anniversary of the dropping of the first nuclear bomb on Hiroshima, Japan. Somehow, the echo of that terrible event had reached me forty years later[62], as fresh and as horrific as it had been the day it had occurred.

Looking back, I interpret this as an example of a moment in the past that is still occurring, and an instance when my 'present' opened a window to that 'present'. It seems that traumatic events not only leave their mark on human memory, but on the corridors of time as well.

Turning from this tragic event and the issue of the past, let us scrutinize the present and ask ourselves how fixed it really is. To do this, I offer a pair of events from my own experience to help examine this question. The first took place while I was still learning many of the basic exercises presented in this book:

I was traveling south from San Francisco with a student of mine and became thirsty. We pulled off the highway into a shopping center that neither of us recalled having seen before and went into a large grocery store there.
Right away we noticed that something was wrong, but neither of us could initially put our finger on it. And then it hit us what was 'off' about the place: there were none of the noises or activities that one generally associates with a busy store.
Instead of begging their mothers for candy, the children in the checkout lines were as soundless as stones. And the women did not chat with one another, or even fumble with their bags looking for coupons. They stood with fixed gazes in a silent line, staring straight ahead.
And over in a corner where greeting cards were sold, stood a strange group of men arranged in a circle, speaking in low voices to one other. As

we entered the store, the men looked at us from over their shoulders, and watched us intently as we found the beverages we had come for.

By the time we reached the checkout line, we both wanted to leave the strange place as quickly as we could. But it wasn't until we were back on the road that we remarked to each other about the people in the market. The event was so odd to us that we finally agreed to look for the place on our way back to the city.

Of course, when we came back, the place was gone. Instead of a strip mall with a grocery store, there was nothing. In fact, there wasn't even an off ramp, just open farmland. We never found the store again.

Certainly, the reader can understand that such an adventure would tend to cause one to wonder at the nature of the present just a tiny bit[63]. I for one, started to realize that the temporal world was not linear or as solid as we like to think it is. But it was another experience I had that fully cemented my understanding that the present is a multi-layered affair consisting of many realities:

Louis and I took a trip to Death Valley National Monument. Instead of camping out, or sleeping in our car as we had on so many prior occasions, we booked a room in a motel in Furnace Creek. When nightfall came, we drove out to Zabriski Point, which had already been the site of several earlier adventures.

After parking the car at the spot reserved for visitors, we headed down into the maze of small canyons that make up the area. As we moved through the largest of these, we both began to notice that a strange phenomenon was taking place.

I had been in the lead, with Louis behind me. But as I walked along, I saw that he had somehow gotten ahead of me. This seemed strange, and I looked back over my shoulder to see him, still walking behind me. I did a double take and realized that he was both in front and behind me simultaneously. For his part, Louis was experiencing the exact same thing.

Finally, we turned around and headed back to the car. At some point on the return trip to the vehicle, the odd effect of seeing these 'doubles' of each other ceased.

But when we returned to Furnace Creek and walked back to our motel room, another weird event occurred. The Furnace Creek Inn had a restaurant that overlooked the surrounding desert and the road we were walking on. As we passed underneath its large picture windows, I looked up and saw a young woman seated at a table near the window at the corner of the building, looking down on both of us with an expression of obvious disdain. But when

Louis looked up at the same window, he saw an older man seated at the table instead, watching us with the same scornful expression.
Neither of us thought much of this until we had returned to our motel room and compared notes. By this time, we were both feeling quite ill, and this distracted us from analyzing what had happened in any great detail. And for some time afterwards, we simply chalked the affair off as something odd, and left it at that.
And so it remained—until I began to understand the nature of time. Then the ramifications of the event became clear. What I realized was that this was a perfect example of two parallel realities—two 'presents' overlapping each other temporarily. In one present, I was leading the way down the canyon, but in another, my companion was. And while in both realities someone was seated at the restaurant table, the sex and age of the occupant were different (even if their apparent attitude towards us wasn't).

To put it succinctly, what I learned from these two experiences was that the 'present' is not limited to one basic plane of existence. It is actually an infinite thing where entire realities like our own not only sit next to one another, but also sometimes collide and intermingle like galaxies in space[64].

These events (and events like them which I encountered from other sources) also introduced the idea to me that the multifaceted nature of time extends to our own personal existence. In addition to 'our' life 'here and now' on this plane, we also possess what I came to term 'alternate parallel existences', each with their own 'present'.

Simultaneous lives like these, which are lived out in parallel time-streams, vary in their level of similarity to our own. Some are near mirror images, but possess subtle features that make them different (such as illustrated in the preceding account where our physical positioning and those of our doubles were dissimilar).

In addition, it would appear that there are also alternate parallel lives that can vary quite greatly from our own, these being polar opposites in every respect: female where we are male, light where we might be dark, and so on (with infinitely varying degrees of difference between them). To borrow from Taoism, these 'negative' alternate lives appear to act in the cosmic sense as the 'yin' to our 'yang', complimenting our existence (as ours does theirs) by their very opposition to our nature.

Appreciated in their totality, alternate parallel lives, negative parallel lives, along with past and future lives collectively comprise our unique being-ness in the greater scheme of things. They are, along with the 'self' we are aware of here and now on this plane, 'us' in the fullest and truest expression of that term. The specific relationship of all of these different selves to our own can best be understood as what Jane Roberts in her famous "Seth" material called the Oversoul. As she defined it, the Oversoul is a group of otherwise individual lives (and realities) that are in fact, merely facets of one another and part of a greater whole.

To view this from an even wider perspective, this same Oversoul, when seen in the context of an infinite multi-dimensional and multi-temporal model of the universe, can be theoretically considered to be only a single element of an even larger 'Superconsciousness' or 'Supersoul' (which is composed of individual Oversouls). And following this same theoretical model a little further, our Supersoul is again potentially a part of something even greater than it, and so on into infinity.

Although this macrocosmic arrangement of existence might seem rather alien and difficult for some readers to appreciate, the fact is that it is in reality quite easy to understand if we simply look to the microcosm within our own bodies as a point of reference. There, our individual cells are interrelated to one another in greater and greater structures that eventually comprise the totality of what we are physically. The difference here is really a matter of scale, and the ultimate entity we are examining, is for want of a better term, nothing less than God.

To return from this somewhat dizzying picture of the self to our humble exploration of the nature of time, let us move on and examine the future. By conventional definition, the future is something that has not occurred yet. As such, it is a potential event that is based on the probabilities of actions generated in the present, and which becomes more and more 'real' as the window of what 'might be' narrows with each passing instant.

If we accept the idea that the past and present are potentially infinite, ongoing and multi-layered, then the only remaining step is to apply these qualities to the future as well--and acknowledge that there is no single future, but rather many possible futures existing simultaneously. What determines *which* particular future becomes 'our' present is then a matter of probabilities, with that future that is the *most likely* to occur being the one that we eventually encounter as the present.

And therein lies the potential to influence future events. **While a particular future may seem to be the most likely, the Magician knows that there are also neighboring futures with probabilities that are *also* high enough to occur as well. The factor that decides which one of these futures takes precedence over the rest is the addition of elements that 'tip the scales' in its particular favor. One of the most pivotal elements, is like so much else in our universe, the influence of energy as expressed by conscious Will.**

In its most basic form, influencing the future is by no means an arcane process. In fact, it is a common procedure, practiced every day by our fellow men on a semi-conscious level.

A good example of this takes place when the outcome of an event is not clear and we are urged by our fellows to 'think positive thoughts' about the result we desire. In many cases, when we do this, the outcome does in fact turn in the direction we want it to. While skeptics tend to ascribe this to mere coincidence, in fact we are actively engaging in the act of influencing the future through the exertion of our Will. Another common instance of conforming the future to our desires occurs when a loved one becomes ill and everyone involved agrees to 'pray' for their recovery—and the afflicted party gets well, sometimes in complete opposition to the outcome predicted for them by the doctors.

The key to success in these cases is the energy put into the situation by the participants at the critical period of time that exists before the outcome has become completely finalized. And this is precisely what the trained Magician uses to accomplish the same thing on a more focused level.

The master of this Art understands that main principle behind influencing the future is the understanding that because an event has not yet occurred that it is only a 'probable' future and that any appreciable application of Will can move it in another direction entirely. The only limitation is that the future that is visualized must be close enough in likelihood (read that: probability) to take the place of what would otherwise be the default event[65].

And this is where we return to the issue of reincarnation and the idea of working with future lives. Just as we can experience past lives, we can also see our next life. But instead of *passively* viewing that life, we can also deliberately create what I call 'event triggers' to ensure that we reawaken the knowledge in that life that we have gained here in this life.

I know that this process works because I have already done it myself at least once. In the first part of this Chapter, I described having had a dream of a former life. The full details of that life are not as important as was the quality of that life, which was neither mystical nor virtuous in any way. In fact, the past life I experienced was the direct opposite of this present one; a life spent in the mindless pursuit of whatever desire came to me, and needless violence.

For many years, I was baffled by the inconsistency of that life with my present one—it seemed so far removed and so much lower on the scale of spiritual evolution that I wondered at how greatly things had changed from it to the present.

Then as I learned the details of other lives, I realized that it was not in fact my last life, but only one of my existences—and perhaps the worst one. In effect, I came to the realization that I had encountered it not because it was the previous life, but because it was a blatant warning to me of what I could become in this life if I did not choose a different path for myself.

But this realization only solved part of the mystery; the greater question that remained with me from that point onwards, was the identity of the agency had placed this warning in my path, and how this feat had been accomplished.

That was until I became familiar with practices in the East. There, adepts in the Art deliberately acknowledge their future lives with the specific intent of reincarnating with some or all of the memories of their former lives intact. As it turned out, the source of this arcane admonition was none other than myself, in a former life, having created the dream event as a 'trigger' to shock me into awareness. It is this very same endeavor that we will now examine in detail, and as a working exercise.

Exercise 2: Viewing a Future Life

We begin by repeating the first exercise in this Chapter in every respect, save in making one key change. When you are in the hallway, instead of walking through a door into a past life, tell yourself to walk instead through the door that leads to the *next* life you are to live after this one.

Make sure to take careful note of all the elements in your initial vision[66]; age, sex, setting and the like. And then, as we did in the first exercise, move forwards to the next significant incident in this future life. In this case, such moments are especially important for the next step in our process.

Exercise 3: Creating Event Triggers for a Future Life

Having determined the significant incidents of your future life, the next step is to exploit their potential as catalysts for the recall not only of former lives (including your present one), but also of the knowledge that you have gained in them. This is a matter of revisiting these moments a second time, but also visualizing an added detail occurring within them that causes your future self to suddenly have a moment of realization or a *déjà vu* experience.[67] This 'event trigger' can cause the future self to recall everything from esoteric knowledge to sexual preferences and even mundane habits. Event triggers are in effect similar in structure to post-hypnotic suggestions based on associations, but ones that span across the very boundary of death into the next life.

An event trigger can be created from an element within the future moment, such as the time of day that it occurs in, a certain landscape feature within it, or anything else that symbolically resonates with your present-day associations. For example, if you always tend to meditate at a certain time of day, you would look for a significant moment in your future life that occurs at that same time of day and create the trigger there. In doing this, we are of course, taking advantage of the potential future realities that lie closely alongside our future life and in effect, weaving them into the fabric of that future life through a process of visualization and affirmation until they become inextricably part of its time stream.

To help illustrate how this is accomplished, I will share from one of my own efforts in this area:

I revisited my future life and found myself in what would be my favorite room. It was late in the afternoon, with that peculiar quality of light that only comes at that time of day. As in my present life, it was a special time, and my future self was using it to relax and meditate after a long day at work.

The moment was perfect, and I saw a parallel possibility where a 'flashback' to the present could occur. It was only a matter of finding the right key in the scene to initiate the memory and make it part of my future life.

Then my future self looked down from the window and over to a small curio—a glass globe with something inside it. It was the kind of thing I tend to collect in my present life, and I realized that this object was also somehow linked to the parallel future I had in mind—and that it represented the very opportunity I had been seeking.

I immediately visualized the image of the globe causing my future self to suddenly have a glimpse backwards to my present, and with this, the knowledge of having had a former life. An instant later, I realized, deep inside me, that the event trigger had 'taken' and that that moment was now set forever as part of my future life.

I left the vision, confident that my trigger was in place and would do its job that very same afternoon—200 years in the future.

Generally, a series of such triggers must be placed at important moments throughout the future life to bring the future self to a point where they have recapitulated enough information to become fully aware. However, I would also add that if they are artfully created, even one or two triggers can be enough to 'do the job'. And, as the reader may have surmised while reading all of this, this same exact process can also be employed with future moments in one's present life, with the same results.

CHAPTER VI: FAMILIARS

"Master, go on, and I will follow thee to the last gasp, with truth and loyalty."---*Shakespeare*

In an earlier chapter on the subject of Faring Forth, I touched upon the concept of working with a Familiar. I also felt the subject of Familiars, in and of itself bore enough importance to explore in detail in its own Chapter.

By definition, a familiar is either an animal or a spirit that works in partnership with a witch, acting in a variety of ways to enhance their magickal Work, protect them physically and spiritually, or which performs specific services for them. It should be noted that the familiar is **not** the 'spirit guide' or 'totem animal' of the Native American traditions, which is essentially an initiatory guide figure[68]. The familiar is instead, an active helper and a direct participant in a witch's day-to-day magickal operations and mundane business.

There are essentially two kinds of familiar. The first is the animal familiar, which the reader will recall, was already discussed in the context of Faring Forth. Normally, this is a pet that enters into a bond with the witch, allowing the witch to work their Will through them. A classic example of this is the witch's cat, which lets their master ride them astrally, or who acts as the platform from which the witch can project a spell (such as in the cases of African Shamans who send their familiar animal out to deliver their spells to their intended targets). A variant of this is where a witch enlists the services of a physical animal that is not a 'pet', but with whom they feel a symbolic association (which is similar in concept to the totem animals of the Native American tradition, but with a different end in mind).

The second kind of familiar, which this chapter will focus on exclusively, is what could be termed the spirit-helper. This is a spirit or supernatural entity that has attached itself to the witch, and which enables the witch to perform certain operations, based upon its unique abilities. Such an attachment can take place at any time, although one of the more common situations is where a spirit bonds with the witch at a very young age and stays with them their entire lives. In modern times, this is often referred to by the uninitiated as the 'imaginary playmate'[69] of little children.

Unfortunately the bond between a child and a willing spirit is often forgotten if the relationship is not allowed to mature and the child transitions into adulthood. But even though such bonds might be forgotten, they are never completely severed. The experiences of many students with whom I have worked with, have showed me that this same bond continues to exist past childhood and can, through conscious effort, be renewed when the child-now-adult becomes spiritually aware enough to do so.

A alternative form of this early bonding between a witch and their familiar is that which occurs as the result of a karmic connection between them, and can span several lifetimes. This was the situation with my own familiar, who has been bonded to me since an earlier life in ancient Rome. In such cases, the familiar follows the Magician through each successive existence, maintaining a continuous relationship with them in each one (up to and including any future lives).

Another type of bonding is where a familiar is attracted to a magician and stays on with them to become a servant. Generally this is the result of some powerful magickal act performed by the practitioner for other purposes, and which attracts the spirit as a metaphysical 'spectator' to the event. This has happened a number of times in my own career, where a spirit made its presence known to me during a magickal operation and it is the way that many magicians wind up obtaining a spirit-helper for themselves.

In other cases, the specific goal of a magickal operation can be to attract a spirit for this very purpose. Such an operation can be anything from an elaborate ritual, or a simple invitation and acknowledgement of the beings presence. For those who are not blessed with a familiar from childhood (or before), this is the most frequent means of entering into such a metaphysical association.

At this stage, the reader might ask what the benefits are for the spirit itself. There are many, but two stand out in particular. The first is the fulfillment of a shared karmic momentum between the Magician and them (such as in the case of the pre-existing bond that spans several lifetimes). The second and more common benefit is the opportunity, through repeated interaction and invocation, to participate in this and other planes of reality, thereby enabling the spirit to evolve to a higher form of being[70].

FIRST STEPS: INITIATING THE RELATIONSHIP

I only became aware of my familiar in the context of a dramatic event as an adult, and it was years before I understood the importance of what I had seen. The catalyst for my meeting my familiar was the Northridge Earthquake of January 17, 1994.

Like many residents of Los Angeles, I was awakened at 4:30 AM to a violent heaving of the earth. After several violent aftershocks, my wife and I went out of our house and into the back yard. As we sat there recovering our wits, a dark mass of energy about the size of a large cat drifted slowly across the yard, flying between us before moving on to circle the house.

My wife, who was still relatively new to such things, saw this and asked me what had just happened. I responded that she had seen a guardian that lived in the home, but I realized even as I said these words that it was in fact something far more profound.

Years passed, and occasionally I saw the same apparition make its appearance. It was only when finally I read Jason Miller's excellent book that it dawned on me that the being I had encountered was a familiar, and that it had actually followed me from a former life into this one. This realization in turn started me on an intensive exploration not only into how our relationship had begun, but also into what our future relationship could be.

In my wife's case, she enjoyed the benefit of having had a childhood spirit companion, but after encountering some difficulties with it in adulthood, parted company with the being[71]. Later, as I explored my own relationship with my familiar, she discovered that she had another spirit that was attempting to make its presence known to her. In acknowledging that relationship, she not only gained one spirit, but several, who were related with one another and who came to work with her as a group, each with distinct personalities[72]. In both of our cases, there was no formal act of recognition or ritual that we performed. Rather, we simply came to acknowledge what we had been subconsciously aware of all along.

For those considering a relationship with a familiar, this is perhaps the easiest method to use. However, if a ritual framework is desired, it will certainly yield the same results. As to the exact elements that such a ritual might employ, I leave it to the reader to decide such details. Whatever the shape it takes, the main thrust of it should be an operation that both invites and recognizes the familiar spirit, and formalizes the relationship.

THE NAME AND THE SPIRIT HOUSE

Whatever the method one employs, once the relationship is begun, the presence of a spirit will become immediately apparent. The next step is the important act of ascertaining the being's name. This action not only makes it possible to exert control over the being (for as the ancient Egyptians knew, the name of a thing *is* the thing), but also makes it more feasible to Call and interact with the being at need.

Like the act of acknowledgement, this can be only a matter of asking the spirit (either verbally or mentally) its name and allowing the answer to come, or a more elaborate affair that employs ritual and tools. In the case of a true familiar, the Name will be revealed immediately and without hesitation to the practitioner as a clear sign of trust between them. Once revealed, the Magician must take care keep this name secret, thereby preventing others from compelling their familiar.

As an adjunct to this, the Magician may also choose to create a 'spirit-house' for their new companion. This can take many forms, from statue, to a framed image of the beings' sigil etc[73]. Jason Miller, for example, describes the use of a bottle as the home for a Familiar spirit (which has interesting parallels to the classic idea of the 'genie in a bottle').

Regardless of whatever object is chosen for this purpose, the function of such an effigy is to act as a focal point for the practitioner to be able draw upon the bond they have with their spirit, and at the same time for it to serve as a direct representation of the vibratory 'frequency' of the spirit itself. The spirit-house can also function as the residence of the spirit (or more correctly as a point through which it can manifest and focus itself in this reality).

In Asia, and especially in Thailand, the concept of the spirit house is quite formalized and even today, many homes in that country have such an object (although it is not intended to house familiars, but rather ancestral and earth spirits). The European magickal tradition is less structured in this regard, however there are many accounts of witches enchanting a specific object for their familiar to inhabit (such as in the classic spirit-in-the mirror of fairy tales)[74]. Some practitioners of this Art were even reported to have generated a brisk income for themselves selling such magickal objects to others, and others were reportedly able to will their familiar over to a family member as part of their estate[75]! In modern times, the spirit house is not considered a place of confinement, but as already illustrated, a point of focus and medium for interaction.

DETERMINING A FAMILIARS POWERS

Familiars, like people, have different natures and capabilities. Once a relationship is established and the Being has given its Name, the next issue is to determine what services it is capable of providing. This would appear to be based largely on the nature of the Being, although it should also be stated that the capabilities of a spirit increase and change with time and repeated interaction.

To draw once more from my own experience, after recognizing that I had a familiar, I then requested different services from the being. Some it was immediately capable of, such as acting as an effective guardian against psychic attacks[76], while others proved more difficult for it to perform. Still others became apparent only after we had worked together for some time[77]. The process of learning a spirit's abilities is an ongoing one, and the skills of a spirit helper change with time, tending to increase in number and complexity as more and more interaction occurs between themselves and the Magician they work with.

FEEDING A FAMILIAR & OTHER ISSUES

In addition to interaction, some familiar spirits also require some form of maintenance, or 'feeding'. This is an ancient magical practice, as the following passage from Margaret Murray's "The God of the Witches" helps to illustrate: *"I meet with little mention of Imps in any Country but ours, where the Law makes the feeding, suckling or rewarding of them to be a felony*[78]*".* Another passage from the same work states: *"The feeding of a familiar was clearly a ritual ceremony, for though Mother Waterhouse's evidence gives the ceremony most completely there are many other instances which show that when the creature had been used for magic it was given a drop of the witch's blood on its return.*[79]*"* and also in Anna Franklin's book, "Working with Fairies" we read, *"..There is always a price to pay for possessing a fairy familiar. The Belvior Witch Margaret Flower, tried in 1619, said that she promised her familiars to fulfill their needs, in return for which they fulfilled her desires. The desires of fairies ranged from bowls of milk and offerings of bread, to human company, music, and even human blood."*

While some familiars are certainly satisfied with an acknowledgement alone, others derive benefit from ritualized offerings. This is based largely on the type of the being one is working with. Familiar spirits thrive not only on attention, but also from such things as real food. While they generally do not consume the food in a physical sense (although this has been known to happen), my observations are that they partake of the energy of the food[80], and derive pleasure, if not a certain level of sustenance from it. Even if this is not the case with a particular spirit, the ritual act of offering a small piece of food at a meal certainly acts to strengthen the bond with the being, and is definitely beneficial from that standpoint alone. And from a purely symbolic perspective, the giving of food certainly shows both respect and care, both of which are necessary elements in such a close relationship.

However, like physical pets, familiars can sometimes be jealous and those aspiring to enter into a relationship with one are cautioned to be alert to this possibility. Jealousy can arise towards other familiar spirits, or towards other people in the Magician's life. In either case, a firm hand and early positive intervention can prevent problems like this from growing out of control. For example, my familiar proved to be quite possessive of me, and while the Being did not have issues with my wife or my physical pets, it did display some hostility towards my wife's familiars when they made any attempt to interact with me. On one occasion, my wife and I were on the living room couch watching television when one of her fairies flew over to me and started to settle in my lap. My familiar immediately appeared and chased the being away. This animosity worsened, with my wife's familiar instigating other events until at last both my wife and I were forced to communicate our stern displeasure to both parties. The events subsided and a peace, however grudging, came to be. The reader is certainly cautioned to take this tale into account. While the relationship between a Magician and its familiar is a special one, and well worth pursuing, personalities *are* involved and can sometimes require careful balance and management.

Play is also sometimes a factor in a relationship with a familiar. Like any physical being, a spirit-helper can sometimes benefit from play (depending of course on what kind of Being they are). Recreational activities can also provide the opportunity to further sharpen the psychic skills of both parties involved. I discovered for myself this shortly after formally initiating the tie with my own familiar.

In that case, I was sitting in my cubicle at work. My familiar, who had come along with me, was flitting about in the air around me as always. On a whim, I created a small ball of energy. Then I threw it out into open space. My familiar immediately flew after it, and quickly devoured the energy. I was delighted and sent another ball, and then another, and soon we were involved in a supernatural game of toss and catch. My familiar visually manifested on several occasions during the event and clearly broadcast a feeling of great joy and excitement. It became a game that we played together often, and strengthened our bond more deeply. If the student has a familiar, this is certainly an area worth exploring, and if possible, developing.

ON THE FEY, OTHERFOLK AND EXPLORING THE HIDDEN WORLD: LORE VERSUS DIRECT EXPERIENCE

One area that certainly deserves discussion at this point is the issue of established lore and belief in the face of direct experience. There is a tendency on the part of those seeking contact with the Hidden World to adhere stringently to the folklore. While conducting research into old ideas is certainly useful, I must point out that not all of the material one might find is completely accurate or useful.

The truth that folklore can offer can frequently be obscured by the actions of time and shifting cultural beliefs---and by the fact that just as in the material natural world, the behavior of a given being can vary depending on its location and local conditions. Therefore, while a study of folklore certainly has its place in magick, it should not be the sum total of one's knowledge and room must always be left for new information.

A good example of this would be the shapeshifters that I encountered early in my studies. Many of the tales about them are rife with warnings about their supposedly evil nature and the dangers of making their acquaintance. And while this can be true in some instances, even older tales than these painted an entirely different picture which turned out to be the truth. Yet another excellent illustration of my point would be the lives and activities of the Fey who interact with my wife.

As in many areas of the Old World, the region of and surrounding Appalachia is home to many types of 'Little People' who were known not only to the Native Americans, but also to the later Celtic settlers who came and made the area their home[81]. Like the Fey of Europe and the British Isles, they tend to the plants and trees, and in the case of the fairies in particular, travel in troupes led by a Queen who calls certain stretches of the woodlands her territory. And, just as in the old tales they are both fierce protectors and lovers of play.

But as I came to understand in my association with them, a great deal of the legends surrounding them, and the practices recommended in books of folklore I read were as strange and as foreign to them as they were to me. I recall many a conversation concerning such beliefs (such as the practice of throwing glove into a fairy ring to rescue a human), where they expressed genuine amazement and perplexity. I found that in my local region at least, that some purported facts simply *did not* apply. In the end, I was forced to sift through the material available to me and compare it to what I was directly experiencing to get to the true heart of the matter.

I urge potential magicians planning their own explorations of the Hidden World to take this into account. While knowledge of folklore is certainly useful, it cannot be a substitute for the invaluable knowledge that direct experience can bring. In reality, it is the marriage of the two, and not the exclusion of one over the other that is the proper approach to understanding and interacting with the unknown. Or to put it more plainly: Never sacrifice what *can* be known for what has *been* known.

TALES FROM THE HIDDEN WORLD: LITTLE COUSINS

Eventually, I decided to leave California for better opportunities elsewhere. I wound up settling in a Midwestern state. I quickly found that not only was the culture and the physical environment quite different, but the supernatural world as well.

Eventually, I attended one of the many pagan gatherings in the area. There, I made the acquaintance of a hereditary 'Granny Witch' who was also visiting[82]. *We had the chance to not only exchange information, but decided to venture together into the forest and explore it together, accompanied by my wife and two guests.*

It was late in the evening, and while the majority of the people attending the event were gathered around a large bonfire, our little group set out on a small path into the woods. The forest was dense and the going was tricky, with many small branches growing into the trail. But after a few minutes we reached a tiny clearing which afforded just enough room for our group to spread out.

The Granny Witch was already quite adept at the Sight and certainly needed no instruction from me, but our two companions, Peggy, who was the wife of one of the events organizers and her teenage daughter who I'll call Nancy, were completely untrained and had to be given a quick lesson.

After a few minutes of this, I decided to call out to the denizens of the woods and the Granny Witch agreed that this was a good idea. She then suggested that I call to beings she referred to as the "Little Cousins". She had explained earlier to me that they were similar to the Fey Folk of Europe and that they were very much a part of her tradition. I was eager to experience them myself and compare them to other beings I had encountered over the years[83].

I made my Call as gentle and inviting as I could, not really knowing what to expect. Then, I began to see movement in the greenery in front of me. After a moment, a diminutive silvery being, not more than a foot tall came out into the open. It didn't have any discernable features: instead it was more the suggestion of a small humanoid form. The Little Cousin regarded me for a moment, then to my pleasant surprise, walked up and hugged my leg.

Then he retreated back into the foliage. I got the impression of great friendliness and the Granny Witch who was standing behind me confirmed this, saying, "They're laughing! They're laughing at you!" In fact, the creatures seemed positively delighted by our presence, as we were by them.

However not everyone in our party shared this joy. After watching the Cousins for several more minutes, my wife informed me that Nancy was becoming increasingly frightened by the whole event (and Peggy didn't seem to be doing much better). My wife tried to calm the girl down, but finally Peggy insisted that we return to camp immediately. Neither my wife, our friend the Witch, or myself felt any need for concern whatsoever, but out of deference to the two women, we reluctantly agreed to leave. When we returned to the campgrounds, they quickly left our company.

We learned later that Peggy didn't want to have anything to do with any of us ever again. She wasn't specific about why she felt this way, but it became clear that even this benign experience had frightened both her and her daughter deeply. Thankfully, I had seen enough of this kind of reaction over the years to take it in stride and cherish the event for its positive aspects instead.

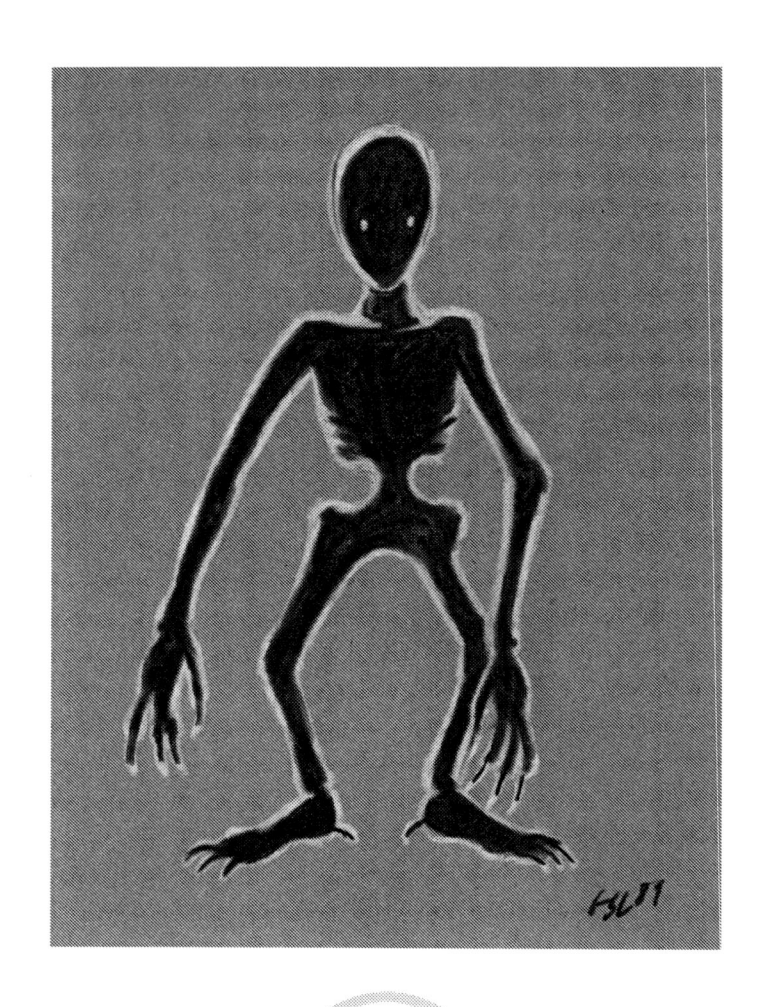

BOLINAS BAY

A SIMPLE CIRCLE FOR
EVOCATION AND A BASIC
TRIANGLE OF MANIFESTATION

THE FEY

A SORCERER'S BOOK OF ART 105

HECKEL AND JECKEL

LADY M

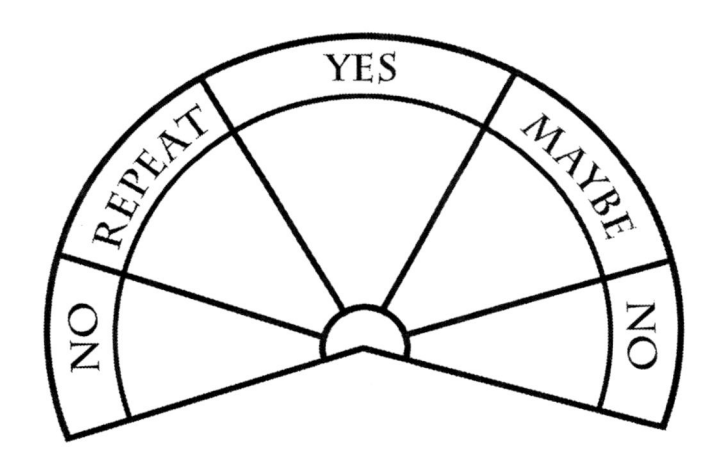

A BASIC PENDULUM CHART
FOR STUDENT USE

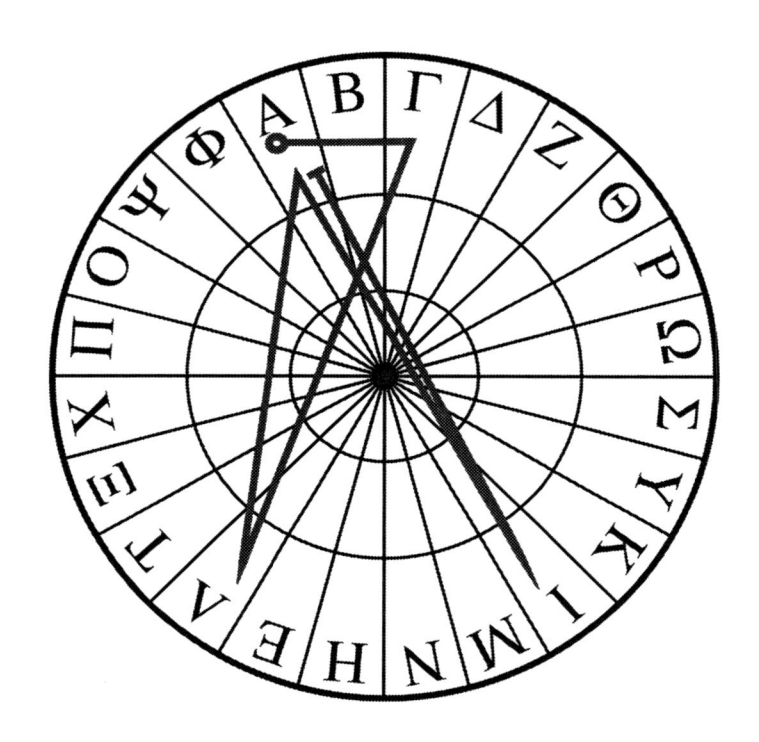

AN EXAMPLE OF A SIGIL
CREATED FROM THE ORACLE
WHEEL

A SORCERER'S BOOK OF ART 109

A FAMILIAR

CHAPTER VII: THE MAGICK MIRROR

"Looking-glass, Looking-glass, on the wall, Who in this land is the fairest of all? The looking-glass answered, 'Thou, O Queen, art the fairest of all!' Then she was satisfied, for she knew that the looking-glass spoke the truth.--*From Little Snow White, by Jacob and Wilhelm Grimm*

Since the first person looked onto the surface of a mirror and realized its possibilities, Magick and mirrors have been inextricably linked. Of all the Tools of Art in the Magician's arsenal, the Looking Glass, as it has sometimes been called, is unarguably the most powerful and versatile.

There are three types of mirrors used in magick. The first is the conventional mirror, which often doubles as a utilitarian device. The second kind is the water-mirror (which uses the reflective qualities of water or a similar liquid in a bowl) and the third type is the black mirror. Of these three, the black mirror is the most conducive to magickal workings, and the most commonly employed for that purpose. It is this last type of mirror that will be referred to in this chapter.

Before I go any further, I must state plainly that while mirrors are a Tool of Art *par excellence*, they are definitely not without their hazards. Magickal mirrors can be powerful portals and if handled incorrectly, can pose real dangers to the careless operator. But not all of the Art is without risk and the rewards that the mirror can offer offset this danger more than enough to warrant a study by the student of its properties and nature.

More than just a piece of reflective glass, mirrors by virtue of their unique physical and energetic qualities, presents us with potential doorways into time and space. Countless magick users have learned that through the proper application of Will, that a portal can be opened in the mirror that will allow matter and energy to pass through. In fact, were modern day physicists so inclined to look, they would find in the magickal mirror a localized version of their famed wormholes. Long before science contemplated the mathematics of time and energy, magick users knew that energy could pass through the Gateway of a mirror and reappear anywhere else (and even *anywhen*), instantly. In the case of mirrors, the 'latest' theories about space and time are anything but theories or real news. And instead of being light-years away, the Magician knows that wormholes are as close to us as a humble pane of glass, properly manipulated.

Exercise 1: Creating a Black Mirror

To create a mirror for magickal use, the list of materials is short: a picture frame with glass and backing, black paint and something to cover the mirror with when it is not in use.

After removing it from the frame, the glass should be painted on one side and allowed to dry. Once dry, the glass is then reinserted into the frame. For added quality, a piece of black matte-paper can also be put in behind the glass to ensure the most opaque viewing field possible.

When the mirror is not being employed for magickal operations, **it must be kept covered**. The reason for this is that magickal mirrors, in very short order, tend to respond to any energy in the room they are exposed to **and will open up spontaneously**. The basic expedient of covering their surface helps to prevent this from happening and also acts to 'shut' the energy of the mirror 'back down' after working. This covering must be light blocking and the construction of a curtain for this purpose, or a bag with ties is recommended.

Exercise 2: Testing for Reactivity

With the black mirror prepared, the next step is a basic exploration of its surface reactive qualities. To accomplish this, you should set the mirror up on a chair and sit across from it. The lighting should be dim.

Fix your gaze on the center area of the mirror and using your Sight, observe for any activity that occurs. Typically this will consist of moving particles of energy, sparks and flashes of color.

Once you have done this for a few minutes, breathe out your Fire through your hand and move it slowly over the surface of the mirror (from a distance no closer than a few inches to no greater than one foot).

While doing this, you should observe for any phenomena that might occur. It is not uncommon for example, to note ripples in the mirrors energy field as the Fire from your hand passes in front of it. Some students may also notice that after a few passes that the general activity over the mirror surface tends to increase dramatically. This is in direct response to stimulation of its energetic field. Be careful to observe the qualities of this reaction and its nature.

When you have had enough of this, your Dagger of Art should be brought into play, and the same maneuvers repeated with it. After several minutes the exercise should be concluded, the mirror covered, and your observations written down in your journal.

Exercise 3: Basic Mirror Scrying

Mirror Scrying, or using a mirror to seek visions of distant places or times, is a type of *crystallomancy,* or the Art of using a reflective surface to produce visions. The use of a mirror for scrying is thought to have evolved from earlier shamanic practices that employed either a calm body of water such as the surface of a lake[84] or bowls filled with water. Black mirrors, such as the one we explored earlier, have long been considered to be the best tool for accomplishing this work, and have been in use for centuries. For example, John Dee (1527-1608), the famous renaissance occultist, was thought to have used one in his pivotal Workings.

Scrying in a mirror is relatively easy to do. The mirror should be set up in front you in a room that is dimly lit. While some sources suggest that a candle be set up in front of the mirror, I do not recommend this, as the direct light can be overly distracting. Instead, I recommend that the lighting be indirect and dim.

The exercise begins with the act of Stilling the Waters, while gazing passively at the mirror. The gaze should be not on the surface itself, but focused instead into the mirror, as if one were looking into the depths of a deep pool. As this is done, it is not uncommon to see mist or smoke-like clouds of energy forming in the mirror and this should be taken as a positive sign that the exercise is progressing properly.

When a level of inner calm has been achieved, the next step is to compose a question, while at the same time formulating and visualizing it in your mind as clearly as possible. Once this has been done, the mirror should be observed using the Sight, and any visions that arise within in it, or in the mind's eye while gazing at it are to be noted.

While some of these images may be quite clear (and even startling), it is also possible that you will notice that the direction of the mists or their color might change in response to your question. The direction and the intuitive feeling that this evokes within you should also be noted, as this can sometimes indicate the answer to your inquiry[85]. With practice, the mirror will become more and more responsive, and generate clearer imagery.

Exercise 4: Scrying a Distant Person or Place

The next level in Scrying involves an attempt to view a distant person or place. In this case, your objective is to look into the mirror, but with the specific desire to see a particular individual or location. Clear visualization of your target is essential for success, as is a relaxed frame of mind, free of all doubt or bias.

Any imagery or impressions that occur are to be noted. Once the exercise is complete, you should then make an effort to determine the veracity of your visions. While this can be a 'hit and miss' affair in its early stages, the reader should be reminded that it is a skill, and as such becomes easier, and more accurate with practice. Even the smallest success in this area should be an encouragement to continue practice.

WORKING WITH A CRYSTAL BALL

An alternative for those who might be experiencing difficulty with the Art of Scrying using the black mirror, there is the crystal ball. Divorced from its Hollywood image, this tool has been in use for centuries to help facilitate the ability to psychically view other people, events or locations. It is a relatively easy tool to use and may aid greatly in honing ones skills.

Crystal balls come in a wide variety of sizes, shapes and colors. While most balls are actually made of glass or lead crystal, there are also many available that are fashioned from pure crystal. When purchasing one, it is best to find a ball that is of decent size and made of the finest quality and materials that one can reasonably afford (large crystal balls, and especially pure crystal balls of any size can be extremely expensive). I myself work with a ball that is 4" in diameter and is made of clear lead crystal. This is just large enough to have a workable viewing area without being too large for my altar of Art.

A stand for the ball to sit in is a necessity. The stand should be able to support the ball reliably and allow the viewer to gaze at its surface without obstruction. It is best to tend towards the simplistic and utilitarian here: I once owned a very fine stand that was a bronze image of Atlas, and while it was certainly lovely enough, it did a poor job of actually supporting the ball.

I eventually replaced it with a simpler stand that proved to be much more efficient at this task.

Some preparation is required before the ball can be used as a magickal tool. The crystal should first be washed clean with mild soap and water. Then after gently drying it, it should be set in its stand.

The next step is the process of 'activating' the ball. This is done by holding ones hands over the surface of the ball while projecting the Inner Fire and then making passes over the ball with both hands (at a distance of no greater than a few inches at most). This action serves to excite the energy field extant in the ball (albeit weak initially) and aids the process of scrying with it.

Once several such passes have been made, gazing can then begin. Like our early experiments in the Sight, ones gaze is not forced and the point of gaze itself should be into the ball at a location somewhere in its center. Obviously, a state of calm should be maintained, and the act should be done with a clear idea of what it is you wish to see.

Results differ from operator to operator. Some experience seeing mist or clouds. Others, like myself, see visions, either in the crystal itself that are similar to holograms in appearance, or receive mental impressions (or experience a combination of these effects).

Once your session with the crystal ball is complete, the ball should be covered with a light-tight fabric. Handling (or viewing) by anyone other than its owner should also be discouraged. These precautions will keep the energies of the ball both attuned to its owner and as psychically free of extraneous energy as possible.

Mastery of this venerable tool can come fairly quickly with a small amount of practice. And even when the student has moved on to other more sophisticated methods, the crystal ball can continue to serve them well and remain a potent tool in their Workings.

PSYCHIC VISIONS AND DISTORTION

One area that begs comment at this stage are psychic visions and the issue of distortion. While some visions may come to the viewer with complete accuracy, it is not uncommon when scrying, faring forth, or through some other method, to receive impressions that are either completely reversed or different in some aspect from what actually occurs.

For example, in one case, I dreamed of meeting a particular person at a gathering. I received a very detailed image of the man, and when I went to that same assembly a year later, I met the person I had seen in the dream. My vision of him was completely accurate down to the last detail.

But in another instance, while I was demonstrating the use of the crystal ball to an advanced student, I took a moment to gaze into it to a moment in the near future. I looked forwards for anything special that the student and I might encounter when we went to dinner together after our class.

I immediately received the strong mental impression of a trailer parked near the restaurant we were to visit, hauling something square in shape that was colored green. I thought it was a camper shell of some kind, and when we went down to the restaurant an hour later I kept my eyes peeled for anything like this.

Sure enough, as we arrived, I drove past a trailer parked along the road. But instead of being a green camper trailer, it turned out to be a square-shaped electronic highway display sign sitting atop the trailer that carried it. And it was also orange in color and sat to the north of the restaurant, and not to the west as I had pictured it. Nonetheless, crucial aspects of the vision were present, albeit in a different form.

This 'reversal effect' is by no means uncommon at every level of mastery. It is important for the aspiring Seer to understand this effect and take it into account when interpreting their visions. Psychic impressions are received by the subconscious mind and like the lens of a camera, which reverses and distorts light waves passing through it, our subconscious deals with the information it receives on a symbolic and interpretive basis that is not always wholly literal.

Therefore, it is important to evaluate a psychic impression with an eye towards critical aspects of that vision that are truly pertinent, and be aware of when and where symbolism--and spontaneous reinterpretation or reversal might occur. At the same time, like ones dreams, constant practice will help to 'educate' the subconsciousness and refine its ability to perceive more accurately and with less distortion. However, it should also be stated that given the nature of this aspect of our being, there will always be some degree of reversal and reinterpretation that can occur no matter the level of talent.

Exercise 5: A Simple Gateway

Moving onwards, the next stage in our Work with the black mirror is the creation of a basic Gateway. A Gateway is exactly what it sounds like; a portal from this side of the mirror to somewhere else. In this case, the portal we will attempt to generate will not be focused towards any particular exit-point, but will be created instead for the student to appreciate its structure and understand the process of its creation.

As with all of our prior exercises, the mirror should be set up across from you. This time, make a downwards-cutting motion with your dagger of

Art across the center of the mirrors energetic surface area (without making physical contact). This cut should be at least 6 inches long.

As you breathe your Fire out of the daggers tip to make the cut, **your must put aside any idea of the mirror being merely a flat piece of glass, but see it instead as an open void. Your Willed intention must be to cut into and down through this void, opening a hole into that same empty space.** Unless your cut is visualized exactly in this manner, your will accomplish little more than disturbing the surface energy field.

Assuming however that the cut *is* completed correctly, you should repeat the entire action several more times over the same area.While this is occurring you should also take your free hand and make a parting motion with it, through the area you have described with the dagger, visualizing the cut that you made widening and moving aside like a curtain. Using the Sight, you may note that the area of the cut does in fact appear to open in response to your efforts. Typically, this action is accompanied by a definite increase in the mirrors overall activity and a drop in temperature at the site of the cut itself. This is a simple energetic Gateway.

Once the Gateway has been created, you are encouraged to move your free hand towards it slowly and gently. As you do so, you should note any changes in temperature, sensation, or overall activity.

The next important step in this experiment involves learning to seal the Gateway shut. This is accomplished by taking your Dagger of Art and turning its blade sideways to the incision you made, and moving from the top to the bottom of it, visualizing the energy coming back together and sealing closed as you do so. A complimentary movement of your free hand (also projecting your Fire) can also accompany this and assist in the action. For the purposes of illustration, the gesture one makes here is similar to what one would make plastering over a hole in a wall (and has the same basic purpose, albeit with energy rather than plaster). This maneuver should be repeated several times and when you no longer observe the energetic incision, the mirror should be covered and put away.

Exercise 6: A Two-Way Gate

After practicing the creation of basic Gates, we will now move on to making a gateway in the mirror with a basic exit point. Once again, the mirror should be set up for working. Then, make a Gateway in it in the manner described above.

But this time, instead of simply picturing your Gate being cut into and opening out onto a formless void, you should visualize it opening up **in and out of** another nearby mirror. Preferably, the second mirror should be a conventional one, somewhere else in the location where the experiment is being conducted. A bathroom mirror is ideal for this purpose and it can be helpful for the student to memorize how their bathroom appears from the perspective of that mirror prior to undertaking this exercise.

Whatever mirror is selected, once the Gate has been cut, you should then create a ball of energy and push it into the opening, visualizing it passing through the first Gateway and exiting out of the one in the other mirror. Once this has been done, and before sealing the Gateway, you should go to the second mirror and observe if the energy ball has manifested on the other side in any manner. Properly done, you should note either the ball itself, or some form of energetic distortion somewhere in space just beyond the exit point in the mirror.

Exercise 7: Fiery Darts

As an adjunct to this experimentation, a particular Fiery Construct can be quite useful. This is the creation of a fiery dart. I have found through practice that shape of a dart-like construct is much hardier than a simple sphere, and better able to make the passage through a Gateway intact.

A fiery dart is created in a similar manner to the energy ball. You will still breathe out your Fire into your hands, but instead of cupping your hands together and creating a ball shape within them, the dart is created by holding your hands approximately 3-4 inches apart from one another. Then, as you breathe your Fire out into the space between your hands, you are to visualize the energy forming an elongated bar that comes to a point facing away from you, similar in shape to a high powered rifle bullet.

One maneuver that I have found helpful in creating this dart is to make a gentle rolling motion with your hands as you visualize the construct (moving in much the same manner as you would to form a physical piece of clay into an elongated, pointed shape).

Once created, the energy dart is launched from its location towards its target by using a gentle push with a free hand (which is projecting Inner Fire) at and against its blunt end. This sounds much easier to achieve than it actually is, as many students tend to push too hard, or push right through the dart, destroying it in the process. But with practice, the dart can be made to move in a straight line away from you towards a Gate and into it. As a separate but related exercise, you should experiment at length with developing and launching this type of Fiery Construct, as it has additional applications that go well beyond basic experimentation with the mirror.

Exercise 8: Focused Gateways

With a two way Gate having been created, the next level of training involves more focused Gateways. In this case, you should pick a target location, such as the home of another person, or another room in your building. This time, while a mirror on the other side can be your exit point, you can also choose **any** reflective surface. Although another mirror might seem the only exit available, the truth is that any surface that acts *like* a mirror can function in the same manner as an actual mirror would.

After creating the dart described above, project this construct through the first gate and visualize it exiting out the second. If a partner is available, they are to station themselves at the exit and observe for the dart's appearance (if not, then a solo student is advised to leave the entrance Gate area and go to the exit point and observe for the dart's presence). Generally, the dart will either manifest as a coherent energetic structure, or at the very least, as a rough area of energy of about the same size or mass as the original.

Exercise 9: Reaching Into the Gate

A variant of the previous exercise involves the same projection of energy I discussed in Chapter 2. Here, after creating the two Gates, the main object is to project energy from your hand outwards into space. Then once this is accomplished, you are to approach the entrance Gateway, continuing to project energy from your hand as you do so. First-time subjects may immediately notice tingling sensations and a pronounced coldness as they move into the actual gateway area. This is the result of the natural changes the Gate itself makes on the energy in the local space around it.

As you make contact with this area, you are to visualize your hand entering the Gate, going through it, and then exiting out the opposite side. Your partner, on the opposite side at the exit location is to observe for any manifestations. If the exercise is successful, the result will either be an apparition of a hand exiting the second Gate, or a mass of energy the same general size of the hand. With practice, this manifestation can become quite visible and tangible.

Withdrawing your hand and sealing the two Gates closed concludes the exercise. It should be noted that your hand might feel somewhat drained of energy afterwards. This is a normal effect, and is quickly remedied by the act of breathing energy through the affected limb until an energetic equilibrium is returned.

Exercise 10: Faring Forth Through the Gate

With the successful projection of focused energy forms through the linked Gateways, the next objective is to travel astrally through a Gate. This begins with the creation of two Gates. However, in this case, you are to lie down, with your head facing the entrance Gate. Then relax your body (using the Cord and Torch method) and once this is accomplished, visualize yourself rising upwards and away from your body, and then going through the entrance Gate, exiting out the opposite side.

If two persons are involved, the second party's job is to observe for any sign of their partner's exit from the second Gate, making sure to note any and all energy manifestations.

Once this short astral flight has been completed, you are to return to your body via the same Gates, then raise and re-circulate your energy using the Cord and Torch method again. The reader should be warned that first-time experiences Faring through a Gate can be quite tiring, and ample time should be given for a full recovery of one's energy before the two Gates are sealed over and the exercise is concluded.

At this stage, the reader might be asking what the potential of all this experimentation is. The following account should give the reader an idea of the possibilities—and the dangers if such technology is misused. The identities of the parties involved have been changed in order to protect them and to avoid fresh conflict with other persons that were involved:

A man I knew had been had been incarcerated in prison for sexually molesting his daughter. During the time he was in the penitentiary, he made the acquaintance of other prisoners who were deeply involved in black magic (it seems that in addition to training themselves to be jail-house lawyers, studying the darker aspects of the Art is the second most popular means of passing the time 'inside').

He told these men about his mother, the fact that she was quite old, and very wealthy. According to what I later learned, they agreed to help him 'collect' his inheritance by using magick to kill her (in return from a 'cut' of the profits no doubt). These men and their associates on the outside were quite adept at working with Gateways and mirrors.

One night, they attacked the home of the old woman using their skills. I was staying there at the time taking care of her, and was in the process of getting ready for bed. I was walking by the kitchen on my way to my room, when I saw the silhouette of a man standing there. I stopped in surprise, and as I did so, the figure gestured and a dark mass of energy shaped like a Fiery dart came flying at me. I responded immediately with several of my own and then pushed the apparition backwards with a burst of pure will.

The figure flew back, disintegrating into an amorphous cloud that went out through a nearby window. I knew right away what had happened and rushed over to a large full-length mirror that was in the next room. Sure enough, a bright line of energy was visible on its surface. It was a Gateway.

I promptly sent another energy dart down into the Gateway and felt it hit a figure that was lying on a bed, surrounded by two other people. Then I sealed the portal.

I later learned that these same people had created a Gateway and had sent a junior member of their group to carry out the assault. No other attacks occurred after this incident.

As unpleasant as this event was, it did highlight the fact that this technology is both well known and widely used by a diverse cross-section of magickal practitioners. It is, in a word, quite effective and a properly trained individual can use the magick mirror as a powerful platform for every type of Working, be it for good or ill. It can enable them to send a very tangible 'fetch' or energy body through to the other side if they so desire. For those who might read this and contemplate mischief, I will only add they should take great care whose home they exit into, as my little tale amply illustrates.

THE MIDDLE WORLD & ITS DENIZENS

The transition time of an energy construct traveling between a Gate cut through one mirror and its exit point appears to be instantaneous at first glance. However, after years of interacting with this magickal tool, I observed that a slight delay actually occurred. In addition, I noticed that a peculiar coldness was experienced when a person's hand partially entered the Gateway proper, coupled with a pronounced drop in life-energy (as observed in the decrease of the auric field accompanied by subjective reports by the subjects involved). The same effect also became readily apparent when Faring Forth through the mirror.

From all this information, I deduced that a 'middle world' of some kind with qualities different from our own potentially existed between the Gateway and its exit point. At first this was purely theoretical, but subsequent experiments with prolonged astral trips through Gateways began to suggest that it might be fact.

Ultimately after numerous experiments had been conducted, the group I was working with, and I, concluded that such a dimension did exist .We also determined that it existed in a space and a time quite different from our own. One of the most compelling research experiments that took place concerning this, occurred in conjunction with an effort to pass through a Gateway physically, and in which I was the test subject:

After years of working with small Gateways, I believed myself ready to try to achieve the ultimate next step—a Gateway through which I could literally walk into another world with my entire body. This ambitious experiment took place during an evening camp-out in Northern California.

After cutting a Gateway in space in front of me, I had proceeded to walk in a straight line into the area of the Gate. This Gateway was a special one: first because of its size and secondly because it had been created out of my own shadow body or double. As I walked into the area, I closed my eyes.

There was the familiar shift in temperature and a perceptible change in the air pressure around me, followed by a sudden cessation of the night's normal sounds.

Then I opened my eyes.

Instead of standing in the open field I had been in, under a starry sky, I found myself on flat plain of immense size. The ground ahead of me was pitted and shiny like the surface of a piece of chipped obsidian. I looked up and realized that the sky was completely devoid of any stars. The only light came from a bright white glow on the horizon.

But as unnerving as the alien environment was, it was nothing compared to the feeling the place exuded. I realized that I was in a place that did not know the Divine Force that many call God! It was place utterly removed from that Force and I instantly understood the archetype of Lucifer being cast down from Heaven-- and knew for myself the awful feeling of being away from that which had created and nurtured me my whole life. It was in a word, a terrible place.

I turned around, closed my eyes, and headed back through the Gate, eager to be shut of the strange scene. When I emerged back into the warm summer night, I collapsed and had to be carried back to a nearby tent by my companions. I was certain that I was about to die and at least an hour passed before I regained a semblance of my strength[86].

But profound loneliness was not the only thing I had encountered on the Obsidian Plain. Despite the isolation from God, that the space was not empty. There had been *things* dwelling there—not human, or even beings as we would know them, but alien entities of an impossible age and possessing nearly limitless hostility to *all* life, whether it was good or evil. And these beings had sensed my presence. I knew as I returned to this world, that had I stayed, *They* would have found me.

This not to be my last encounter with these eldritch creatures. As the years passed, I had occasion to visit what I came to call the Middle World again however briefly. I discovered through additional study and research, that these beings were nothing less than impossibly ancient forces that had somehow been imprisoned there by other, greater forces that were beyond our wildest reckoning. I learned that *They* had been sealed into that dimension by some incomprehensible action, since before time was even a concept--or mankind even its most primitive form had ever existed. From what I determined, it is well for our world that they are locked in there, for they represent energies that transcend any notion of evil that we could ever conceive of[87]. *They* are literally anti-life itself in its most fundamental expression.

In another experiment with the Middle World, I called to its inhabitants through a magick mirror, deliberately making my presence known. As I expected, They came, and as They did so, I pulled back from the Gate and let Them come out a ways, unopposed. The result, which truly horrified a student who was working with me, was a mass of black shapes that could only be described as tentacles writhing wildly into the room we were Working in.

After a few moments of observation, I pushed the shapes back into the Gate and sealed it shut. Although this endeavor might sound reckless, the exercise was actually quite controlled and its purpose a very serious one. From this event, I was able to determine more of Their shape and nature—and confirmed conclusively both Their essential temperament and great age.

It also served as an excellent warning to my student to take care when working with the mirror. Certainly, having seen the real thing myself, I can now appreciate the genius of H.P. Lovecraft and the veracity of his visions as never before. Some 'fiction' it seems, is well grounded in fact.

Despite all this, it must be stated emphatically that normal passages through the mirror offer little danger aside from the energy drain created by the process. Most trips through are generally too brief and make too little contact with the Middle World to offer *any* appreciable hazard. This information was presented here simply to stress, as I have stressed with my students over the years, that the Magick Mirror is a serious magickal tool, and worthy of great caution. It is only when *extended* journeys are taken within the Middle World itself and the traveler *loiters* in that place that any real risk arises. And I would add that it is also equally dangerous to open a Gate simply into that void for any great length of time. My account therefore is intended as a caution to those who might be tempted to experiment recklessly in this area or be fool enough to treat with these Beings: Do so at your own risk.

TALES FROM THE HIDDEN WORLD: HECKEL AND JECKEL

Going into the Field was never without its surprises. This was especially true when it came to escorting new students out on their first few trips.

I had gone with a group of associates out to Death Valley National Monument, which for many years was one of my favorite spots to explore. The Valley is steeped in history and filled with locations that can offer incredible supernatural experiences for those hardy enough to venture into it.

And one of the best areas I found was the rugged badlands of Zabriski Point. The barren landscape is itself a paranormal experience, and the things I experienced there never disappointed me. For my newest student, a girl named Lisa, it was the perfect spot for her second trip into the Field and ideal for her to attempt what we called a 'solo'—(this being a short time spent by the student using the Sight and providing both an opportunity for them to experience some of the Hidden World on their own, and the chance to build up their confidence in working with paranormal phenomena).

I escorted Lisa down to a small promontory over looking the valley, and as I always did on such occasions, advised her to use her Sight, and to remain where she was until the event was over. I then retreated back up the hill to wait until it was time to go and retrieve her. There was no fixed time period for this. Instead it was matter of waiting and listening to my own Little Voice to intuitively 'know' when the student was ready to end their solo—and I was never wrong about when this was.

In Lisa's case, the event ended quite suddenly and on an alarming note. I was suddenly filled with a sense that she was in grave danger and immediately headed down to where I had left her. At first, I didn't see her on the promontory, but then I managed to pick her out, standing with her back to me. But what really got my attention was what was hovering in the air above her and out some distance into space.

Two disembodied heads floated there, each about 3 feet in height. Neither was human. Instead they appeared to be more bird-like than anything else, with what resembled beaks and huge dark eyes. I only saw them for a moment, for as I approached the scene, they looked at me and quickly vanished.

I called out to Lisa, who backed away from the promontory at the sound of my voice.I asked her what had happened, and Lisa informed me that she had been standing on the outcrop when the two strange creatures had manifested in front of her. She told me that they had telepathically tried to convince her to walk off the ledge into space—apparently promising her that it would somehow be safe for her to step out into thin air. For her part, Lisa had almost been convinced to believe them when I had arrived and scared them off.

It had been a close call—but fortunately it proved to be the only time in my career that a 'solo' was ever remotely dangerous. I never forgot the event however, or the two creatures that my companions and I came to refer to as "Heckel and Jeckel" (from their loose resemblance to the two mischievous magpies of the Terrytoon cartoons). That, and the fact that the supernatural can always hold hidden dangers for the gullible, or the unwary...

CHAPTER VIII: GOING INTO THE FIELD

Life is either a daring adventure or nothing. Security does not exist in nature, nor do the children of men as a whole experience it. Avoiding danger is no safer in the long run than exposure. --*Helen Keller (1880 - 1968)*

Perhaps one of the most useful learning experiences in my own career happened when I decided to venture into the field; to go into a natural setting with my skills and experience the entities and the magick that is inherent in the world at large. Not only did this give me invaluable insights into the nature of supernatural forces, but it also allowed me the opportunity to stretch my magickal abilities to their limits. Certainly, the prospect of going out into the field can be a daunting proposition (as it was for me in the beginning), but the rewards this offers can far outweigh any of the potential hazards and difficulties.

Some readers might wish to defer this endeavor to a later stage, citing the relative newness of their abilities, but I must urge them to reconsider such a stance. I went into the field with far less 'under my belt' than even the reader, and the process complimented the growth of my knowledge base exponentially. For those up to the challenge, this short chapter is presented to help them navigate the experience safely and realize the greatest potential returns.

PREPARATION

The first step is to find an area for exploration. Books on local hauntings and regional lore are valuable tools in this regard and will present locations that may prove worth a visit. In addition to this, a working knowledge of your areas geography is also quite helpful. Local parks and other natural sites, while not necessarily noteworthy or famous, can provide excellent locations for exploration and magickal Work.

Once a location has been chosen, it is always advisable to scout it out during the daytime. This will reveal the lay of the land and any possible hazards that would otherwise be hard to spot at night, not to mention revealing possible routes into and out of the area. The next issue is proper equipment.

TOOLS AND EQUIPMENT

Even though the objective is spiritual in nature, the would-be explorer cannot forget that any trip into a deserted area can present physical challenges and hazards. They must also ensure that such necessities as a first aid kit are present along with any magickal tools. In addition, training in basic first aid and the essentials of backpacking and hiking safety are highly recommended.

One piece of equipment that has proven useful to me in the field is a heavy-duty flashlight capable of accepting colored lenses. Although a person with developed Sight will not use this item very often, it can be quite handy in certain situations. I have also found that while white light will interfere with night-vision, that blue light is just as effective in illuminating a trail, and with far less disturbance to this vision[89]. A helpful accessory is the traditional red-lens flashlight, although I have found this to be the most effective where reading maps and observing small details are required.

Proper clothing is another concern: a good jacket and strong, comfortable shoes are very important and for obvious reasons, so are gloves. But another item I also recommend is a hat with a brim, with a baseball style cap being my headgear of choice. Not only will it provide warmth, but the brim also allows the user to shield their eyes from the bright light of oncoming vehicles, the full moon, the lights from buildings and by doing this, helps to preserve night-vision.

There are many other items that are worthy of inclusion, but I will leave them to the student to pick and choose from, based on their experience and the nature of the location they choose to explore. In addition to whatever equipment is selected, the Tool of Art should also be included in one's kit, but only after careful consideration. While a wand is easy enough to pack into any location, there are some places where a dagger would be problematical and even illegal. For this reason, the prospective adventurer may choose to create a wand for just such occasions. I do not endorse any specific action, but merely point this out as a factor to be taken into consideration.

SOME RULES OF THE FIELD

- The use of stimulants other than coffee, and drugs of any kind is not recommended. Not only is this dangerous and illegal, but any phenomena that is witnessed will be in doubt because of the potential influence of such agents. If any type of photography is being performed, smoking should also be discouraged, as this can produce 'false positive' results.
- Get permission whenever possible: the very last thing a group needs is to be arrested for trespassing.
- Because this is a mystical exercise, horseplay and excessive talk should also be discouraged. The participants should keep a focused, serious fame of mind at all times. Not only does this help to ensure a successful outcome, but it also increases the safety factor.
- The most seasoned person (if this is a group) is in charge. Experience, not egos is what is needed most and while group members should express their opinion, every group needs a leader to function properly and their decisions should be followed.
- At any time that the group leader feels that the situation has gone too far, or has become dangerous in any way that is beyond the group's capabilities to handle, they should end the event, and withdraw. This should be a non-negotiable consideration.
- Once the event is over, there should be no conversation about what occurred until the group has left the area completely. This rule is derived from the Navajo custom that forbids discussion of the dead out of the concern that such a conversation will attract negative entities. Certainly, after a particularly intense experience, the very last thing a group needs is to have to deal with the forces that they were involved with on the way out. Any examination of the event should take place in a safe location, away from the site where it occurred—and not beforehand.
- When it is time for discussion, everyone should contribute any and all details no matter how trifling they might have seemed at the time. Often it is the small elements that turn out to be the very thing that confirms an experience for someone else. A good example of this would be where someone sees a glow around a particular tree, and in sharing this information, confirms this phenomena for another person who saw the same thing and thought they had simply imagined it.

By following these rules, journeys into the field such as I have talked about in this book can be enjoyable, educational and rewarding.

CHAPTER IX: THE ELEMENTALS

I will first make an offering and send a voice to the Spirit of the World, that it may help me to be true. See, I fill this sacred pipe with the bark of the red willow; but before we smoke it, you must see how it is made and what it means. These four ribbons hanging here on the stem are the four quarters of the universe. The black one is for the west where the thunder beings live to send us rain; the white one for the north, whence comes the great white cleansing wind; the red one for the east, whence springs the light and where the morning star lives to give men wisdom; the yellow one for the south, whence come the summer and the power to grow.--*Black Elk*

The ancients divided the basic components of the universe into four basic elements: Earth, Air, Fire, and Water. Each element was considered to be *both* a physical substance *and* a spiritual force. Eventually, these same elements became part of the classic magical circle, with each assigned a specific quadrant. While there have been many ideas about which element occupies what direction, it is generally accepted by most practitioners of today that the northern quadrant of a circle is assigned to the Earth, the east to Air, the south to Fire and the west to Water (although I myself follow another set of assignments based on my own beliefs).

When collectively invoked as part of the circle, the elemental spirits add their essence to create what is in effect a complete energetic model of the universe, with the Magician at its center. As I stated earlier in this work, the magickal circle has two basic functions; it acts as a protective enclosure and secondly as an energetic lens of sorts to help focus the Magician's intention in a ritual.

But while most Magicians of today are capable of drawing a serviceable enough circle, I have seen from my own observations that the real connection between the Magician and the elements they call to the Circle are generally not present, nor fully realized. Most modern practitioners certainly have varying levels of empathy with the elemental forces, but very few in today's mechanized society have any practical understanding of them in their pure spiritual form. As a result, I contend that they are unwittingly robbing themselves of the full power that a magick circle is truly capable of.

I believe that it is vital that the calling of the elements to a circle be more than a purely ritual act and I assert that the only way to truly ensure this is for the practitioner to gain direct experience with each element of the circle before they can truly lay any claim to an understanding of the magick circle as a whole. This is accomplished by working with each element individually, and gradually building up a rapport with the elements (and also an understanding of their true nature). A secondary benefit of this effort is that it also introduces the practitioner to a new level of interacting with the denizens of the Hidden World—while also ushering in the possibility of a genuine working relationship, rather than an open-ended encounter.

I first saw the classic magical circle when I was exposed to Wicca and ceremonial magick. I was already aware of the basic protective circle (which was discussed in Chapter 3) and I was intrigued by the inclusion of the four elements as part of this construction. Towards this end, I asked various people with magickal experience about the elementals themselves, but quickly realized that few (if any) of them had any real working knowledge—and those that I suspected did, would not divulge their information. Not being satisfied with these impediments, I embarked on a study of my own.

I quickly learned that there was very little written about the elementals and what there was of it was sparse at best. This left only one path open to me—direct experimentation, coupled with adaptations of existing rituals. The result was as follows:

In a short amount of time, I devised a ritual for calling an elemental and made arrangements with my student Louis to go into the field to try it out.

The location we picked was Vasquez Rocks County Park, just north of Los Angeles. This area offered easy access and plenty of lonely spots where I knew I would be able to Work undisturbed. Not knowing precisely what would or would not occur, I had Louis go into a small valley that neighbored mine and started my experiment.

I began by drawing a simple Triangle of Manifestation[90], followed by a basic circle around myself. I then proceeded to call out to the elementals of Earth demanding that one of them appear in my triangle in visible form. At first, nothing happened and I repeated my call with more intention.

At this point, the wind began to pick up and I realized that something was responding to my efforts, so I continued to demand that a spirit appear. Then suddenly, the very dust in the air congealed into a basketball sized shape that spiraled right into the triangle. I was so amazed by this that my concentration broke. At the precise instant that happened, the swirling ball exploded outwards in all directions with such force that it knocked me off my feet.

As I struggled to stand back up, the mass shot away from me and went up and over the hill towards Louis. For his part, Louis saw it coming and quickly deflected it with an act of willed intent. The mass veered away from him and went towards some homes a few miles away. Seeing this, Louis ran over to my location and told me what had happened.

I redrew my circle and the triangle and called out again. The swirling cloud returned a few minutes later--and this time I made sure to keep myself focused. Once again, I commanded it to come into the triangle and once it was there, I ordered it to give me its Name. It responded, and once I had the Name, I told it to leave, harming no one. The mass obeyed and we left the area satisfied that we had succeeded (albeit a bit shaken up).

This account highlights several important points. The first is that the elemental forces are by their very nature, wild things that will not necessarily obey unless they feel a sure hand is on the reins. This is a basic principle that many magical texts through the centuries repeat again and again and it is not to be taken lightly. In my case, I got off comparatively easy, but there are many tales of would-be Magicians who did not fare as well and even paid with their lives.

The second point is that while a spirit may represent a certain element, it may not always appear in the manner that the magician might expect it to. Certainly, the information I had gleaned from the grimores I had read about earth elementals did not describe anything like what I had actually encountered. I only realized after many years of Work that the descriptions such arcane texts give can be allegorical, or are presented with the intent to deliberately mislead those who are not worthy of pursuing this area of the Art.

And the third point, which has proven to be critical time and time again for me, is that the Magician should always be ready for surprises, no matter how well they might have prepared for their Working, and react accordingly. A good example of this comes from another Calling I conducted, many years later, involving a spirit of Fire.

I had long since mastered calling the basic elements to a Working Circle, and as part of my ongoing efforts to improve myself, I went on to Calling spirits of greater power and complexity. One series of Workings I undertook involved Calling the Elemental Kings and Queens (which are of a higher order than the elements themselves and embody their collective essence).

I chose the Queen of Fire for my first Calling and went out into the Mojave Desert for the Working. The desert, with its searing heat seemed to be the ideal backdrop for this particular ritual and I made my arrangements for the trip. Part of my preparations involved the creation of a special oil which was formulated to be in harmony with the element of fire---and flammable enough to help start the bonfire I planned to use for my summoning.

I arranged to stay with my brother at a small cabin deep in the desert. We had been given it to use by a friend of his for the weekend, and had driven there in my brother's 4-wheel drive Jeep.

On the evening of the ritual, I packed up my supplies and a rifle, and drove up alone into some nearby hills. Eventually I managed to find a fairly open and level spot, and after parking, quickly set up the wood for my fire. Then, after pouring on the special oil, and encircling both the fire and myself, I lit the wood ablaze and began to call out to the flames.

After a time, the Elemental responded, taking shape in the fire as a dancing figure. I was moved to tears by her beauty and watched her dance, enraptured by the event. She called to me to join her in the flames, and although a part of me wanted to leave my Circle and do so, I stayed where I was and gently declined the offer.

Then I suddenly realized that I had an audience standing behind me. I turned to see what it was. A figure was standing there.

She was as tall as I was and dressed in a long dark green cloak that seemed to be made from velvet. Her skin was as white as chalk and her hair was jet black. But it was her eyes and her teeth more than any other features that clearly announced that she was not human. Two sharp canines protruded over her lips and her eyes completely lacked any whites. Instead they were black and slanted at an extreme angle.

She smiled at me and I heard her voice in my mind, asking if she could step across my circle and join me. I laughed aloud and denied her request, knowing that to have agreed to it I would have sealed my fate. She responded to this with a mental laugh of her own and shrugged as if she had known I would do this, but had felt compelled to at least test me for weakness.

I then asked her out loud what her business was and she telepathically stated that she had been attracted by the Circle and wanted to conduct business with me. I replied by asking that she leave and promised to contact her at a later date to discuss the matter. This seemed to be agreeable to my uninvited guest and the apparition departed.

Except for the modern context, this could have been a story from any ancient book on magic, and like the subjects of those tales, I accepted what happened and was careful in my responses. **I cannot stress enough that if the reader embarks on a program of calling spirits, that although the early levels are benign enough, that such operations can become quite dangerous later on. Calling Spirits is not a part of the Art to be taken lightly, nor performed haphazardly**[91]. With these examples—and cautions in mind, we will examine the basic elements themselves and undertake several exercises in which we can interact with them.

SPECIFIC CHARACTERISTICS OF THE ELEMENTAL SPIRITS

Each elemental spirit not only possesses an appearance that is specific to the element it embodies, but each also has a unique temperament that can influence how it is Called and dealt with in the context of a ritual. Certainly there are many variations on how an elemental might appear, and what I present is based only on my own experience, but hopefully my information will provide the reader with insights that will be useful for their own experimentation.

EARTH

Earth spirits, like the element itself, tend to be heavy in form and solemn in demeanor. In my experience, they tend to appear visually as black shadows, often humanoid in shape. But even if they are not immediately visible, one sure sign that the earth elementals have responded to a Call, is the smell that many practitioners have noted of fresh turned earth.

While there are times that the earth elementals will appear without great effort, there are others where their Calling will require some exertion of Will on the part of the Magician. As the reader has already gathered, they can, if they feel there is any uncertainty on the Magician's part, break the bonds of their Calling. Therefore, it is incumbent on the practitioner to be firm and resolute with them during the operation. Once they have been called enough times however, they will be quite cooperative and appear fairly easily.

AIR

Air will generally respond to a Call with little effort, and I have found that the best way to do this is more in the manner of an invitation, than a command. Tending towards an almost sensual nature, Air could be called friendly, although a firm intention is sometimes required to get compliance from it.

In appearance, air will often take the form of misty shapes, or small moving bodies that are either light or dark in appearance. A sure sign of their presence is the reaction of the wind around the summoner, particularly when it rises and falls in time with the Magician's Call or gestures.

FIRE

In my experience, Fire is perhaps the hardest elemental to Call and work with. Just as Mankind is still learning to harness Fire for mundane purposes, this element can be just as wild and unpredictable in the magickal context. Calling Fire requires a firm commanding intent that is strong and unwavering during the entire operation. Many practitioners have remarked that Calling Fire is similar to trying to tame a wild horse and I agree wholeheartedly. There can be no break in concentration once Fire has appeared, and no lapses in ones confidence.

In terms of its appearance, Fire manifests itself in exactly the same way it physically occurs. It is its actions once it is Called that announce that the spirit has manifested, specifically the reaction of the Fire to the magicians commands or gestures. On some occasions, practitioners may notice that the flame takes on various shapes, but tends to stay amorphous the majority of the time.

WATER

Water is as subtle as its physical manifestation. Generally all that is required is a Call that invites its presence, but there can be a tendency for it to be seductive. Many practitioners working with larger bodies of water often report that the element tends to try to lure the summoner out into it. This makes it important that the person Calling maintain their focus and avoid deviating from their operation no matter how great the temptation (which is in itself a good general rule to follow). As for its appearance, Water, like Air, tends to manifest as misty clouds over the physical water, sometimes accompanied by luminous shapes moving in the water itself and in more advanced operations, may even take on a humanoid appearance.

THE BENEFITS OF WORKING WITH THE ELEMENTALS

With all of the above taken into account, the reader might ask what makes these potentially risky operations worthwhile. The first benefit was stated at the beginning of this chapter: by learning to Call the Elementals, the aspiring magician moves from the basic level of mere encounters with supernatural beings to the higher level of a working relationship. This relationship not only allows for a deeper experience and understanding of such forces, but also makes it possible to employ the Elementals to assist the magician in their rituals, and in their daily affairs as the following example illustrates:

I had applied for a job at a local hospital and a promotion at my present place of employment. But for various reasons the hospital was not hiring, and my efforts at advancing myself were being thwarted by numerous obstacles and delays that were seemingly beyond my control.

Finally, frustrated with the impasse, I called upon the Earth Elementals to assist me, asking that since they were reputed to govern material success and riches, that they aid me by removing any and all obstacles in my way to gaining this for myself. Within 2 days, word came to me that the hospital was suddenly making plans to hire people and a promotion was suddenly offered to me at the job I had. I took the promotion and received a commensurate raise in pay.

Interestingly, during the time this was happening I kept noticing what I first thought were people walking by my desk at work, only to look over my shoulder to see no one passing by. I quickly realized that these dark shadows were none other than the Elementals working their special magick.

In Classical times, each elemental force was believed to govern a specific area of material affairs and I have found that this is certainly true. An understanding of these qualities allows the magician to Call the right spirit for the task at hand.

Just as the ancients believed, Earth tends to govern material wealth, protection and growth. Air is involved in communications and matters of the intellect. Water acts in the area of emotions and Fire in matters of energy, creation and destruction. With this in mind, the aspiring magician will have little trouble formulating the proper ritual for a given situation once they have achieved basic mastery.

But while material success is certainly an important aspect of the Elementals assistance, it is not the only one. Another set of benefits involves the process of learning and spiritual growth. The act of Calling the elementals imparts a deeper understanding of the spiritual essences that exist behind the material world and also helps to establish a deeper connection with these very same forces. Not only does this lead in turn to greater abilities with which to work with such forces, but at the same time brings the Magician more in harmony *with* the natural forces they are working with. And as this process gains momentum, it ultimately opens the door to the knowledge and interaction with even greater forces beyond these.

We will now examine the specific operations of calling the Elements as I know them.

Exercise 1: Calling Earth

The first step is to find a private place to conduct the Working, free of unwelcome interruptions. Preferably it should be in a natural environment that is in harmony with the element you are Calling. In this case, a forested setting is ideal. As always, lighting is important and the ritual should be conducted at dusk, or full nighttime.

Very little is required in the way of equipment; your dagger of Art, possibly some chalk for drawing the diagrams along with whatever you need for your comfort and survival.

The ritual begins with the act of drawing the physical representations of the Triangle of Manifestation and your own working Circle (although some practitioners like myself eschew this step, preferring to create them solely from pure Inner Fire). The Triangle should be anywhere from 5 to 10 feet from your Working Circle, in the north of your working area[92]. Your Circle should surround you and be large enough to accommodate you and your supplies comfortably.

There is one addition to the Circles design that should also be introduced (or reintroduced) to the student at this point, which they will immediately recognize from their earlier primary exercises working with the Inner Fire. This is the addition of a pentagram within its boundaries.

The pentagrams apex should point towards the Triangle[93] and it should be drawn so that all its' points touch the Circle. It should also be large enough so that there is enough room for you to stand in its center. Without going into great detail (which other books on magick will amply supply), the basic purpose of this added graphic is to further empower the magick Circle, by evoking the elemental forces expressed by its fundamental shape, thus aiding a Magician in focusing their Will within the Circle. This 'encircled pentagram' design should be employed in all Workings from this one onwards, which require a magick Circle.

Once your have physically laid out the Working area, it will be time to charge the Circle and the Triangle. You should begin by breathing out Fire from your dagger and draw the Triangle first; visualizing it as an enclosure and a place of manifestation for the spirit you are about to Call. Then draw your Working Circle around you and finally the pentagram within it.

Once you have completed this, relax and let yourself meditate on the element of earth and all that it means to you. Then when you are ready, extend the point of your dagger and call out to the spirit.

The exact wording you use is of little importance—what matters instead is your intention, which is that a spirit of earth come into your Triangle of Manifestation and make itself visible to you. A basic script for this might be: "Element of Earth, I Call to you! Come into the Triangle of Manifestation and make yourself visible to me. I command you to visible appearance! I command you to obey me in all ways and to appear to me in a pleasing form."

As you do this, *it is imperative that you do not let doubt enter your mind. The Magician only succeeds in their magick where absolute certainty has supplanted doubt entirely*. If you are free of uncertainty, focused and put all your power and belief into your command, the spirit will appear.

The 'trick' is not so much getting the spirit to come into the Triangle as much as compelling it to stay there, and making itself known to you. There have been many cases where a spirit was called, but the Magician failed to demand that it make itself visible—and the spirit obliged them by remaining invisible. Keep in mind that the spirit of earth may appear to you in a variety of ways including the scent of fresh earth, a dark amorphous shadow or simply a heavy presence in the area. Recognizing these signs may be the key to knowing that you have succeeded in your endeavor and the entity is present.

Once you are aware of the spirits attendance, you must then compel it to stay in the Triangle, and more importantly, to give you its Name. To recite the ancient formula once more, the name of a spirit is the key to controlling it—and to calling it again and again.

You may not hear its reply with physical ears. Instead it may be something that you hear in your mind, and in fact this is far more likely as most spirits communicate on a telepathic basis. Many students, new to this type of communication find this the hardest part of the operation and I can only suggest that the easiest way to 'hear' is to relax as much as possible and let the spirit's words come to your mind free of doubt or interference. This is where the skill of Stilling the Waters becomes a critical ability. Once you have the Name, commit it to memory.

The next step after this is to banish the spirit. One formula for this is: "Spirit of Earth, I command you to depart from here. May you leave in peace and may there be peace forever more between us."

This command should be as forceful as the initial Calling, and should be repeated until you are certain that the spirit has in fact departed. **An important safety point needs mentioning at this juncture: under no circumstances are you to venture out of your Working Circle until you have banished** the spirit. Keep in mind that just because you cannot see anything does not mean it is not there; as many would be magicians have learned to their ultimate regret.

When you feel that the spirit has departed, it will be time to banish the Triangle and the Working Circle. The best method for this is to go back over the lines of energy that comprise the Working Circle and the Triangle in reverse and then cross through the designs with your dagger to disrupt their patterns completely.

With this step completed, make sure to police the area and remove all traces of your Work. Not only is this action friendly to the environment, but also helps to ensure that the area will be available to you in the future. In our society, nothing attracts attention to a place like the remains of a magickal ritual.

Exercise 2: Calling Air

In this case, the setting of choice should be a mountaintop, or some large open area that allows for the wind to move freely about. The Call should be forceful, but tempered with a sense of invitation. One method of determining if Air has responded is to demand that the wind around you rise or fall at your command. In the past, when training student's, I often required that they make this command while simultaneously raising and lowering their arms. This gesturing helped the student and all observers to see if the spirit was in fact responding to the practitioner's Will.

Exercise 3: Calling Fire

The most basic method for calling Fire utilizes a candle, or a bonfire. Which one depends of course on the resources and circumstances of the summoner. In the case of candles, the reaction of the flame to the summoner is of primary importance and attention should be paid to this particular detail. My own measure of Fire's response is the raising or lowering of the flame to my commands. A variation of this often involved having the student walk around the flame (or from side to side within a Circle), while visualizing the desire that the flames follow their movement.

Exercise 4: Calling Water

A large body of water is preferable for this operation, either a lake or the ocean. If this is not feasible, then a container of water can suffice and this should be set out in the Triangle of Manifestation. Care should be taken to remain at the shore of any large body and under no circumstances should one actually go into such a body while the operation is being conducted. Water, although lovely enough to look at, can be unpredictable.

CHAPTER X: GHOSTS AND EXORCISM

My utterance is mighty, I am more powerful than the ghosts; may they have no power over me. --*Egyptian Book of the Dead*

In my book, "Crossroads: the Path of Hecate", I described my self-initiation as a Priest of Hecate. For those who are not familiar with Her, She is, among other things a Goddess who leads the spirits of the dead into the Afterlife. Not surprisingly, my initiation involved a ghost:

My Work was done, and I had left nothing behind me to cause me any possible problems. What I did not know was that the evening was far from over. I had one more task planned for me.
I returned to my car (making sure I had not been followed) and started back for my motel. It was still quite early however, and I was not eager to return to my room and simply sit there watching television.
In what seemed a spontaneous moment of decision, I elected instead to drive to a nearby road that I had read about in a book about haunted sites to see if I could find the ghost the book had mentioned. Most people would probably not have done this, but again, I had had enough years of exploration into the supernatural that I regarded this as simply a recreational activity to enliven the evening a bit more.
I followed the road signs and quickly found the highway that I was seeking. Once there, I parked in a local campground, and got out of my vehicle. The being that the guidebook had mentioned had been described as

a terrible creature; a horribly deformed man, who had allegedly died in a local forest fire and now haunted the roadway, scaring the odd teenager or lost motorist.

I had no specific plan in mind; I just intended to follow my curiosity about this local phenomenon and learn what it might be. To be sure, I was somewhat skeptical about the tale, as it sounded like so many local tales told by people with overactive imaginations or a propensity for tall stories, but I had time on my hands and I was willing to explore whatever possibilities there were.

I began to walk the length of the road, shielding my eyes now and again from oncoming cars and watching for any sign that something strange was afoot. After a time, I began to suspect that the tale of the gruesome ghost was just that, but I remained committed to completing my journey at least to the roads end.

A sensation that I was not alone came over me, and I looked behind me. Something moved in the darkness, but it was gone before I could fully register what it had been. I pushed onwards, knowing that something was following me.

Then when I came around a bend, I saw my companion. The apparition was fairly large this time; it appeared as a blue-white cloud-like formation of energy, taking on the rough shape and size of an adult male. It hung suspended in the night air, just in front of what I realized was a crude wooden cross set at the side of the roadway.

As I approached, the being retreated and then vanished, leaving me alone with the marker. I stopped to read it.

A satisfied smile came to my face. The name on the marker was the same as that of the 21-year-old accident victim from the graveyard. I realized then that this was the exact spot where he had died. And with this knowledge came an understanding of what I had just seen: the apparition had been his restless spirit, still wandering the 2-lane blacktop.

I also knew why I had been led here. I had one final act to complete in my Initiation as a servant of the Queen of the Ghostworld.

Visualizing a brilliant, but comforting light that led to the next life in my minds eye, I spoke aloud to the being (whom I knew was hovering somewhere nearby).

"Wandering spirit," I said, "in the name of the Mighty One, Queen Hecate, I charge you to leave this place and follow Her light to your reward. It is time to move onwards."

A moment later a soft breeze caressed me, and the feeling of something lurking nearby vanished entirely. The spirit of the young man had found his rest at last, and I had found my true calling.

It was certainly not the first time I had dealt with a ghost, but it was the first time that I experienced a genuine sense of compassion for one. I came to understand that for all the mystique surrounding them, ghosts are simply disembodied people and in most cases, are the victims of tragedy. This event profoundly changed my attitude towards them. I came to see what is nowadays referred to as 'ghost hunting' as an opportunity for crisis intervention in an area that is for the most part, spiritually neglected.

Most ghosts are beings that for a variety of reasons cannot move on to the next life. In many cases, they are bound to a particular spot because of fear, a trauma, or through their inability to let go of something they had in life. As a Magician, a Priest, and a human being, it became impossible for me to ignore their suffering, or to minimize it in favor of the cheap thrill of merely seeing one. I believe now that the highest calling one can undertake is to help a spirit, be it in a body, or out of one, to find its peace and the path to knowledge. I invite the reader to share this point of view with me.

This chapter deals with some of the ghosts I have encountered before and since my Initiation and the means to handle those among them that are either troubled, or are causing harm to others.

TYPES OF APPARITIONS

There are four basic types of apparitions that people generally experience in their brushes with the Hidden World that are collectively referred to as ghosts. These are the True Ghost, the Shade, the Echo and Otherfolk. While most people tend to lump them all together and classify them simply as 'spirits', in realty, they are quite distinct from one another. And of these four, only one is what can be considered a ghost in the classic sense of the term. We will examine this type first, and through that, gain a better understanding of the other types of beings and their natures.

DISEMBODIED SOULS OR TRUE GHOSTS

The first class are disembodied souls or what I call 'true ghosts'. They are sentient, conscious and can interact with their environment. Frequently, they are unaware (or in denial) of the fact that they are dead, or have unfinished business of some kind that they need to attend to before they can move onwards to the next level of existence. The determinant is largely their emotional connection with the world of the living and their desire to interact with it, or their fear of the unknown that the afterlife represents.

Like the living, true ghosts come in all shapes, sizes and ages. They can range from infants, through children and into adulthood, based either upon the time they died or on their self-image of themselves at the time of their death.

They can also possess varying abilities based on their level of residual Will and consciousness. For example, some ghosts can influence material things around them (such as opening a door or touching the living), while others are incapable of this kind of action.

True ghosts can also manifest themselves in many ways, appearing as everything from full-figure apparitions to cloud-like mists or bodies of light. Again, this is based on their abilities and the level of energy they have retained after death.

The color a ghost takes on when it manifests can also vary. It can range from what we could call 'normal' coloration (that is, possessing the colors we would equate with the living), to white or blue-ish, black, and sometimes even green or other colors (these being the rarer). The reason for these different colors is not fully understood, however one theory I heard, and which I tend to agree with, is that the coloration occurs as a result of the energetic frequency that the ghost most closely corresponds to (in much the same sense that color itself is a frequency of light). Another theory that has equal merit is that these colors are the result of the ghost's emotional or energetic state, but to date there is no agreement on which color corresponds to what.

While certain colors have had specific values ascribed to them by observers, i.e. white being 'good' and black being 'bad', I must state that from my own first-hand experience, that these notions are purely cultural and have no actual bearing on the true nature of a given spirit whatsoever.

Like the living, some true ghosts are solitary apparitions, while others tend to haunt a location as part of a group, with the temperament and activities of its members varying just as they would in life. There are many reasons such groups come together, but we will look at several of the main causes.

The first is a group that comes together as the result of a shared trauma, or as the result of the co-dependant relationship that the spirits had with each other in life. Here we can see a direct parallel between their activities and the co-dependant relationship they had while living.

In these cases in particular (although it also occurs in other, more positive groupings), it is not uncommon for a particular spirit in the group to be dominant over their otherworldly companions, tending not only to make the most appearances to the living, but also suppressing or limiting the activities of their fellows.

A good example of this occurred in a case which is detailed later in this chapter (and resulted in an exorcism): the problem spirit had in life been a domineering male who had mercilessly lorded over his wife. The same situation continued in death between them--while he was seen frequently, his wife remained an unknown figure.

However after his banishment, she made her appearance, and when asked, stated that she had been unable to fully manifest because her husband had 'kept her' from doing so. It was only after his influence was removed from the equation, that she was able to make herself known and enjoy the home that they had both resided in.

How exactly a dominant ghost accomplishes the suppression of another ghost is unknown (but is thought to be the force of their personality acting in combination with an exertion of their Will). Whatever the mechanism might be, determining if a dominant spirit exists in a group can be the key to dealing with a ghost group and the removal of that same dominant entity can be the linchpin that not only changes the dynamics of the group, but can also help to facilitate its removal or management.

Another type of ghost group can come together not out of a negative relationship, but out of the basic need for companionship. A good example of this are child ghosts, who tend to stay with one another for much the same reasons that living children congregate—to satisfy their need for play, company and a sense of security.

A third type of ghost group that can tend to confuse paranormal investigators occurs where ghosts who were not related in life in any manner, come together in the same location. In this case, the causes for their appearances are from separate incidents that took place at the same site, or due to the nature of the site itself.

Some locales tend to be 'attractive' to wandering spirits either because the area is a natural collection point for psychic energy, or the occupants who reside there are especially receptive to spirits in general. The result can be a cluster of apparitions with no pre-death relationship with one another who are manifesting to the living as a group nonetheless.

True ghosts also have a 'lifespan' if you will, just as they had before death. As with everything else about them, the amount of time they can haunt a location in a coherent form is dependent on two things: their karmic obligations and their basic energy levels.

Karma is a factor where a ghost has made its appearance as the result of unfinished business in the world. As a rule, once this business has been concluded, many ghosts tend to cease their haunting and move on to the next life. How long a process this is, depends on their task and its nature. Perhaps one of the most interesting examples of karmic obligation and a ghost took place with a man who was career criminal:

The man and his 'wife of the moment' (he had been married several times and she was the third in the series), had been traveling from San Francisco to Los Angeles. It was Christmas Eve and raining heavily. As a result, there were almost no service stations open, and when he began to run low on gasoline, he pulled into the first one he found.

After pumping his gas, the man went inside the station to pay. The attendant on duty was an older man, who greeted him by saying a rather odd thing. Reportedly he stated, "I'll bet you're surprised to see me open tonight."

The man replied affirmatively, and the attendant smiled cryptically and responded with "I'm always open for travelers on Christmas Eve".

The man thought this was a little strange, but paid for his gas and left. It was only when he reached his destination that he discovered that a small private journal he had kept in his jacket that night, was missing. After searching his car and possessions, he realized that he had lost it at the service station. So, when he was on his return trip north, he searched for the station and managed to locate it.

Once there, the man sought out one of the employees on duty and asked after his notebook, thinking that it might have been found and put in a lost-and-found box. The employee knew nothing about it, and rewarded the man with a strange look when he told him when exactly it had been lost. Then, when the man continued to insist that the notebook had been lost on Christmas Eve, the attendant went and got his manager.

The manager who came out to meet the man was a younger version of the attendant he had met, and clearly a relative. The man told the manager his story, and the manager responded by demanding that the man leave his station immediately or the police would be summoned.

Baffled by this, the man started to obey, and on his way to his car, asked the first employee about the manager's strange reaction. The attendant, who also appeared to be agitated by the whole inquiry, responded by telling the man that the gas station had been closed Christmas Eve, and that the last time it had been open on that holiday had been five years earlier—when the current manager's father had still been alive.

The man left the station, mystified by all this. Although he had dabbled with spirituality, he was not given to great belief in the occult and this ghost story was well beyond his understanding. So he put it out of his mind. It was not long however, before his luck changed. In short order, he was caught for his crimes, put on trial and served a lengthy term in prison. Undoubtedly his journal had played some role in this reversal of his affairs, falling as it had into the hands of a supernatural agent of justice.

If karma is not the main dynamic of a haunting, then a ghost can appear for an indeterminate period of time. But generally, however, the maximum amount of time a ghost can sustain itself appears to be a few hundred years before their energy is completely exhausted (or they transition onwards[94]).

One exception, which has been noted by paranormal experts, is where the ghost seems to prolong and replenish its energy by draining sources of electricity, thus reenergizing itself. This has been observed in cases where the batteries used to power the investigators equipment are unaccountably drained during a haunting, or where the ghost tends to appear near obvious sources of power. With the bounty of electrical sources available in our modern age and in the times to come, one can imagine that the ghosts of the future will last much longer than their predecessors did, perhaps even thousands of years.

But regardless of a ghost's lifespan, there comes a time when the ghost ceases to appear and stops interacting with the world of the living. This occurs when it has at last made its transition onwards to the next world either due to a lack of energy to sustain itself on this plane, or as the result of concluding its business here in the world of the living. Although a variant of it can still be called after this point through the use of the Art, and even communicated with, what will appear is something entirely different from a true ghost. It is now the second type of 'ghost', or what the ancients referred to as a 'shade'.

SHADES

Shades can be loosely defined as a spiritual remnant of the soul of the deceased. They are an eternal 'after-image' that goes on long after the main body of the soul has transcended this world. Unlike true ghosts, shades do not haunt the living or a specific location and are generally only encountered when the living seek *them* out.

The ancient Egyptians, who made an extensive study of the soul and the afterlife[95], offered up a model that helps not only to explain this type of spirit but also to help us better understand the nature of many other important aspects of ghosts and of the afterlife in general.

For the Egyptians, the soul was not a single being as contemporary Westerners view it (this modern notion being a by-product of Judeo-Christian ideas[96]). Instead, they saw the human soul as being composed of nine specific parts, each with their own role in the process of death and rebirth.

The first part of the soul was the *Khat* or *Kha*. This is the physical body.

The second component was the *Ka*, which was the double of the deceased and which could live on, inhabiting the tomb with the *Khat* and even statues of the departed. This same *Ka* was independent of a person and did not only appear after death, but could appear to others while one was still alive. The *Ka* could also travel forth while a person slept, and the ancients held that everything in our world had its own Ka, or spirit[97] (which of course should be immediately familiar to modern readers as being exactly the same concept that other cultures such as the Native Americans, hold to be the case).

The next element was the *Ba*, which was depicted as a bird-headed being that stayed near the tomb during the day. The *Ba* acted as the connection with the Divine, and accompanied the God Ra on his solar barque at night.

The fourth component was the *Khaibit*, which was the shadow of a person and stayed near the *Ba*. It was believed that this shadow could also partake of funerary offerings.

The next three elements were the *Akhu (Akh, Khu, Ikhu)*, the *Sahu* and the *Sekhem*. The *Akhu* was the immortal part of the soul that came into being after final judgment in the afterlife had occurred (and the *Ka* and *Ba* had united with one another). The *Akhu* lived on with the *Sahu*, or intellect, along with the *Sekhem*, which was the life force itself.

Then there was the *Yb (Ib, Ab)*. The *Yb* was the heart of a man and was regarded as the source of all the good, or evil, that one perpetrated. It was the *Yb* that the Gods weighed when a person was judged. Looking back at the tale of the ghost of the gas station manager, it should be clear to the reader that this same heart is not so much the literal heart responsible for pumping blood (although that organ having a *Ka*, would be by that very fact, part of the overall soul), but that part of the spirit that accumulates karma. Certainly in that particular case, one can have little doubt that the man in the story will have a hard way to go when the Gods finally weigh his particular heart.

Finally, we have the *Ren*. The *Ren* was a person's true name. As the reader will recall from earlier sections, for the Egyptians, the name of a thing was the thing itself. For this reason, naming ceremonies in ancient Egypt were highly secret affairs and in fact, ancient Egyptians went through their lives using the equivalent of 'nicknames' and kept their true names a secret. The act of destroying the names of pharaohs on stone monuments was therefore nothing less than an attempt to destroy the very soul of those rulers utterly.

To add to these ideas, the ancients also believed that each component of the soul lived its own existence, with some portions of the soul residing in heaven, while others went about their business here on this plane. But as complex as this model might seem on the surface, if we take it into account and apply it to not only the subject of ghosts, but such phenomena as 'daytime' ghosts, doppelgangers and the like (and even refer to it when examining the idea of simultaneous existences), it emerges as being quite practical and to the point--and makes our conventional view of the soul seem rather quaint and simplistic, if not entirely incomplete.

A good way that I have used to help students understand the Egyptian model of the soul is to use the analogy of an egg. As a living person, all of the nine components of our soul are intact, just as our hypothetical egg's shell is unbroken with its yolk still contained within. At death, this shell is broken and if all goes well, our soul emerges in the afterlife in a new form, just as a chick emerges from a fertilized egg.

And just as in the case of our theoretical chick, the remnants of the egg that created it are left behind (these being the *Khat* or *Kha,* the *Ka, Ba* and so on). One by-product of these soul fragments are shades, which could be considered to be composed of the *Ka* or the *Khaibit* (or both)[98]

But where a true ghost occurs, we see where the transformative death process was interrupted and like an unformed yolk, a ghost is only half of what it could be (being composed mainly of the the *Sahu,* the Sekhem and the *Ka).* But, unlike the egg, a ghost can resume its evolution onwards to become something greater, the *Akhu.* What is required for this to happen is that either the ghost be guided back on its journey by our efforts, or realizes its own way there when the time is right.

With this all in mind, let us return back to an examination of the shade. Although the shade might appear as the person had in life, shades are in realty only the 'representative shells' of their former selves and not the entire soul. A shade is the end result of a process where the greater soul essence has become detached from its former existence and has transformed to a higher state of being.

For the living, this manifests where a true ghost initially has emotional connections with its loved ones and actively interacts with them, but then gradually becomes more and more detached until these connections are gone completely. While their spiritual body can still be interacted with after this point, the essential essence that was the former person is no longer accessible (having become the *Akhu*), leaving the shade behind like a footprint in the journey it has made.

The point where a true ghost makes this transition and leaves a shade appears to depend on the particular person involved, their karma and their emotional connections with the world they left. There appear to be no fixed periods or conditions that are universal to this process and it seems to vary from case to case.

'ECHO' GHOSTS

The third type of apparition that is frequently mislabeled as a true ghost is what could be referred to as an 'echo ghost'. An echo ghost is an apparition that has no consciousness, and is in fact merely an energetic recording of an event that took place at a particular spot. It appears on a regular basis and mechanically performs the same actions over and over with no apparent awareness of its surroundings and it does not interact with the living in any meaningful way[99].

Numerous theories abound concerning this kind of ghost, but there are two that I find to be the most convincing. The first is that these apparitions are the result of a time-slip[100], and are not in fact ghosts at all, but living beings experiencing what for them is the present.

The second theory is that they are the by-products of the energy of an event that has impressed itself into the physical structure of things around them (such as a building), which is then sporadically released by the structure itself. This release produces a vision of the 'ghost' similar to a movie being projected--and with the same level of self-awareness. A good example of this was something I witnessed in a small coastal cemetery in California:

The cemetery was old, dating back to the mid 19th century, and housed the remains of what were mainly Italian immigrants. As a result, although the site was small, the monuments were classic examples of graveyard sculpture and included a stone statue of the Madonna.

At some point in the recent past, vandals had pulled off the upper half of the statue, leaving only the lower half of the figure. But at night, one could clearly see the entire figure, which would only vanish when the lights of passing cars illuminated in it. Clearly, the years of devotion it had seen had imbued the statue with an energy that transcended its ravaged physical form.

OTHERFOLK

The fourth type of ghost is, like shades and echoes, not really a ghost at all, but a non-human entity that is mistaken for a ghost and is not really dead in any sense at all. A good example of this is what is commonly referred to today as a shadow being[101] or poltergeist phenomena.

In reality, these apparitions are either other forms of life, or are thought forms that have been created psychically. The latter can occur as the result of the spontaneous collection of stray energies in a particular location[102], as the unconscious creation by a particular person (such as in the cases of poltergeists who are the end result of the uncontrolled psychic energy of the living), or through a process of deliberate visualization. Our world is full of such beings and they are frequently misidentified as true ghosts. I experienced one such entity in a local occult bookstore I frequented.

After teaching a class at the store, I had remained behind to socialize with the owner who was also a witch and the leader of her own coven. Almost as soon as everyone (except for her closest students) had left, she confided in me that 'something' was attacking her and her group.

She told me that she and several of her students had had dreams, followed by waking encounters with a strange black, hooded figure[103]. The beings appearance seemed to coincide with a series of accidents and disasters that had visited her group and I learned that the hooded apparition had made its appearance shortly after the woman had had a falling out with a rival coven. I knew right away that she was not dealing with a ghost at all, but rather an 'egregore' or thought form, probably created by her opposition. She was, in a word, at war and under direct assault.

I asked more questions of her, particularly about how the being would manifest itself, and what she told me gave me the key to defeating it. The woman stated that the figure would appear in the main room of the bookstore, and walk across it from one wall to the other, without variance. When I examined the room, I observed that the 'exit' wall had a decorative mirror hanging on it that faced the opposite or 'entrance' wall. The entrance wall it turned out, had actually been a door at one time, but which had been walled over. I told the woman that egregore was following what is called a Ghost Path (or Ghost Road).

This is actually rather typical for some ghosts and entities like this one. The Ghost Path is a line of travel that follows the line of least energetic resistance through a space. In some cases, this will follow a local ley-line, and it allows the apparition to expend a minimal amount of energy to traverse an area. I explained this concept to the bookstore owner and suggested the remedy of removing the mirror. The mirror was, by its presence, helping to create a flow of energy from the former door to itself and allowed for an exit point for the being to depart through. This suggestion was itself a variant on an much older idea of driving iron spikes into a ley-lines to quash negative hauntings.

The mirror was removed and the apparition was never seen again, either at the store or anywhere else (evidently the focus of the attacks was the bookstore, and once this was denied to the egregore, the assault lost its focus and completely dissipated).

THE PROCESS OF DEATH AND THE CREATION OF A GHOST

After lingering in ill health for some time, my wife's grandfather became terminal. The family was summoned to his bedside. After a hard passage, he died.

Several minutes after his death, I volunteered to go downstairs to the hospital cafeteria to get everyone some coffee. I found the elevator and got inside.

As I pushed the button for the next floor, I felt someone behind me. I glanced over my shoulder, and saw the old man standing there, still in his hospital gown, complete with IV's still hanging from his arms. He looked both angry and frightened. I spoke to him aloud, telling him that everything was well and that he needed to move onwards. After a few seconds, he departed.

How does a ghost come to be? For all the people in the world who have died, ghosts are in fact, comparatively rare. And to understand them, we need to understand the basic process of death itself.

When a person dies, their spirit separates from their body and by its nature is able to transcend the physical realm and move onwards to another level of existence. As I stated in the preceding section on Shades, here in the modern West, we generally believe the idea that this spirit is a single entity. As I explained, the ancient Egyptians, among others, believed quite differently.

I personally subscribe to the Egyptian model, and believe that what we refer to as the soul is in fact only a portion of the energetic construct of a being, and that it is this part that moves onwards to the next life, while the remaining elements either dissipate, scatter or remain on the material plane.

Many cultures also feel that this transition to the next world is not an instant event, but rather a process that takes a specific period of time and only *begins* with the moment of separation from the body. The consensus among most of these societies is that a period of time elapses after death where a spirit is between our world and the next, generally ranging from the old magickal fortnight of two weeks, to as long as a month. It is during this time that most religions perform their funeral rites, which are in fact as much to help guide the spirit of the departed onwards as they are to provide comfort for the living. And it is in this critical period where a ghost can be created.

There are several major factors that can be involved (and a host of lesser ones). The first is where the person suffered a trauma, either in life, or as the cause of their death. And because this event remains unresolved, they cannot emotionally separate from this reality and as a result, remain bound here.

One example of this was a ghost I encountered in the Presidio Military cemetery in San Francisco. I had come to this historic locale as part of a project to photograph memorial art. I wanted to capture the classic line of graves that one sees so often in a military cemetery and to get the shot, I was forced to cross over a section of graves reserved for the wives of former officers. I personally hate walking over graves as a rule because I feel that this disturbs the dead, but I had no choice in this instance and made the trip as quickly and as respectfully as possible.

When I reached the other side I readied my camera, but as I went to take the picture, a cold wind blew over me. I looked over my shoulder and saw a man standing there out of the corner of my eye.

I knew him for a ghost right away. He was tall, and well proportioned with heavy 'mutton chop' sideburns. He was also very pale and dressed in a

19th century navy-blue military uniform, complete with brass buttons down its front. And he was angry with me. He stood there clenching his fists in rage and I intuitively realized two things: that he had died violently and that I had trespassed on the grave of his former wife whom he still had an emotional attachment to. I promptly spoke an apology aloud and the ghost vanished.

This tale also illustrates the second reason for a ghost coming to be: a profound attachment to another person or thing and a reluctance to leave it behind. Even if limitless possibilities exist in the next world, some spirits refuse to depart from what is familiar or held dear to them. I, for one, cannot really blame them for wanting to stay under such circumstances.

The third reason for a ghost can be fear of the unknown or a reluctance to face it. Given the imagery of hideous retribution and judgment that exists in some major religions, this certainly should come as no surprise—after all, who wants to report for punishment for real or imagined wrongs?

And the last major cause is ignorance or disorientation from the death process. Many ghosts are simply not aware they are dead, or have no idea how to find their way from this reality to the next. I have met many beings like these. They are generally the victims of sudden trauma: people who died so quickly that they are unaware that they have actually passed on.

Whichever the root cause for a ghost, it is during the critical time period of the fortnight to a month that they come to be. Here is a good example of this process:

The brother of a student of mine suddenly committed suicide. He had battled with bouts of depression for a number of years, which he had suppressed with excessive drug use. Unable to take the pressure any longer, he went to an open field near his home and shot himself in the head. His friends and family were shocked and saddened by the event and his funeral was held not long afterwards. But the story did not end there.

Two weeks after his death, his friends and family began to report visitations by him. At first they were dreams, but as the days progressed, he began to appear to them while they were in a waking state.

And to make matters worse, he was changing with each visit. Initially he had appeared as he had in life, and had even seemed happy to those who observed him. But this was soon replaced with ghastly visions of him as a corpse with the bullet hole in his head clearly visible.

His friends, all 'rocker' types, were deeply shaken by these events and went to my student, asking him to ask me to intervene. To be honest, I was initially disinclined to help them—these same people had looked down upon me for years because of my 'strange' esoteric beliefs and I would have been quite happy to have left them to wallow in their own terror of the unknown.

But I cared for my student, and felt compassion for his brother and finally agreed to do what I could for him.
At my instruction, my student got a picture of his brother and met with me at my home. We then proceeded to visualize the brother (using the picture both as an aid and an energetic link to him) standing near a bright white light. We collectively urged him to move onwards into that Light, seeing him do so. No more appearances by his ghost were reported after this.

This tale clearly shows a ghost in the making and one of the more common remedies for the situation. However, the operation I employed in that case is by no means the only method of exorcism. It is simply one of the most common ones and the simplest to perform. There are, like other acts of Magick, different levels of Working, designed to deal with different types of circumstances.

THE CASE FOR AND AGAINST EXORCISM

I have performed many exorcisms over the years. Some were basic 'house cleansings', while others were both more elaborate and dangerous. From this experience I have come to feel that exorcism is an operation that should be approached with a conservative frame of mind.

Far too often, people who are simply afraid of the supernatural and want the ghost banished for that reason alone, have approached me. I do not feel that this is ample cause to intervene; education and accommodation are a much better approach to take in such cases and I have turned many such invitations down for that very reason. Not all ghosts *need* to be moved on; instead some will take care of the matter on their own and without any aid.

I believe that it is only when the spirit in question either wishes to move onwards and is unable to accomplish this, or poses a direct threat (either physically or psychologically) to the living that such an operation should be undertaken. When this is the case, there are various levels of exorcism to consider, based on the magnitude of the problem. The choice of employing one over another should be proportionate to the strength and level of resistance that the spirit exhibits, and the level of hostility and aggression that they are capable of.

THE HOUSE BLESSING OR CLEANSING

This is the simplest form an exorcism can take. In this case, incense (most commonly sage or frankincense) and salt-water[104] (or blessed holy water) is taken around the home where a haunting has occurred. With accompanying prayers for the spirit to depart, each room of the home is ritually cleansed by fumigating the area with the incense and sprinkling the water in key areas. In addition, some practitioners such as myself, also employ a bell or gong[105] to further purify an area, and also draw banishing symbols on every window and door with specially prepared oils.

For this operation to be truly effective, all entrances and portals to the home must be sealed against the spirit. This includes not only windows and doors, but also and **especially any mirrors, drains and any other area that is determined to be a Ghost Path for the spirit.** This can be determined either from sightings of the spirit by the home's occupants, or from the content of any dreams they have had of the residence. Like ghosts, when the living are Dreaming True or Faring Forth, they tend to enter and travel through a residence using the same paths of travel a ghost would.

Another area that deserves attention are closets, attic spaces and basements. These are not only potential habitats for negative spirits, but also collection points for generalized negative energies (which naturally accumulate in homes as what the Chinese would refer to as 'bad *Sha*, or negative *Feng Shui*). In addition to all of this, any locations that the spirit is known to linger in or occupy should be cleansed as well.

The basic objective of this cleansing operation is to move the spirit out of the home and then seal it against any reentry. And this method certainly does work—but only if the spirit is not terribly strong, or deeply bound to the location.

In such cases, all that really results is that the spirit is psychically 'stunned' for a short period of time and simply pushed out in to the street, only to return later[106]. And sometimes, the return of that spirit ushers in a situation that can be worse than the original haunting. I know of one case, where shortly after being expelled in this manner, the entity returned and engaged in throwing furniture and other objects at the inhabitants, obviously enraged at being ejected by the priest they had brought in to expel it.

I personally encountered a situation like this myself when I was enlisted to exorcise a mansion in Malibu. A malevolent spirit had been tormenting some workers that were living there. The being had assaulted several of them, even going so far as to lie on the chest of one to the point he was nearly unable to breathe. My partners and I engaged in a classic 'house cleaning' and did manage to expel the spirit from the home—but not the general neighborhood.

Although I warned the occupants that they would need to fill the space with positive energy and urged them to use prayer to support this, they did not do so. Within a fortnight the being returned to the residence, admitted back in by their lack of belief in themselves (or any greater power) and their fear.

It renewed its attacks and continued to torment them to the point that they finally were forced to leave.

Because of this incident, and other cases where I have either used it or heard of it being used, I take the stance that 'house cleansing' is a good method for cases were a light haunting has occurred, but that it is not sufficient for handling more serious situations. It should be employed when possible, but definitely not be the exclusive means of effecting an exorcism.

MOVING A SPIRIT ON TO THE LIGHT

Another method that has become quite popular in recent times is the action of moving a spirit to the proverbial Light, and as I illustrated in my tale of my student's brother earlier in this Chapter, it can certainly be effective. However there are two issues that bear examination.

The first is that while the method certainly works, it only does so when the spirit in question is *willing* to depart, or can be convinced to do so. In cases where they do not wish to comply, and where the spirit is hostile, force, and not persuasion, is what is called for. This is why so many cultures and religions have a formal ritual of exorcism that transcends operations like this one.

The other issue that surrounds this method is more troubling, and this concerns the 'Light' itself. When I studied Latin American Shamanism, one of the things I encountered was the notion that the Light was *not* considered the proverbial gateway to Heaven, but was thought by some shamans to be a metaphysical trap for unwary souls.

Coming from a New Age Western belief system, this point of view initially shocked me (especially having previously employed the Light as a place to move spirits on to).

But more and more Western practitioners have begun to wonder, as I did, about the nature of this Light, and to doubt that it is what it seems to be. Even stanch adherents of using the Light admit to its 'one-way' nature, and to the fact that what is within it is completely unknown—except to those who go into it.

If the Light is in fact a trap as the shamans of Mexico contend, we can easily see a parallel in nature among insect eating plants, which make their livelihood by making themselves as attractive as possible to their prey. It is certainly possible that the Light may be the same thing in a spiritual sense—after all who can resist something that seems to be populated with loved ones and is so easy to enter? If this is the case, then the Light must be considered a place for the dissolution and consumption of souls and *not* their redemption[107].

This idea has certainly proven food for my thoughts, and a part of me has suspected since I first heard the notion that there is some truth to what the shamans assert. For this reason, I no longer employ this method, at least not for loved ones. Instead, I now prefer to send wayward souls to the heaven of their belief-system. There at least, faith, coupled with generations of affirmation in something positive being there waiting for them, gives me some assurance of their ultimate redemption. But, as always, I leave it to the reader to decide the case for themselves.

EXORCISM BY DREAMS

Modern parapsychologists have often observed that dreams bear a definite significance in relation to hauntings. Oftentimes, the subjects of a haunting experience an entity not only in the waking state, but also during sleep. It has also been observed that the dreams of investigators can have importance as well; oftentimes clues to the haunting will come to them during these times which ultimately lead to understanding the root causes of the event. This is, of course, a fact that ancient shamans knew long before the term parapsychology was even coined.

But the use of dreams for interacting with spirits goes much deeper than this. Ancient cultures also knew that dreams are the middle ground between our world and the Hidden One and that a shaman could use them as a vehicle to effect magick on a scale that was sometimes greater than what they were capable of during the waking state (owing to the free conditions their astral self enjoyed during this state). One such magick was the Art of Exorcising a spirit through dreams. I have used this particular method to great effect myself, as have my students. The following is an account of one such operation:

I was tired of teaching. I had been actively instructing students for over ten years and I had come to realize that in the process, that I had neglected my own training in the Art. And so, I quit: I disbanded my small group and had gone off in search of new lessons to learn. One of my initial steps in that direction was to go back to where things had truly begun for me—the field.

Years of practice had taught me to research a new area before going there. In this case, I chose the coastal region of Ventura County, not far from Malibu (where I had spent time as a patrolman). Finding information was easy enough. The market was filled with books on ghosts and strange events and I found one that suited my purposes well, "Ghosts of the Haunted Coast: Ghost Hunting on California's Gold Coast" by Richard L. Senate.

One of the more interesting tales in the book concerned the ghost of a Chumash Indian girl named Hueneme, who killed herself as the result of a curse placed on her by an evil witch. According to the book, in punishment for her deed, the witch was said to haunt the area as a vengeful spirit. I wasn't particularly interested in hunting this entity down per se. Rather, I filed it away in my mind as something to be alert for when I made plans to camp out in the area.

The campgrounds I chose were close to the Point, and well-maintained trails led up from the area into the nearby hills. After a small meal, and the coming of nightfall, I headed out in search of whatever adventure I could find.

After a few minutes, I reached a wooded area and the wind began to blow through the tall trees there. I noticed immediately that there was a strange quality to the noise the wind made, and as I listened, I realized that it sounded like someone whistling a strange tune. A chill went up my spine and I knew that the wind was not a normal one. It was then that I recalled the tale of the witch, and other stories I had heard concerning malevolent bird spirits that according to the coastal tribes, whistled strange songs and attacked travelers in the forest. I knew, deep inside, that these forces were there and that the witch herself had somehow called them.

The eerie song became more distinct, and with it a feeling of great danger. Then an inspiration came to me and I began to whistle the same tune. Once I had it perfect, I changed the song a little, and then a little more. Gradually, the sounds around me altered until they matched my song. I continued to whistle for a time in harmony with the sounds and then let my song slowly fade away. As I did this, the wind followed suit and died away altogether.

I turned back at that point and returned to the campground.

Once I was there, I went immediately to bed and had a vivid dream. In my dream, it was daytime and the sun was shining down on the campground. I saw myself coming out of my little tent and encountering a Native American woman. She was incredibly old, and her eyes were filled with anger and hatred towards me. But then a rainbow came down out of the sky and the woman turned and walked into it. As she did so, she transformed into a lovely young girl, who raised her arms and vanished up the rainbow into the sky.

I awoke to find that it was indeed morning. I broke camp in high spirits, knowing for certain that the witch's ghost had found her rest at last.

As I stated, I am certainly not the only practitioner to use of dreams for exorcising spirits by any means. Here is another instance, in which a friend and student of mine used the dream-state to remove a troublesome spirit. He did so on his own, without any suggestion or urging on my part, as a spontaneous response to the problem he was dealing with, and inadvertently discovered this ancient technique for himself:

On Saturday April 28, 2007 I performed an exercise that is still influencing my perception of reality. I had recently been reunited with an old friend who had become employed at my work. I had not spoken with him for several years, so it was exciting to get to work with him and catch up on old times.

One of the things that he told me about was his purchase of a new home. The house was in the area that he had grown up in and was near the same location where I currently reside. Having lived for only two weeks in his new home, my friend told me about some strange, yet oddly familiar, occurrences that were rationally unexplainable to him. He stated to me that from the onset that something about the appearance of the house had depressed him deeply. He told me that he would arrive home from work, and would not even want to go inside. And once he did go, he felt as if the air itself seemed to be alive with some kind of energy.

Then he told me that something had shaken him while he was sleeping there, and that his wife had thought that she had been punched or kicked in the leg one night. He also added that the bed would seem to shake by itself while they lay awake. In addition, he reported that the glasses in the kitchen would sometimes fall to the floor for no apparent reason, and that drawers there would open up by themselves at night.

He also stated that his children had begun to complain to him about the house. His three-year-old daughter had reported that she had been scared by an 'old man' in the hallway and that this figure would not let her go into her room. And other things had been going on as well: something had begun throwing and breaking their possessions and all the cabinet doors in the kitchen were being found open in the mornings.

I knew all too well what he was going through. I had had to deal with something just like this in my own home, and at one point things had gotten so bad there that my wife and kids had been forced to leave for over a week. In our case, we had gone to the Catholic Church looking for help and when that had failed us, I had been lucky enough to make the acquaintance of two people who were skilled in magick. They had been able to eject the evil spirit that was causing all of this, and as a result of that event, my wife and I had started to work on sharpening our own magickal skills.

As a result, I took a deeply personal interest in my friend's situation. I understood his frustration and his sense of helplessness and I wanted to help if I could.

At the end of our conversation, my friend wound up giving me an object that held personal value to him, a coin. Neither of us knew it, when he presented it to me, that the coin would be instrumental in the removal of the spirit I was certain was haunting their house.

I heard again from my friend over the next few weeks. He reported that the strange occurrences had continued and had become even more severe. From this, I determined that the spirit he had in his house was a strong one, and skilled with whatever powers it had. We discussed my suspicions and he and I agreed that something had to be done, but I didn't know what that would be.

On the following Friday and Saturday, I carried the coin in my pocket and handled it as much as possible. I wanted to feel its energy and any energy it had absorbed from my friends house.

Then on Saturday night, before I went to sleep, I focused on the coin again, and the energy within it. I went to sleep after this with the intent of going out of my body and traveling to the house to confront the ghost directly.

As I had intended, I 'landed' right in the living room of my friend's house. As I focused on my surroundings, I observed the old man screaming at me to leave, and then saw him charging at me.

In a blink of an eye we engaged in a fight. The fight itself was both a physical thing, with me striking the figure and a psychic one, as I projected my energy at it at the same time. We fought like this together for an undetermined amount of time, but it felt as if it went on for at least an hour. We ran through walls and I chased him around the house throwing more energy at him. Each blast knocked him backwards. Somehow, I seemed to be stronger than he was and faster, and I had no fear. The only thing I did feel was the desire to kick his ass for the trouble he had been causing my friend.

The climax of our fight was reached when, in a single fluid motion I thrust him down the hallway and out through the wall with what sounded like a loud explosion.

I woke up laughing.

The next day at work, my friend told me that he and his family had had a wonderful morning. There had seemed to be a real difference in the air. His family had gotten along with each other and there had been none of the tension that had been between them in the previous weeks. He added that his youngest daughter had gone into her bedroom to get her blanket and teddy bear and that nothing had bothered her there.

This was the confirmation that I had been seeking from him and I told him about what I had done the night before in my dream. Being a skeptic, he was excited at the fact that I had accomplished this feat, but he was still not totally convinced that I had really managed to eject the ghost for good. He needed confirmation and he went home that night, alert for any sign that the haunting had resumed.

I received a phone call from him the next morning. He had stayed up all night, but he told me that nothing extraordinary had happened. His daughter had slept peacefully in her bed, and his possessions had stayed where he had *put them, untouched. By six o'clock he knew for certain that the affair was truly over and he thanked me for my help. We were both excited by this news, and any doubts he had had about my abilities were now gone.*

FORMAL BANISHMENT: THE RITE OF APOPOMPAI (EXORCISM)

In cases where a spirit has proven dangerous and harmful, and where it will not leave of its own accord, or by gentler methods, formal exorcism is required. There are many such rituals, including the famous Catholic one, and all are valid, provided that true faith exists in the hearts of those performing them.

I present the following rite that is derived from my own beliefs and has proven to be quite effective at achieving the desired results. The student will immediately appreciate that this operation is not for the casual dabbler in the occult, and that it employs elements that must be thoroughly mastered before it can be undertaken:

RITE OF APOPOMPAI (EXORCISM)

First, clean water is taken and purified with fire, saying
"*Kherniptomai!* (Κηερνιπτομαι) May the sacred flame purify this water!"

The Circle is then purified and consecrated by sprinkling the purified water around the circle three times, saying:

" Hekas, hekas, este bebeloi(Hεκασ, ηεκασ, εστε βεβελοι); Let the profane ones depart!"

Calling the Quarters[108]:

South: To the Spirits of Fire: I call to the denizens of Fire. Burning Flame that purifies the world and burns away all evil. Fire, blaze forth and be with our Circle. Kalos irthes (Καλοσ ιρτηεσ); welcome!
Then to the God: Lord Hêphaistos, Lord of Fire and Mighty Smith stand with us and guard this circle with Thy mighty Hammer. Shield us against all evil and smite any who would dare to trespass.

West: To the Spirits of Air: I call to the Denizens of Air. Eagle of victory whose sight is keen and whose talons grasp up the aggressor, fly through the skies and be with our Circle. Kalos irthes (Καλοσ ιρτηεσ); welcome!

Then to the God: Lady Athênê, Ruler of the Winds, Wise and Fearless Fighter, stand with us and guard this circle with Thy Spear and Aegis. Shield us against all evil and smite any who would dare to trespass.

North: To the Spirits of Water: I call to the Denizens of Water. Oh powerful wave and mighty river that sweeps away all resistance before it flow forth and be with our Circle. Kalos irthes (Καλοσ ιρτηεσ); welcome!

Then to the God: Lord Poseidôn, Lord of the Waters, stand with us and guard this circle with Thy mighty Trident. Shield us against all evil and smite any who would dare to trespass against us.

East: To the Spirits of Earth: I call to the Denizens of Earth! Solid rock that stands as a bulwark against which the aggressors sword is smashed, rise up and be with our Circle. Kalos irthes (Καλοσ ιρτηεσ); welcome!

Then to the God: Lady Demeter, Ruler of Earth, stand with us and guard this circle with all the Forces of the Earth at thy Command. Shield us against all evil and smite any who would dare to trespass against us.

Above: To the Aethyrs of Spirit: In the name of Lord Zeus I call to the Gods and Goddesses of High Olympus and to the Denizens of the Subtle Planes! Join and surround us. Kalos irthes (Καλοσ ιρτηεσ); welcome! Stand with us with Your mighty powers as You stood together to meet the Titans. Shield us against all evil and smite any who would dare to trespass against us.

Below: To the Chthonoi: In the name of Lord Hades and Lady Persephone, Rulers of Tartarus, I call to the Denizens of the Underworld. Kalos irthes (Καλοσ ιρτηεσ); welcome! Stand with us with your mighty powers. Shield us against all evil and smite any who would dare to trespass against us.

Priest: Let us pray together. Oh Mighty One, Kurotrophos, Nurse of the Children and Protectress of mankind, protect us, your priests during the prosecution of this righteous Work. Guide our actions and empower us to complete our task to a successful ending.

Then to the assistant: May the Lady bless and protect you. May you be resolute and your mind clear. May your eyes see true and may your heart be strong and without doubt. May your ears be stopped against lies and your person shielded from all harm.

and without doubt. May your ears be stopped against lies and your person shielded from all harm.

The Spirit is then called to the Triangle and addressed:

Priest: In the name of Queen Hecate—Queen of all Ghosts and Mighty Mistress of the Underworld, Anassa Eneroi, Queen of the Dead, She who has dominion over Heaven, Earth and the Underworld, I command thee oh spirit as Her servant and in Her ancient and ineffable Name (name of departed) to appear in the Triangle set aside for thee. Be thou constrained and confined within it.

As the children of Chaos, the Titans, were expelled from heaven by the noble Olympians and our Great Lady, so too art thou banished from the world of the living! As She smote them down with Her fiery brands and compelled them to retreat, so too art thou laid low and compelled to obey. Withdraw lest ye be struck down by Her to thy utter and eternal destruction.

In the name of Lord Hermes, Guide of the Dead, may the road to the underworld open up before thee now. May thou (name of departed) be drawn down its shadowed length into the bosom of the afterlife and brought to Lord Hades and Lady Persephone, whose judgment awaits thee. Oh (name of departed) by thy name you are commanded and compelled! Be thou expelled from this home and this world, never to return to either precinct.

May the doorway be sealed against you and may you find no purchase anywhere upon it. May you be imprisoned instead in the land of shadow until the Gods decide your fate! In the name of the all-powerful Goddess of the Underworld, She who commands all shades to obedience be thou rendered harmless against us and obey our command forthwith. Hekas, hekas, este bebeloi! (Hεκασ, ηεκασ, εστε βεβελοι) Be thou expelled and exorcised!

Assistant: May the Goddess bless and protect us in this righteous endeavor. Be thou harmless against us and compelled to obey our command, oh (name of the departed). Hekas, hekas, este bebeloi! (Hεκασ, ηεκασ, εστε βεβελοι) Be thou expelled and exorcised!

Priest: Phosphoros, Great Lightbringer show this spirit the path to depart and drive them to it with thy illimitable Light. Prytania, invincible Queen of the Dead, aid us now and command this spirit to obedience. In Thy Name, Hekas, hekas, este bebeloi! (Hεκασ, ηεκασ, εστε βεβελοι) Be thou expelled and exorcised!

Then to the God: Lady Athênê, Ruler of the Winds, Wise and Fearless Fighter, I thank you for your presence and protection this night! May we always honor thee and thy name!

North: To the Spirits of Water: I call to the Denizens of Water. Oh powerful wave and mighty river, thank you for your service. I bid thee depart now from our circle and may there be peace forever between us!

Then to the God: Lord Poseidôn, Lord of the Waters, I thank you for your presence and protection this night! May we always do honor to thee and thy name!

East: To the Spirits of Earth: I call to the Denizens of Earth! Solid rock that stands as a bulwark, thank you for your service. I bid thee depart now from our circle and may there be peace forever between us!

Lady Demeter, Ruler of Earth, I thank you for your presence and protection this night! May we always honor thee and thy name!

Above: To the Aethyrs of Spirit: In the name of Lord Zeus I call to the Gods and Goddesses of High Olympus and to the Denizens of the Subtle Planes! I thank you for your presence and protection this night! May we always honor thee and thy names!

Below: To the Chthonoi: In the name of Lord Hades and Lady Persephone, Rulers of Tartarus, I call to the Denizens of the Underworld! I thank you for your presence and protection this night! May we always honor thee and thy names! I declare this rite done. Fiat!

For comparison and additional study, I also present the text of a ritual my wife created for an exorcism that we conducted together (which is presented in the section following this Chapter). The reader will note that the symbolism is quite different than mine (being derived from the Northern Pre-Christian belief system), but has the same basic intent of the previous rite:

LINDA'S RITUAL

Allfather, Odhinn, Father of Gods and men, God of Seidhr and magick, please come and guard the North. Help us in this working to rid unwanted beings from this place. Share your knowledge and protection where needed. So Sei Es![109]

Lady Frigga Goddess of home and hearth, Consort of Odhinnn, please be with us, offering your knowledge and protection of the east as we rid this home of unwanted beings. Please bring happiness health and prosperity to the family that lives among the living in this home. So Sei Es!

God Thor, Protector of God and man. I ask that you be here tonight protecting us all, guarding the south and lending Your Hand and Hammer as needed to rid this home of unwanted beings. Please help us move this being to Helheim to reside and learn what he needs to do. To pay any debts he owes. So Sei Es!

Lady Freya, Goddess of Seidh and Magick please guard the west share your protection and knowledge with us this night as we clear this house of unwanted beings. So Sei Es!

Tyr, God of victory I ask that you watch and protect us from above offering your help and protection as needed as we rid this home of unwanted beings. So Sei Es!

Goddess Hella, Goddess of the Underworld and of the crossroads between life and death, I ask that you guard us from below and open your gates to Helheim. Draw this being to Your world to live, learn and pay any debts he owes.

I ask that You guard him well in Your realm that he may not ever come back to cause pain, friction or fear. As You know, he has been reasoned with and shown respect. Everything that we could think of to appease him has been done. He has ignored us, and most of all, You. I ask You to send guides and guards to take him to your realm. So Sei Es!

TALES FROM THE HIDDEN WORLD: AN EXORCISM

A co-worker of my wife's, a man named Rob, complained to her that his house was haunted by what he believed was the ghost of the former owner. According to Rob, the man had died in his 80's from a fall from a ladder while trimming a tree on the property. The spirit had manifested itself to them in several ways: in cold spots and strange noises and they were very interested in an exorcism.

Initially, I was disinclined to intervene, feeling that as no harm had occurred to that point, that an exorcism of any magnitude was not warranted. Instead, I counseled that the couple attempt to determine what the spirit wanted from them, and if possible find a way to accommodate him.

Rob's wife, Paula did this by trying to speak with the spirit one day in their kitchen. But while she got an impression that he was possessive of the house, and disliked the overcrowded conditions created by its new tenants, she did not reach any conclusive settlement.

The haunting increased in intensity. The ghost began to shake the couple's bed every morning at 5:30 am and pulled the blankets down to their feet on several occasions. In addition, a box of pictures of the former owner and his family were found upstairs, along with a 1930's era merchant marine medal. In an attempt to placate the spirit, I suggested that the couple return the box to the ghost's living relatives, but this only seemed to aggravate the spirit. Not only did it continue to shake the bed, but went on to grab Paula by her ankle while she was sleeping.

The couple's unease increased, and Rob began to sleep with a loaded firearm. He told my wife about this, and asked her if she thought that a stun gun might be better protection (reasoning that since the spirit was an energetic being that the electrical charge could conceivably injure it). Both my wife and I counseled against his sleeping with the gun (and the stun gun), and we suggested instead that we come to the residence to conduct a further investigation. A date was set and we went to meet with Rob and his wife.

When we met with the couple, Paula's fear and concern were palpable. The events to that point had frayed her nerves completely. And as we spoke with the pair, I learned that a second incident of the ghost assaulting someone had occurred. This time it had happened with Rob and had been connected to the medal found in the box. He had apparently tried to hide the medal on his person and had gone to sleep with it in his hand. According to him, the ghost had tried to pry his hand open in an apparent effort to retrieve the object. I was also informed that the family dog had refused to come inside the home for the last 6 months, choosing to go completely around the building instead to get his food.

All of this new information increased my level of concern, but as no harm had happened to any of the residents, I was still reluctant to expel the entity. I asked instead that Paula, who was friendly with their neighbors, find out more information about the being. I knew that if things progressed any further, that we would need to know as much as possible about the spirit, and I was still hoping that something would come to light that would help the couple in reaching some form of agreement with it. I explained to them that exorcisms are a drastic measure, and compared the situation to a conventional domestic disturbance; one does not call for a SWAT Team when street officers can handle the problem. Paula reluctantly agreed to find out what she could.

While we were there, I was also waiting to see if the ghost would react to our presence and to the discussion. The being did, making several strange 'bumps' and at one point was sensed coming down the stairs into the living room where we were (my wife and Paula both reported seeing the ghost as a body of energy and I sensed his presence and felt a distinct cold spot when he came near us). But beyond this, he did not exhibit any overt aggression, heightening my belief that the entire matter could ultimately be settled in an amicable fashion.

That following week, Paula spoke with the neighbors and learned several things that proved of interest. It turned out that the former owner had been in the Navy, and married. According to the neighbors, the man had been the literal 'master of the house', coming home every day and waiting in his car for his wife to come out and open the gate in the yard for him before exiting the vehicle. His rule over her, and the home, had been absolute. He had also apparently hated children and the neighbors related to Paula how he had forbidden their children to come within three feet of the property line for any reason (although he did allow them to come over to retrieve lost balls). He had even built a fence beyond the property line to keep visitors from entering.

In addition, she learned that the man's wife had died of complications from a stroke, leaving him alone and a widower until the accident occurred that took his life. 5:30 AM turned out to be the hour that his wife had always arisen to start her day.

As we were digesting all this information, Paula decided she had had enough of the situation and invited her grandmother to come to the home and attempt a house cleaning (using some holy water they had secured from their local Catholic Church). According to Paula, the ghost had reacted to this attempt by manifesting briefly before running into a wall to hide from them. But it was not expelled, and the haunting continued, largely unabated.

Finally unable to stand it any longer, Paula left the house with her children refusing to return. This was the final 'straw' for my wife and I. Although no physical harm had been done, we all agreed that the psychological harm and the disruption to the family had reached a level that required intervention. We informed Rob that we would conduct the exorcism after all.

My wife and I had already conducted several astral 'fly-bys' of the house and had made contact with the spirit himself. We had found him to be resistant to any reason and downright arrogant about his claim on the house—and his supernatural abilities. We knew that we were in for a fight.

I proceeded to conduct research into improvements on prior exorcisms I had performed in an effort to ensure that our work would achieve complete success the first time. As I had explained to the couple, exorcisms were not always 'one shot affairs', nor effective 100 percent of the time. Now that we had agreed to expel the entity, I wanted to narrow our margin as much as possible.

One issue that I addressed was finding a more efficient means of creating an energetic link to control and drive out the entity with. My solution was to request a picture of the man (borrowing from other magickal operations) and in particular, his full name. Rob and Paula supplied the name, and agreed to supply a picture from the box they had found.

Once I had the ghost's name, I was able to create a sigil of it using the Oracle Wheel (which can be studied by the reader at greater length in my book "Oracle the Sacred Wheel of Becoming"). The sigil, which is normally *used in spirit evocation, corresponded to the energetic 'signature' of the ghost himself. In creating and employing this, I had a direct link to his energetic vibration. In addition, I availed myself of exorcism rituals from other faiths, and tightened up a number of details in my own ritual that in my estimation, needed attention.*

My wife also conceived an exorcism ritual that involved Norse symbolism. I promptly modified my own so that the two rites could operate within one another and be complimentary. Our plan was that I would initiate the event, and that she would use her rite as our first esoteric 'volley', dropping back to my ritual if required.

With all of this accomplished, we were ready to perform our operation.

The couple was instructed to leave the residence for the evening. They had already endured enough, and given the fact that the ghost was recalcitrant, and had become physical in his assaults, we did not want them to be subjected to any potential danger. We also asked that the residence be left unlocked, even though we had already been given keys. This narrowed the possibility that we would arrive to find the home locked against us by the spirit and any keys that had been left behind for us, conveniently 'missing' (which has occurred in other cases).

My current student, who had never been on such an operation, was asked to accompany us, and was given strict instructions to do exactly as we requested. She was told that while on the premises, that she was be the last one up any stairs, and the first one down them. This admonition was for our group's safety and came from prior experiences where the spirit assaulted the weakest (read that 'least-experienced') person. I for one did not want to wind up under her if she was shoved down a flight of stairs by a ghostly hand.

In addition, she was instructed to stay with us at all times, again out of concern for any attack that might occur were she left alone. Her main job, as I explained it to her, was to lend energy to the event, and assist us with the lengthy task of cleaning and sealing the residence after the spirit had been banished.

Although I knew it would tire me, I also insisted on driving to and from the home. I had experience as a professional driver, both with an ambulance driver and as a patrolman, and I had driven in all road conditions and in all weather. I reasoned that my being at the wheel offered the best chance of our arriving safely. Some readers might wonder at this particular requirement.

I had learned long ago that physical safety during the entire event, from start to finish, is a legitimate concern. On prior exorcisms I had encountered sudden and dangerous events on the road while traveling to and from them. For example, on the exorcism in Malibu, after expelling the entity, I had been about to enter an intersection down the street from the location. The light had been green, and the roadway had appeared to be clear.

But an intuitive feeling of danger came over me and I had hesitated. A split second later, a car raced through the intersection against the red light at over 100 miles an hour. Had I gone through, my companions and I would have surely died. As I saw it this 'coincidence' was too close to the event to be anything other than a demonic attempt at revenge. Although I did not plan for the present spirit to be left hanging around for its own version of this, a last ditch effort by it to de-rail us from arriving was still a distinct possibility.

The weekend for the event arrived. My student had come up to my home on Friday, and I had used the extra evening to familiarize her with the rite and go over the safety requirements in detail. We were as ready as we could ever be.

Before leaving for the residence, each participant on called on his or her personal spirit-helpers. In my case, this was my familiar. In addition, each member was anointed with protection oil and protective sigils.

The drive to the home proved largely uneventful. Only two things occurred that are worth mention, these being a pair of cars that tried to back out in front of our vehicle, and a driver in front of us who drove at an unreasonably slow pace. If either events were related to the spirits intervention, they were feeble obstructions at best.

When we arrived at around 8:00 pm, we did not waste any time.

As we had instructed, the picture of the former owner had been left waiting for us. I quickly drew the sigil of the man's name on the back of it with a ballpoint pen, and placed this on a spot on the floor between the living room and the kitchen. The medal that had also been left for us was placed in the same spot, under the picture.

I then created a protective circle in the living room, which was to serve as our 'safe spot' and the area for our ritual. Once this was done, a small end table was commandeered to serve as our working altar. Two black candles (traditional for rituals involving the dead) that had been previously 'dressed' with protection oil were then set there, along with a charcoal censer containing vervain (an herb commonly employed by the ancient Greeks for exorcisms) and stick incense made of frankincense (another ancient scent used in Europe for the same function). A container of salt needed for creating the salt water that we would need for ritually cleansing the home, joined these items.

With the basic circle created, I then drew an energetic triangle of manifestation outside of the main circle, using my Tool of Art. This was intended for the spirit to manifest in when we called it. The triangle was drawn so that it was between the living room where we were, and the kitchen, where we had sensed the ghost was attempting to hide (and where the ghost had been previously noted to travel through).

I was determined that there would be no repetition of the ghost concealing itself from us as it had with Paula's grandmother, and together with my companions, we called our familiars to astrally 'corral' the ghost in the kitchen area until we ready to deal with it. This measure proved effective in limiting the ghost's mobility considerably. He remained in the kitchen area.

As the Operation was getting ready to commence, I realized that a glass of water was needed (to make the salt water). My wife volunteered to get the glass from the kitchen, and I 'cut' (and then resealed) the circle so that she could do so.

The ghost's presence was very strong in the kitchen and as she retrieved a glass, it attempted to follow her back towards the circle. As it passed the triangle, we all felt it stop for a second and attempt try to retrieve the medal in the triangle. It failed to do so and tried to follow my wife once again.

But she had already been readmitted to our circle and I had resealed it. The result was that the spirit slammed into the energetic wall, causing a visible ripple in the air. I had the distinct impression that the ghost was surprised by its inability to penetrate the area, and for the first time, I sensed that his confidence in being able to resist our efforts was slipping.

We began our work.

I started with an invocation to the Gods and the elements of the four directions, using my ritual notes. With the circle further fortified, my wife then engaged in her own rite.

We sensed that the ghost was beginning to struggle very hard to not only resist our efforts, but to escape if possible. We redoubled our efforts, and visualized the ghost being forcefully pulled into the triangle of manifestation. At one point, we all saw the entity manifest, being dragged by our combined efforts literally by its heels into the magical diagram. But it was unable to prevent us from imprisoning it within the triangle.

Once it was secure, my wife proceeded to call upon the Norse Goddess, Hela (who presides over the Nordic Underworld) and asked that She send helpers to take the spirit down into Her realm. My student and I joined her in this visualization, watching as these beings arrived and dragged the ghost through the gates to the Underworld.

As the gates closed shut, my wife addressed the spirit. She told him that he had lessons to learn in the Underworld--and debts to pay for things he had done in his life, and his afterlife, before he would be allowed to move on to the next life.

With that, the rite was completed, but certainly not our labors. The circle was dissolved and the cleansing of the home began.

My wife used sage incense to fumigate every corner of the home and ritually sealed all windows, doorways, TV and computer screens, and mirrors. My student followed her, anointing these same places with the protection oil we had used earlier for ourselves. I took up the rear, sprinkling every corner with salt water and using my brass gong to disrupt and banish any residual negative energy.

The entire house received this attention. We started in the combination loft/Attic/bedroom upstairs and worked our way down to the basement. We also took special care in cleaning all the air conditioning vents, plumbing pipes and drains.

The only negative energy found to be remaining in the house was in the closets and the worst of this was in the closet where we later learned, the ghosts' box of personal pictures and mementos had been stored.

After over an hour of work, the home was finally cleansed from top to bottom. We then policed our equipment and left the residence. For just a minute after all supplies were loaded back in the car, we all stopped for well-deserved cigarettes. Each of us noticed how peaceful the home suddenly seemed. As my wife stated, it was like seeing the residence for the first time.

Rob came home later that night and called us the next day. He told us that the house had been so quiet and serene that he had actually had trouble sleeping, and that he had even gone so far as to turn on a fan make a little noise and movement in the home.

Later the same day, Paula returned with their children and also noticed the profound change. But the most dramatic reaction to our work was from the family dog, which immediately bounded into the house in joy.

In gratitude for our work, Paula sent us a homemade cake and a card, which summed up the family's sentiments. It read:

"I can't even begin to thank you for giving us our life back. You are truly 'special' friends and this is an experience I will never in my life forget. Linda, thank you for being there at my breaking point. Your friends, Rob & Paula"

Since this event, there have been no further disruptions of the family's life by supernatural entities.

CHAPTER XI: MAGICK, INITIATION AND THE GREAT WORK

We wake, if ever at all, to mystery. --*Annie Dillard*

There are many reasons why a person becomes involved with the Art. Many come to it out of curiosity, or to satisfy a material need. Others seek a thrill from the unknown, and a few, such as like myself, take up the study out a sense of destiny.

Regardless of the reason for coming, only a few persist in their journey long enough to achieve any appreciable level of mastery. The quote 'For many are called, but few are chosen' is particularly apt when it comes to the Art.

The journey to true knowledge of the Art is an arduous one and many tend to drop off the Great Road at various points along the way. The forces of distraction, laziness and fear often waylay the student and terminate the process long before the ultimate destination is in sight.

During my many years as a teacher, and a student, I have seen this occur over and over again. And yet, no one I have known or have taught, has ever emerged from a study of the Art without being changed by it in some way. The Art is, by its nature, not merely a set of skills or abilities, but a living process of self-transformation.

If the student has applied themselves and followed the path which I have pointed out in this book, then much more than an exploration of the strange and the eldritch has occurred. Each skill area is expressly intended to open up different aspects of human consciousness as well. Assuming that this Work was approached with the proper diligence and seriousness, the end result can only have been a simultaneous evolution of the student's spirit. This, I feel is the true intent of studying the Art; material desires and base curiosity can certainly be satisfied by magickal knowledge, but those things are nothing compared to the inner growth that comes from the process of self-initiation the Art embodies.

We will now examine the final level of our training, which in turn opens up onto an even greater world than the one that we have been exploring. This is what has been referred to as the Great Work, and once this Work has been achieved, the reader will have to draw their own map of the road forwards from that point onwards.

Like any student, I embarked on my own magickal journey years ago, mastering skill after skill. It was only after many years of doing so, that I realized that my true destination was nothing less than a rendezvous with the Divine—an encounter with the great force that we refer to loosely as the Godhead. And once I understood this, all of my original reasons for taking my journey seemed empty by comparison.

There have been many approaches conceived for achieving this worthy goal, ranging from intensive periods of meditation, to ecstatic prayer, to vision quests and complex rituals. And each one of these methods has their merits.

But it was a Jewish mystic in Spain, Abramelin the Mage, who authored a ritual centuries ago, that is regarded by many, including myself, as being one of the most effective ever created. He called it the Great Work and it is referred to in many occult circles today simply as the Abramelin Working.

The Great Work that he described is a process of daily prayers and devotions that increase in intensity over a set period of time and end in a ritual where one comes face to face with the Divine, or as Abramelin put it, the Knowledge and Conversation of the Holy Guardian Angel. As magickal studies go, nothing transcends such an objective and as an enterprising young student, I eventually took up the Great Work myself, not knowing what, if anything, would occur at the end of that endeavor.

It should be stated at this point, that the ritual I preformed was a highly modified version of the original, and not nearly as elaborate. I therefore do not offer my Working as a definitive account of the Great Work as Abramelin revealed it, but as a variant and one that was performed with substantial additions and changes. I therefore beg forgiveness in advance from those occult scholars who might read my account and take issue with any inaccuracies or omissions on my part.

THE TOMB OF MEMORIES

Before the Great Work can even be embarked upon, I believe that another task must first be completed. The philosopher Martin Buber once said "There is no room for God in him who is full of himself" and certainly no truer a statement could have been made in the context of the Great Work. As long as a person is impeded by their own inner limitations, ecstatic Knowledge of the Divine certainly cannot find its way into their soul.

One mechanism for making way for this Knowledge is achieved through the act of Recapitulation. Carlos Castaneda described this in his books as the act of taking back the personal power we have spent throughout our lives, and in the process of doing this, not only achieving a break with that same past, but empowering our spirit to move forwards into the future.

Certainly, each of us has experienced events that have affected our souls for better or worse. As a victim of childhood abuse, I know this better than many. Not only can the past shape what we become from a psychological sense, but traumatic events also rob us of our Magickal Will and power, and impede our spiritual development. Therefore radical steps must be taken to lighten our spiritual load in preparation for the Great Work.

The exercise that Castaneda suggested for this was a simple one, but like all great acts of Magick, it can be difficult to perform. It consists of revisiting the past while in an isolated state, and taking back the energy from each pivotal event in our lives, using specialized breathing maneuvers. Before I embarked on my own version of the Great Work, I performed a variation of what Castaneda proposed, and later, when my students reached a point when they were ready for their own Work, taught this to them.

The act of Recapitulation begins with a special journal. This journal is to contain all of the major events that one can recall from their earliest childhood to the present. Composing this can be difficult for some people; revisiting certain events can require a great level of fortitude, but in order to perform the task effectively, the list must be thorough and complete. I also believe that critical events of a positive nature should also be included in the same journal. Although they are benign, there is no question that they still required a certain level of emotional involvement and personal energy when they occurred.

Once the journal is completed, the next stage is to create an isolated space, free of all distraction and specific to this purpose. My own choice was a cardboard prop-coffin I purchased during Halloween. As macabre as this item might sound, my reasons for selecting it were well grounded. Not only did it offer me a small isolated chamber to work in, but at the same time, by reason of its symbolism, it ritually invoked the death-like process that some consider Recapitulation to be.

In another case, a student of mine chose to dig a special hole in the ground for himself, which he covered with a board, again borrowing on the idea of death imagery. But whatever the form or the symbolism one employs, isolation is the key.

With a chamber arranged for, the actual process of Recapitulation can then be undertaken. The exercise should take six months to complete (with another six set aside for the Great Work that follows it). Each night, the student is to select a small portion of their past from the journal (perhaps one to three incidents at most), starting with their earliest memories, and then go and lie inside the chamber. Once inside, their task is to recall these events as clearly as possible and to attempt to re-experience the emotions that they felt at these times.

As soon as these events are clearly visualized in the minds eye, the student is then to perform the specialized breathing maneuver. It is begun with the head turned to the right. Taking a deep breath, the head is slowly turned from right to the left while simultaneously visualizing the power and energy of the past event being drawn into the body through the solar plexus.

Then, covering the solar plexus with the hands, the student exhales while turning their head slowly back to the right again, simultaneously visualizing the connection with the past event being severed. This maneuver acts to extract the personal power that was originally invested in the past event, and releases whatever connections might still exist to it in the present. In cases where a particularly painful event is being recaptured, several 'passes' like this might be required before a sense of completion is felt.

This process is performed each night until the events listed in the journal have all been addressed. As an adjunct to this activity, I also highly recommend that some form of conventional counseling or therapy be engaged in as well. Certainly, between the two actions, a tremendous amount of personal growth and spiritual healing will occur that will prove beneficial regardless of the outcome of the Great Work itself.

THE GREAT WORK

The Great Work, in its original format, was based on Judeo-Christian archetypes. While this ran contrary to my personal religious beliefs, its 'engineering' is universal to any belief system, just as the Divine is itself, is universal to all beings. I learned in my conversations with those who had attempted this Work that it could be adapted to any belief system, and that if followed properly, would yield the same results for anyone.

My own version was based on my belief in a Goddess, and because my resources were vastly different than what Abramelin proposed, the rite was changed to fit my circumstances, while remaining true as possible to the spirit of the original.

The first step that one must take is the decision to undertake the Work. This is harder than it sounds; the world around us offers many enticements to waste our time on smaller pursuits, and it is very easy to procrastinate. I myself did not.

The next stage is carrying the rite out to its finish. Abramelin warned that whoever chose to attempt the Work would encounter distractions and temptations all along the way, and counseled that fierce determination was needed when, as he called it 'the dark night of the soul', eventually descended. But as he also stated, if the rite, which is carried out over a period of months, is pursued to completion, then there could be no doubt of its ultimate success.

For those interested in studying the original work, S.L. MacGregor Mathers wrote a splendid translation, "The Sacred Magic of Abramelin the Mage". It is worthy of study by anyone who is considering taking this next step forwards in the Art and I strongly recommend that it be read in preparation for the same.

I also present my own account here in this book, to serve as both a guide and a potential model for the reader to base their own rite upon. I defer of course to the original for any final form that such a rite might take:

I began by composing my rite and gathering the few things needed to perform it. Abramelin had suggested many items, including a ritual robe and a special Temple area set-aside for the Great Work, but as my material resources were rather limited, I was forced to adapt his requirements to my station in life. The Temple for example, was to be none other than my working altar, and the terrace that he prescribed for the final day, was changed to an outdoor location. The scarlet robe he suggested became a colored sash.

And not subscribing to Judeo-Christian religion, the prayer I composed was to my Goddess. While it prayed to Her for the knowledge and conversation of the Holy Guardian Angel, I viewed that archetype in a looser sense than someone with Abramelin's beliefs might have had, and saw it more in the context of my spirit guide as it interfaced with the Divine. The Tatvic imagery (which was used to visualize that intercessory force during my daily prayers) came to me in a series of meditations, and was painted on a piece of cardboard.

The time length of the ritual was divided into three periods of two months.

I began my Work before dawn on the first day. I was at a campground with a group of people involved in mysticism, and used the communal Temple area that had been set aside for general usage by the celebrants.

I tied my sash about me, and in the quietness of the space, recited my opening prayer. It was an entreaty to the Goddess to grant me success in my Work, and to reveal to me what some writers had termed, 'the holy perfume' that represented greater knowledge. I was, like many who embark on this Work, uncertain as to what exactly all this meant, but I was determined to see the task through to its completion.

When I finished my prayer, I went outside and up onto a hillside to watch the dawn, thinking on how in six months, I would be rising for another dawn, and facing an unknown outcome. The Goddess must have smiled on my efforts, for as the sun rose, I was filled with tremendous sense of fulfillment and wholeness.

After a time, I went back down to the encampment.

The next six months were a daily affair of saying my prayers in the morning and in the evening. I also meditated on my Tatvic image, and as the time progressed, reached the point that Mathers had suggested, where I could call up an energetic vision of it clearly and crisply at a moment's notice. The ability to do this, I had learned, was required on the Final Day as part of the last prayer.

There were times, just as Abramelin had warned, that I was tempted not to complete the Work. My own 'dark night of the soul' was more of a process of resisting the distractions that the world wanted to throw in my path, and of staying true to my goal to see the Work through instead of anything dramatic. Certainly there were moments when I wondered, as many before me had wondered, if the entire effort would lead to naught, but I kept to my routine, and did my best to withdraw from affairs of men as the final period approached. My operating motto became a saying I had learned in Spanish: "Ser en el Mundo, pero non del Mundo", or "Be in the World, but not of the World."

On the last day, I had a student drive me to Red Rock Canyon, a wilderness area an hour or so outside of Los Angeles. I had chosen this spot for its remoteness, and its great beauty. The journey began in the pre-dawn hours, and we raced to arrive at the location before sunrise. This place was to be my Terrace.

When we arrived, I tied my sash around my waist and left my student at the car. I hiked some distance into the desert until I found a spot that offered a spectacular view of the eastern sky.

I recited my final prayer. This was basically an expansion on my original prayer and the daily ones that had followed, said spontaneously and from the heart. At that moment, I truly wanted to achieve success and know at last what Abramelin had been writing about for myself. Then I let go, and as the saying goes, let God.

Language cannot adequately describe what occurred next, and I will stop my narrative here, rather than attempt any crude recounting. Suffice it to say that as the sun rose, I did come to know the 'holy perfume' that Abramelin had spoken of and achieved Knowledge and Conversation. Anything beyond this, I leave to the reader to experience for themselves. In the end, when they stand on the Terrace of their Final Day, they will understand completely what I mean, and why it is that I can say no more....

CLOSING COMMENTS FROM AN APPRENTICE

I feel very blessed to have studied in a system that is as active as this one is. When I first met Greg, he told me that he was a serious magician, and that much effort would be required on my part.

This was just what I wanted to hear. I'd always been the adventurous type, and I wanted to see what the Hidden World he described had to offer.

What I've encountered amazes me to this day. I've seen spirits, felt the Elements inside my soul, and traveled to Astral places that were both terrifying and beautiful. I've faced my innermost fears and came in contact with the purest, most spiritual part of me. The knowledge that magick has brought me is worth its weight in gold. I had set out to see if a Hidden World existed, and I can tell you with certainty that it does.

The Art is definitely not for the faint of heart. Among other things, it requires that you deal with your emotional baggage and face your inner demons. It is like an alchemical process: you go in a piece of lead and come out shining like gold! It is not material wealth by any means, but rather a process towards a golden enlightenment. Such a transition is hard to achieve and takes a lot of work, but the reward is wisdom, and that, my friends, is priceless.

I believe that a magician who has a good heart and inner courage will go far with this system. The lessons can be difficult, even if they seem simple enough. I, for one, am not that great at holding visualization in my mind due to ADHD. But I've learned to keep at my magical tasks, knowing that the Queen of Witches was smiling on my efforts.

And as any good teacher would do, Greg was there to guide me. The Work was frustrating at times, but he encouraged me to keep trying if I couldn't do something to my satisfaction.

Another frustration was dealing with the abuse I had suffered as a child. I never realized just how much junk I had tossed away inside my subconscious, and how deeply it had affected me. It's hard to face that Shadow that represents our fears and hurts, but by doing so, I came out a stronger, more confident person. Contrary to the Judeo-Christian system, this system does NOT seek to make sheep. You are expected to think and to believe in yourself. In studying the Art, I've become a different person and I would absolutely do it again in a heartbeat.

There are some things I have personally noted in doing the exercises listed here that I feel I should also mention. For one, my cat has no interest whatsoever in magic, despite him being a black little "witchy kitty".

Secondly, mirrors take a lot more effort than you will initially think. The third thing is to make sure you push yourself ALL THE WAY back into your body after Astral traveling...trust me on this one. Finally, don't expect to be perfect at everything all at once. I'm still not the best at visualization, but I'm much better than I was when I started. Be patient. Results will come in their own time.

I wish you luck and hope you enjoy the Art as much as I have. Hecate's blessings be upon you,

--Lady Carissa Stormbringer

APPENDICES

THE GREEK ALPHABET AND ITS MAGICKAL USES

In addition to their usage as an alphabet, the Greek letters also have specific magical qualities like the Norse runes. But unlike the runes, Greek magical letters derive their power not so much by their shape, as by their phonetic vibration and their specific linkage with a God, and that God's particular nature.

The use of a Greek letter in magic is in fact an invocation of the God themselves to act in a specific way in a given situation. Numerological values of combined letters also play a role (as seen in the Greek Gematria) and help to create an overall vibratory influence that can be supportive of a magickal endeavor.

As stand-alone sigils the Greek letters are employed in much the same manner as one would the Norse Runes or any other magickal alphabet; either as stand-alone energetic magickal sigils, or for inscribing a tool or charm.

The following are the letters of the Greek alphabet and some of their magickal associations, based on my research in writing *"Oracle: The Sacred Wheel of Becoming"* and from other sources, including Nigel Pennick's work, *"Magickal Alphabets"*[110]:

Letter: A (Zeus)
Mastery over a situation and success, triumph over a lesser force, inner and outer strength. Worldly power. Wealth. Authority and leadership. Dominion and power. Pennick: Mobile wealth, society and its foundations

Letter: B (Hera)
Development, attainment, trust, home, family, birth and renewal. Specifically a letter for the family as a group and not of the home, per se. The second, the challenger of God

Letter: Γ (Artemis)
Independence. Swift justice, protection. Righteousness. Freedom for the innocent. Matters concerning childbirth and children. Virtue and honor.

Letter: Δ (Demeter)
Fruitfulness, bounty and abundance, the Life Force itself and the process of growth. Nurturing influence. Adaptation. Also a blessing upon the home and its occupants. Abundance and plenty. Reversed, this letter signifies famine and scarcity (as symbolized by the season of winter).

Letter: E (Kore)
A fertile base from which growth can arise. Virtue and honor. Hope. Preparation for new horizons. Reversed, this letter signifies something precious being removed from a person or situation, but in accordance with their Fate.

Letter: Z (Hestia)
Neutrality and impartiality, nurturing, the home and domestic life. Patience and accommodation. Frugality, moderation. Protection in times of danger; a secure place. A parental influence. Mercy, kindness and compassion. Another letter that blesses the home and its occupants. Reversed, it can signify sacrifice.

Letter: H (The Pleiades)
Completion of a stage of life, a temporary pause. Introspection, completion, solitude, withdrawal from a person, situation or thing.

Letter: Θ (Helios)
Command and control, a position of responsibility, illumination, inspiration and cosmic knowledge. Triumph. Reversed, this letter signifies the downfall of those whose mastery of a situation is fueled by pride and arrogance.

Letter: I (Hephaistos)
Craftsmanship, skill, building and creation, a favorable influence for engineers, builders and craftsmen of all types, and their works. Overcoming limitations. A sigil to be used before a creative project or constructing anything.

Letter: K (Kronos)
Time, passage, the inevitable, destiny and fate, the force of change. It can be used to accelerate or decelerate an event or to instigate change.

Letter: Λ (Atlas)
Responsibility, challenges, an oracle of the future, insight and knowledge. Maintenance of order, stability. A symbol to bring order into chaos. Reversed, it is sign of servitude and captivity.

Letter: M (Hades)
Material wealth, hidden treasures, secrets and things hidden. That which is past. Inevitability, culmination and conclusion. The end of a problem, or the resolution of a question.

Letter: N (Hecate)
Purification, renewal, magic, magical powers and inspiration. A divinatory omen; Destiny and fortune. Luck and chance. Also matters concerning travel and transition; a positive outcome or a safe journey. Past foundations that contribute to the present. Rest.
An unpleasant necessity. Also, charity towards the downtrodden, secrets and things hidden. This letter can be used as a powerful sigil against negative occult forces.

Letter: Ξ (Astraea)
Purity, cosmic justice and balance, a sense of order is brought to a situation, a just outcome, truth and fate. Decision, determination.

Letter: O (Aphrodite)
Love, infatuation, and romance. New relationships, desire, beauty and pleasure, popularity, excitement.

Letter: Π (Apollo)
Truth and its revelation, clear choices and foreknowledge. Good advice. Matters concerning music, the arts and healing are well favored. Destiny and fortune. Knowledge, but more in the form of a revelation of a truth.

Letter: P (Dionysus)
Rebirth, renewal, reincarnation, laughter and joy, a special blessing for actors, actresses and playwrights. Friendship and friends. Celebration.

Letter: Σ (Hermes)
Transformation and rebirth, occult power and mastery, mastery of a life situation, union with an opposite resulting in a greater whole. Alliance. A truth revealed. A surprise event.
Also: Concealment from an enemy. Knowledge (of things previously hidden). Secrets kept. It can also be sigil to protect oneself during clandestine dealings.

Letter: T (Selene)
Sexuality, fertility, possible pregnancy, desire and union. A blessing upon a woman for a pregnancy, ensuring fertility.

Letter: Y (Ares) An unavoidable conflict, revolution, or struggle. Action. Defiance. Conquest. Triumph. Attainment despite perils. Reversed: War and conflict. Difficulties.

Letter: Φ (Athena) Courage and bravery. Wisdom and knowledge (in the worldly scientific sense). Judgment. Common sense. Impartiality. Justice and the force of law. Fairness. Mercy and forgiveness. A favorable outcome in a matter of law, a just cause, reason and intelligence, invention and craftsmanship. A sigil for knowledge, wisdom and clear-headedness.

Letter: X (Kosmos) Divine union and Knowledge, Order and physical boundaries, a gift or an exchange among men, Harmony in both a cosmic and material sense. Satisfaction.

Letter: Ψ (Poseidon) Inner forces come to the surface, a revelation of the unknown, and a glimpse of the inner-self. Voyage or journey. Also: Protection on a journey.

Letter: Ω (Omegas) Endings, enclosure, prosperity and completion of a cycle. Synthesis. Perfection. Fulfillment.

THE PHOENICIAN ALPHABET AND ITS ATTRIBUTES

Greek, Etruscan and Hebrew all have their common roots in Phoenician. This is true not only of their graphic shapes, but also as some scholars contend, their symbolic meanings. This seems to be especially true with regards to Hebrew, which is with the exception of some minor differences, is nearly identical to Phoenician in both the names of its written characters and their esoteric meanings.

𐤊 Aleph: Ox. Meaning: Money, possessions. Phonetic value: a, Numerical value 1

𐤁 Beth/Bait: House. Meaning: Home, family, dwelling place. Phonetic value: b, Numerical value 2

𐤂 Gamel/Gimel: Camel, alternately, an oil lamp. Meaning: Travel, transportation. Alternate: Illumination, revelation. Phonetic value: g/c, Numerical value 3

𐤃 Dal/Daleth: Door, alternate: fish or day. Meaning: a doorway, transitions, threshold, a barrier. Phonetic value: d, Numerical value 4

𐤄 Heth/Hait: window, or alternately a salutation. Meaning: a glimpse or vision. Alternate: a message. Phonetic value: h/e, Numerical value 5

𐤅 Waw: hook. Meaning: Acquisition, accomplishment. Phonetic value: w/f. Numerical value 6

𐤇 Hait/Heth: wall. Alternate: a ladder. Meaning: Barrier, protection. Alternate: ascent or descent. Phonetic value: h. Numerical value 7

𐤉 Yad/Yod: Hand. Meaning: Order, creative force, control. Phonetic value: y/i/j. Numerical value 8

𐤊 Kaph: Hand. Meaning: Force, protection, energy. Phonetic value: k. Numerical value 9

𐤋 Lam/Lamedh: Ox-Goad. Meaning: Motivation, purpose, drive. Phonetic value: l. Numerical value: 10

𐤌 Mai/Mem: Water. Meaning: flux, change, movement. Phonetic value: m. Numerical value: 11

𐤍 Nun: Fish. Meaning: adaptation, change, mutability, a solution. Phonetic value: n. Numerical value: 12

𐤏 Ayin: Eye. Meaning: Sight, wisdom. Phonetic value: o. Numerical value: 13

𐤐 Pe: Mouth. Alternate: opening. Meaning: Expression. Communication. Alternate: an opening or way. Phonetic value: p. Numerical value: 14

𐤒 Qoph: Monkey or alternately the back of the head. Meaning: Playfulness, trickery, greed. Lower order desires. Alternate meaning: that which is not seen, or that which is seen by others. Phonetic value: q. Numerical value: 15

𐤓 Resh/Ras: Head. Meaning:?. Numerical value: 16

𐤔 Sin: Tooth. Meaning: Consumption, breaking down. Phonetic value: s. Numeric value: 17

𐤕 Taw, Tah: Mark. Alternate: sunrise. Meaning: The life force. Influence. Beginnings. Phonetic value: t. Numeric value: 18

𐤅 Waw: Hook. Meaning: Impediment and obstacles. Also possessions and order. Phonetic value: w/u/v. Numeric value: 19

ܫ Samekh/Sheen: Fish?. Meaning: Hidden aspects, contemplation and adaptation. Phonetic value: s/x. Numerical value: 20
Z Zayin: Sword. Meaning: Force, aggression, protection from danger. Phonetic value: z. Numerical value: 21

NUMEROLOGICAL CONVERSION CHART

1 2 3 4 5 6 7 8 9
A B C D E F G H I
J K L M N O P Q R
S T U V W X Y Z –

To determine the numerological value of a Name, each letter is assigned a numerical value, which can be based on the chart above. The numbers are then added up, and the sum, if it is two digits or greater, is added again until only a single digit remains. This number is then the numerological expression of the Name. An example of this would be:
John= J (1), O (6), H (8), N (5), or 1+6+8+5= 20= 2+0= 2. In this case, 2 would be the numerological value for the name John.

There are however, several numbers which when they are part of a sum, are exceptions to this. These Master Numbers, as they are called, are: 11, 13, 22 and 33. They have their own specific meanings and are not added together to create a single digit sum.

BASIC NUMBER MEANINGS

The following are basic number meanings. They are by no means the only interpretations of the numbers, and the reader is invited to exchange them with other sources as they see fit.:

1: Unity, Male, beginnings, solitary, self-reliance and Will. Tarot Card: The Magician, Planets: Sun, Aries, Mars, Mercury, Uranus

2: Duality, The feminine, cooperation, service, gestation and fertility, partnership. Tarot: High Priestess, Planets: Moon

3: Trinity, Union of the Divine with the Human, matter, manifestation, expression. Tarot: The Empress. Planet: Jupiter, Venus

4: Order, practicality, stability, earth forces. Tarot: The Emperor. Planet: Saturn, Earth.

5: Adventure, exploration, learning, traveler, the five elements and harmony. The interplay between matter and spirit. Tarot: The Hierophant. Planets: Mercury, Venus.

6: Love, healing and nurturing, order, duty and service. Tarot: The Lovers. Planet: Venus.

7: Stoic, inventor, seeker of wisdom and perfection. Desire. Considered lucky in the West and unlucky in the Orient. Tarot: The Chariot. Planet: Jupiter, Neptune.

8: Achievement, abundance, wealth, authority and the intellect. Tarot: Justice. Planet: The Sun.

9: Humanitarian, mystic, idealist, spiritual. A number of magic and power in the East and among the pagan Europeans. Tarot: The Hermit. Planets: Sun, Moon, and Mars.

11: Messenger, teacher, visionary. A Master Number. Tarot: Strength. Planets: Uranus, Neptune, and Mercury.

13: Lunar cycles, change, transition, gestation and cycles, elimination of excess, considered unlucky by some and magickal and lucky by others. Considered by some to be a Master Number. Tarot: Death. Planet: The Moon

22: Idealist, builder, expansion, genius and inspiration. A Master Number. Tarot: The World. Planet: Jupiter, Saturn.

33: Healer, compassionate, blessing. A teacher. A Master Number. Tarot: The Star. Planets: Jupiter and Venus.

SECRETS OF THE ORACLE WHEEL

In addition to its use as a divinatory aid, the Oracle Wheel that I wrote about in *"Oracle: The Sacred Wheel of Becoming"* has deeper magical applications. The Wheel can also be employed in the same manner as a conventional 'magical square' to calculate sigils for calling daimones[111], determining the God associated with a particular hour of the day, and to determine compass headings.

CREATING SIGILS WITH THE ORACLE WHEEL

To create a sigil, the daimon's name is first determined by the Magician. The sigil itself begins with the letter that corresponds with the first letter of the daimon's name, and continues through the remainder of letters, creating the final graphic design of the sigil.

This sigil is then used for invoking the spirit. For accuracy, the summoner can also refer to the sums provided by the Greek Gematria. For example, Tau is equal to 300, as opposed to its mundane sum, which would only be 20. I have reproduced the chart for this to make referencing this source easier:

GEMATRIA NUMEROLOGICAL VALUES FOR THE GREEK ALPHABET

A Alpha	1	B Beta	2	Γ Gamma	3
Δ Delta	4	E Epsilon	5	Z Zeta	7
H Eta	8	Θ Theta	9	I Iota	10
K Kappa	20	Λ Lambda	30	M Mu	40
N Nu	50	Ξ Xei	60	O Omicron	70
Π Pi	80	P Rho	100	Σ Sigma	200
T Tau	300	Y Upsilon	400	Φ Phi	500
X Chi	600	Ψ Psi	700	Ω Omega	800

For example: AGLAIA= ΑΓΛΑΙΑ
The sum is: 1+3+30+10*=44=8= Theta/Helios
*This sum is arrived at by dropping repeating letters.

The sum of daimon's name, when rendered to one of 24 possible sums, can subsequently supply the letter of the God on the Wheel that has direct influence over it (starting with Alpha as one, Beta as two and so on). This is useful in rites where a daimon must be compelled to obey a command from the Magician and is otherwise reluctant to do so.

In addition the same numerological sum will also supply the hour of the day that is best for summoning or commanding the spirit (with Alpha being midnight, Beta being 1 o'clock and so on). And if they are needed, compass headings can also be determined using Alpha as due north and working around the wheel clockwise, with the Magician viewed as being in the center of the arrangement.

BIBLIOGRAPHY AND RECOMMENDED READING

Briggs, Patricia, *"Bloodbound"*, Penguin Group, 2007
Casteneda, Carlos, *"The Teachings of Don Juan: A Yaqui Way of Knowledge"*, Simon & Schuster, 1968
Casteneda, Carlos, *"A Separate Reality: Further Conversations with Don Jaun"*, Simon & Schuster, 1970
Casteneda, Carlos, *"Journey To Ixtlan"*, Simon & Schuster, 1972
Casteneda, Carlos, *"Tales of Power"*, New York, NY: Simon & Schuster, 1974
Crowfoot, Greg, *"Crossroads: The Path of Hecate"* Aventine Press, 2005
Donahoe, James J., *"Dream Reality: The Conscious Creation of Dream & Paranormal Experience"*, Bench Pr, June 1979
Franklin, Anna, *"Working with Fairies: Magick, Spells, Potions & Recipes to Attract and See Them"*, The Career Press, 2006
Jameison, Brian, *"Exploring Your Past Lives"* Astro-Analytics Pulications, 1976
Kaplan, Stephen,*"Vampires Are"* ETC Publications, 1984
Khalaf, Saleem George, *A Bequest Unearthed, Phoenicia, Encyclopedia Phoeniciana*, http://phoenicia.org/
Kriss, Marika, *"Werewolves, Shapeshifters and Skinwalkers"*, Sherbourne Press Inc., 1972

MacGregor Mathers, S. Liddell, *"The Sacred Magic of Abramelin the Mage"*: Digital Edition: Joseph H. Peterson, http://www.esotericarchives.com/abramelin/abramelin.htm

Miller, Jason, *"Protection Magick & Reversal: A Witches Defense Manual"*, New Page Books, Franklin Lakes, NJ 1972

Miller, R. Michael, Harper, Josephine M, *"The Psychic Energy Workbook: An Illustrated Course in Practical Psychic Skills"* Aquarian Press, 1987

Pennick, Nigel, *"Magical Alphabets"*, Weiser Books; American Ed edition, May 1992

Senate, Richard L., "Ghosts of the Haunted Coast: Ghost Hunting on California's Gold Coast" Pathfinder Publishing, 1986

Scott, Dr. Gini Graham, *"The Shaman Warrior"* Falcon Press, 1988 (First Edition)

Scott, Dr. Gini Graham, *"Secrets Of The Shaman: Further Explorations with the Leader of a Group Practicing Shamanism"* New Falcon Publications, 1993 (First Edition)

ABOUT THE AUTHOR

Both teacher and a student of Rune Magic, Shamanism and Ceremonial Magick since his earliest years, Greg Crowfoot is the creator and founder of the Temple of Hecate Online, one of the Internet's oldest and largest free interactive temple sites. He has lectured for numerous organizations including the California Club of San Francisco, the Unitarian Church and the Elverhoy Danish Museum. He is also a practicing priest of Hecate, having entered Her service in 1990.

Greg is the author of two other books *"ORACLE: The Sacred Wheel of Becoming"* (Page Free Publishing, 2004), and *"Crossroads: The Path of Hecate"* (Aventine Press, 2005). Greg lives quietly with his wife Linda and their cats, and continues to study and practice the Art.

ENDNOTES

1 The reader may be unfamiliar with the term 'magick' as opposed to the more conventional term 'magic'. Magick refers to events and skills that are purely occult in nature, whereas the word 'magic' refers to the art of illusion practiced purely for entertainment.
2 Not more than a week after my encounter with the ball of light, I was back in the woods again. This time I was hiking near the encampment of some fellow residents. Although I knew that they had gone north to Oregon for the weekend, I heard the distinct sounds of people laughing and talking in the small clearing their Indian-style teepees were pitched in. Certain that they had returned early with friends, I went to the place. But when I reached it, the clearing was deserted and silent.
3 I tend to refer to myself as a sorcerer, although many have called me a shaman. While the distinctions between the two terms can be hazy at times and even intertwined, I define them as being parts of the same thing, as divided by the magick user's activities. Shamans tend to work their Art on behalf of a community, healing its members and interceding with the forces of Nature on their behalf. Sorcerers are by contrast, largely solitary and either use their abilities to explore the universe around them, or for personal issues. The common understanding therefore is that because the shaman is generous with their abilities they are therefore 'good' and the sorcerer, being seen as miserly, is 'bad'. It is also assumed that both types of magician remain static within their roles.
In reality however, there is no 'good' or 'bad' magick, only Magick itself. It is how its effects are perceived by the society around the magician that determines which label is applied. And a true magician is neither the shaman nor the sorcerer, moving instead between the two poles as the situation demands. In my own case, I have used my Art to help, and to harm, for the good of a community and for my own purposes interchangeably. Being called one or the other is something I leave largely up to the person addressing me, although to be fair, my solitary nature makes the term 'sorcerer' the most accurate of the two.

4   While Castaneda referred to the ability to perceive psychic phenomena as "Seeing", the term 'the Sight' having originated with the Scots, is more prevalent in western culture. For that reason, I prefer to refer to it with what is in essence, a more understandable label.
5   This is not only a good location for the hands, but also a helpful indicator of stress levels. When we are too caught up in our internal chatter, there is a tendency for the thumbs to push forcefully against each other and noticing this action can help to remind us to disengage any inner dialogue we might have inadvertently become involved in.
6   The reader might think me something of an ascetic with my constant references to materialism. I am far from this, and enjoy material things like anyone else. But with one exception—to me posessions are only 'things' and not the be-all and end-all of my existence. This is the dividing line between the practitioner of the Art and most men. The practitioner of the Art knows that ultimately, that all we truly possess is our consciousness and our spirits. The rest is only on loan to us in this life.
7   This group of exercises should be familiar at once to students of the martial arts, and is used for much the same purpose: to refine, sharpen and re-awaken the senses.
8   Candlelight is certainly one option. However, the candle should be placed in such a location as to not interfere or cause distraction, and be situated in an area that is relatively free of crosscurrents that might cause it to flicker. Exercises in the Sight are 'light-sensitive' and natural, indirect light, preferably as dim as possible is recommended for them.
9   For those who experience difficulty with this, it should be pointed out that human beings normally hold their eyes open for long periods without discomfort and that some of what the student might be experiencing is more psychosomatic than any actual dryness of the eyes. With that in mind, an effort towards maintaining a calm inner state and ignoring discomfort will go a long ways towards getting around this problem area.
10 This prohibition comes to us from the Tibetans, whose own experiments in this area revealed some of the hazards that could exist with the use of this powerful tool.
11 With one notable exception: my brother. Instead of disinterest, he was actively hostile towards me when I told him the story. For years, I could not account for this. Finally when we talked about the event, he confessed that the reason behind his anger had been that he and some friends of his had encountered the same creatures, just a few weeks earlier. According to him, they had been riding their motorcycles, and having cut the engines to save gas, had been coasting down the same general stretch of roadway. He told me that the creatures had appeared the same way as they had to us, and that they had tried to grab him and his companion. He and his friend had escaped by engaging their engines and driving off. The very last thing he had ever expected was to hear about something he had desperately wanted to forget, and coming from his own brother.
12 Skeptics of course, were not long in making their appearance. My second trip into the field occurred on Mt. Diablo, which is located roughly east of San Francisco. One of the groups members, a fellow named Chris, spent most of the

night discounting the experiences everyone else was having. He did his level best to find a 'rational' cause for everything. But this dreary person eventually received his come-uppance. As the group was walking up the road to the summit, a nebulous cloud of energy came flying up the road and hit him squarely in the shoulders, sending him flying head over heels. He landed on the ground and looked up just in time to see the cloud and watched incredulously as it promptly disappeared into thin air. Although he tried to ascribe the cause of his fall to a loose backpack strap, everyone had seen cloud and even he knew better. This was Chris' last trip: he never returned to class.

13   The Fire can be roughly divided into two components: the Inner and Outer aspects, with the Inner Fire being that energy that animates the body's core, and the Outer being that which extends away from the body proper into space in layers of lowering density.

14   Some students may, in the course of their earlier exercises, have already have seen it and they are encouraged to continue doing so and to perform the following nonetheless as a way of strengthening their Sight.

15   Some theorists have argued that this dense layer might be the layer of air that is known to surround the body. Others have contended that it might be water vapor, evaporating off the body. However, this same layer is quite thin and would not account for the larger field one sees in this exercise, nor as one person pointed out, does a shadow have any water to evaporate.

16   Students may note a heavy sensation in their solar plexus, or experience some gastric upset. This is common to this exercise, and they should not be alarmed. This sensation is the result of the body's energy gathering together in this place, and will pass shortly after the exercise is concluded.

17   For those who are still experiencing difficulty with their Sight, a special maneuver with the Fire can be employed at this stage that may help. It is begun by projecting the Fire out of the hand, and then while this is being done, facing the fingers towards the third eye area and making a downward motion, cutting the energy of the aura in this region. Several repetitions of the motion should be performed. The result is often a dramatic increase in psychic perception as the student's energetic blocks are quite literally cut away.

18   If two persons are involved, it is not uncommon for one person's third eye to become spontaneously stimulated while the other person performs the exercise on themselves. It can also sometimes occur when one member merely thinks of performing it on their partner, or simply starts to approach this center.

19   For this exercise it is preferable that it be performed with as much of the body exposed to the sunlight as possible. For those who enjoy the proper setting, and are not bothered by the concept of nudity, this same state is recommended.

20   This is due to the fact that all material things in our world are ultimately composed of energy in varying states of density and agitation. Conventional science actually helps make the case for this on the atomic and sub-atomic level by showing us that 'solid' items are in fact collections of particular atoms in a constant state of motion, which are themselves composed of smaller and smaller particles, which ultimately appear to be composed of pure energy. As atomic energy shows us, this can be released, transforming formerly solid nuclear fuel into pure energy expressed in the form of heat and light.

21 Some find that rubbing the objects' surface with the fingers helps with the act of reading it. Certainly I have found that this is an almost instinctive action when I read objects.
22 This gesture has only one real purpose and this is to expose the maximum amount of body surface to the solar or lunar energies so as to derive the greatest benefit from these sources.
23 Dr. Gini Graham Scott, in her book *"Secrets of the Shaman"* (itself part of a series of books she wrote about studying with me) gives an excellent account of one such trip she took with me and I recommend it to the reader for the details it will add to this exercise. The reader will note that the main character is named "Michael Fairwell", a fictional one that I requested she use at the time due to my aspirations to become a paramedic.
24 I remember hearing the tale of fellow martial artist who knew a couple that ran a store that specialized in old weapons, including many Japanese swords from the feudal era. He told me that the owner was often sick, and that his wife (who was Japanese herself) was urging him to give up the business. According to her, the negative 'spirits' or energies contained within blades, which had seen centuries of bloodshed, were the source of her husband's maladies.
25 This action has gotten the nickname of 'radar' by some for the similarity of the seekers movement to the sweep of a radar dish.
26 Use caution with plants, as too much energy can prove harmful or even lethal to them.
27 This exercise can heighten this basic ability to discern the unique energy of an individual and their true mood. Those who have developed Seeking to a fine degree have often reported that the ability to Seek and Read is similar in sensation to the physical sense of smell and taste. For this reason experienced practitioners often refer to a person's specific energy as their 'scent' or 'taste'.
28 I knew one young woman who engaged in this and claimed to derive energy from the blood she drank (gathered form willing donors--or so I was told).
29 I discovered that I was a 'natural' energy vampire myself. This trait came to light when I first started teaching and noticed that my students would fall asleep during my class. At first, I thought I was simply boring them, but after speaking with a wide cross-section of my audience, I learned that while they were certainly interested in what I had to say, that they became physically drained to the point of total exhaustion. Once I realized that this was occurring and why, it was only a matter of stopping the process by the application of conscious Will, and the result was that this phenomena ceased altogether.
30 Which brings up the wider issue of the 'morality' of Magick. Viewpoints have differed widely depending on the society that addressed the issue. Some cultures in the past, such as pagan Rome, even attempted to impose legislation forbidding certain acts, or even the Art as a whole, but with little lasting success in the context of history. Like many other human activities, magick, by its very nature, cannot be effectively regulated by a society. The only real limitations that can be imposed are those set upon it by the individual, based on their personal moral codes and religious beliefs.

31 In this situation, a true illness such as the flu represents an excellent source of "ammunition" to send out, however other sources also exist in its absence such as simple fatigue, headaches and other discomforts.
32 There are of course, other methods one can employ in cases of energy vampirism, but I will reserve these for another work, and my private students. For the reader, I suggest that in addition to studying this book, that separate research be conducted on the general subject of magickal self defense.
33 As a defensive tactic, the initial process is the same, except that instead of letting the energy dissipate, it is consciously sent outwards directly at the attacker.

34 For those readers who might point out that wolves are not native to Yosemite, I am fully aware of this fact. Nevertheless, it changes nothing of what I saw. Wolves are certainly not part of that regions fauna, but then, neither are shape shifters.
35 One of the most interesting things I found was that our experience had strong parallels with some of the oldest tales of the shape-shifter, mainly from Eastern Europe and Russia. There, the werewolf was not portrayed as the fearsome killer that Hollywood presents, but is seen more in the context of a competitor or at least a 'co-habitator' of the forest with man.
Many of these stories have similar themes. Usually such tales tell of a young woman who is described as a 'foreigner', who meets a shepherd who subsequently marries her. And after a time, the shepherd's livestock begins to fall victim to what he believes is a wolf. In these cases, the shepherd hunts the animal, and wounding it, follows its blood trail back to his own cabin. There, he finds his wife, dying of the same wound that he inflicted on the wolf and she is revealed to him as a werewolf.
Taking these old stories into account, and the relatively benign treatment my companions and I received on this and other occasions, it would seem that these creatures are not the fearsome monsters they are thought to be, any more than normal wolves are. It would seem instead that they are one of the many races that mankind shared the planet with in his very early days (like the Fey of Ireland) and are a race that has not vanished with our disbelief, merely adapted to modern times.
Another noteworthy finding in my researches was the complete absence of any mention by the Native Americans of such creatures during the period they inhabited the Valley. On the basis of this, it would appear that this phenomenon is fairly new to the region, highlighting the fact that not all supernatural events are necessarily ancient in origin.
As for other modern reports of the shape shifters, none I encountered was as colorful as ours. However I did manage to gather the accounts of several campers who reported having had encounters either with luminous wolves, or strange people that they met while hiking in the forest.
36 Looking back now, I wonder if the girl was the same one I had met on our first trip in. Certainly her age was the same as the first one.
37 This last tale showcases a different kind of shape shifter; one that is purely human but has mastered the Art of changing their form. Marika Kriss in her book *"Werewolves, Shapeshifters and Skinwalkers"* gives some excellent detail

on the subject of human transformation and the various means by which this is accomplished.
38 In the East, this concept is quite familiar. Items such as swords are believed to have a 'spirit' within them, which is simply another way of saying that such an item has a stored field of energy that has been added to and modified by its users. Many old swords have had multiple owners, and the spirit of those owners, and of their families, are imbued into the very steel. As such, a family sword is more than an icon of a family, but is in a sense, the spirit of the family itself.
39 It is generally considered to be extremely bad form to touch a magickal tool owned by someone else in the same manner that it would be to touch or handle anything else considered intimate. Novices beware! **Always** ask before handling anything magickal!
40 Not all Witches clean a newly acquired Tool, especially one with a history behind it. Just as swords in the Orient are allowed to accumulate then energies of multiple users, some practitioners feel that the energies left over from prior owners are complimentary to a Tool. They opt to retain and add to such energy instead of trying to remove it. The determinant whether to clean or not to clean is the nature of the prior owner and the circumstances surrounding the object. While the reader might agree with this philosophy, they are urged to at least study the proper method of cleaning an object, if only to add to their store of knowledge of the Art.
41 Many cultures around the world believe that the magickal Name is not only the seat of a Magician's power, but were it known by others, the key to potentially controlling the Magician against their will. For this reason, most Magicians keep their Name a secret. Students are cautioned to observe this custom. Novices beware!
42 Many researchers (the writer included) agree that Hecate had Her origins in Caria in Southwest Asia Minor (now Turkey). The Carian people were familiar with Greek characters (although they spoke Greek with what was known of as a Carian accent). But these people also wrote and spoke Phoenician. Each village in the Carian region had its own local variants of Phoenician script (in much the same way that regions in Germany and Scandinavia once had their own individual rune-rows).
43 Many cultures regard blood as a magickally powerful substance. Not only does it nourish our body's cells, but in the esoteric view, it is infused with the very essence of our Inner Fire. Certainly in Northern magick circles, this is the case, and no proper rune-spell is done without the caster putting some of their own blood into the runes they carve. In this way, the energy of the runes and that of the caster are made one and the item carved is considered spiritually linked with the carver.
44 According to many occultists and many cultures around the world, sound is the ultimate expression of Universal energy.
45 For best results the dagger should be approached from no less than 2-3 inches away from the physical blade, and from no more than several feet. The same holds true for the bare palm.
46 If this persists, or becomes unpleasant, the simple act of breathing energy through the effected area will generally remedy the situation.

47 Which should make reason for needing a sheath rather obvious.
48 Once the two-week mark has passed, not only does the Fire within not increase, but in some cases, it actually decreases. In addition, students who exceed this time period often note sleep disturbances that can include insomnia and nightmares.
49 One effect that some students may note is that when they complete the drawing of the pentagram, that there is a momentary increase of energy, which can manifest as the sigil temporarily increasing in brightness or presence. This 'snap' comes when the design, having been completed, becomes energetically active.
50 This is similar to the Pythagorean idea that everything in our world is only an imperfect expression of its perfect cosmic counterpart, but is by extension, an aspect of that perfect thing. As an aside, the Pythagorean school used the pentagram itself to express the concept of *Pentemychos*, which expressed among other things the five elements and as an expression of order being imposed on chaos in order for our universe to come into being.
51 One of perhaps the best examples of proof when it comes to visualization occurred with the Tibetan Buddhist mystics. When asked to describe the shape of the universe, they meditated. When they finished, they described what they had seen in the form of images. These images, still popular in Asian art today were swirling, multi-armed graphic forms, which at the time they were created, made little sense. Later, with the advent of high-powered telescopes, some observers realized that these designs appeared to be stylized representations of spiral galaxies. Of course, hardened scientists dispute such a notion as ridiculous, but the similarity of the Asian designs to those astronomical bodies is unmistakable. In my opinion as a Magick user, it is not simply a matter of mere coincidence, but the product of advanced practitioners using their skill accurately.
52 Initially, an alarm clock can be used to facilitate this. However, the student will find that after a very short period of time that they will wake up at the same time without such an aid. This is one of the signs that the effort to train oneself in Dreaming is taking its effect on the subconscious mind.
53 This method, while effective, can take some practice to perfect. It is quite easy to disturb the process of falling asleep if the statement is made with too much emotion or intensity.
54 The process of 'reading' in an astral library can be a bit of a trick. For some students, the process of maintaining the imagery can be distracting from the secondary act of taking in knowledge. The only real solution is for the student who is experiencing this problem to relax and to let the information come as it will. Thankfully, I did not have this difficulty when I was training in this area. However, I was surprised to find that instead of interpreting words on pages that were in turn translated into mental concepts, that the concepts came directly into my consciousness in the form of complex feelings and images. This process did take some getting used to.
55 These are by no means the only uses or purpose for an Astral Temple. The possibilities go far beyond this, but in the interests of training, I have kept things on a relatively elementary level.
56 I heartily recommend his book, "Exploring Your Past Lives" for those interested in this subject as being one of the finest available on the subject.

57　This exercise will not only make the process of Faring Forth much easier for those who are struggling with this particular Art, but also provides additional practice in working with and moving the Inner Fire. This same practice with the Inner Fire also offers another benefit to the student by stimulating the healthful movement of energy throughout the body, thus removing blockages which as any practitioner of traditional oriental medicine knows, can lead to disease and stagnation if left untouched.

58　I use this term for literary purposes only. Pets, and especially cats and dogs, tend to see themselves as part of the family and not as a piece of living furniture. And most 'owners' see the relationship the same way.

59　As with the Astral Temple, the possibilities go well beyond this stage. Tales of witches projecting their power through their familiar—in effect having their animal partner act as a platform for Willed energy is one such example. But as for the exact manner this is accomplished, I will keep silent out of deference to the safety of the familiar and leave it to the clever student to put the pieces together for themselves.

60　Unlike many who claim to have been Cleopatra, or some other historical figure of importance, I was never anyone particularly famous. Nor was ever I terribly enlightened. In fact, many of the lives I lived were the direct opposite of this, and as is the case in history, many of these lives were short and brutal compared to the relative ease we enjoy in these times.

61　This area is often the most difficult part for someone who is new to exploring past lives, mainly because doubt tends to enter the situation. Try not to let it interfere with any answers you receive.

62　The number 40 has particular occult significance. For example, in the Bible, it is the number of 'probation and trial'; Moses was on the mountain for 40 days, there were 40 days between Jesus' death and ascension to Heaven etc. It would seem that unlike any other anniversary, that the 40th was a time when the veil between the past and the present, was at it's thinnest.

63　I am by no means the only person with a report like this. There are many accounts of travelers encountering places that seem initially like our world, but soon reveal themselves to be somewhere--or more correctly, *somewhen* else. Whitley Streiber in his series dealing with extraterrestrials, details a similar event.

64　Which offers an opportunity to reexamine the Sight for a moment. One theory about the Sight is that we are not simply seeing otherwise invisible aspects of the world around us, but are instead seeing alternate neighboring realities overlaid on our own. Being realities, they are sharable, and therefore visible to multiple parties. Another even more intriguing idea is that the Sight, as an act, does not so much reveal things around us, but literally opens up a doorway to them. In this model, the Sight is not a perceptive ability, but is instead a manner of changing the fabric of reality itself.

65　However, successive futures can be introduced which contain a degree of potential for something utterly different. Like water flowing in between a boulder and eventually wearing through it, these futures can eventually turn the outcome into what would otherwise be a completely unlikely result were it introduced in one large component. This is the concept of using incremental futures to turn the course of reality.

66   The first vision had of a future life (or of any life for that matter) generally represents the actual 'entry point' into that life from former ones. It is a moment when the basic soul of that life unites for the first time with the greater super-soul and is a time when that soul can be considered truly 'complete'. Such a moment generally does not occur at birth, but rather at some time after this (usually in early childhood). The specific event can be recognized as an instance where one is, for the first time, not only fully aware of self, but also of a greater purpose for that particular life. I believe that it is from this initial entry point that the life in question truly begins in the spiritual sense.

67   One theory I have is that moments of *déjà vu* are in fact moments we have experienced before—having created them in former lives as triggers to potentially remember these previous lives and their wisdom. I know that this has certainly been the case in my own life, and I venture that the same may hold true for many other people as well.

68   As one person who was versed in both Native American shamanism and the Art put it, the totem animal is present to provide a specific lesson, whereas the familiar acts as a partner in general Magickal Works.

69   Some experts in the paranormal hold that 'imaginary playmates' are the ghosts of other children who are attracted to a relationship with a living child in much the same manner as any child would to another—seeking companionship in play. However, while there are certainly many cases of this, there are equally as many that occur between a child and a being that is not a ghost, but is instead a disembodied entity.

70   In the case where a true ghost is involved, the relationship can provide the same benefits, and potentially allow them to work to resolve whatever issues might have hindered their moving onwards to the next state of being.

71   Their parting was later reconciled and they reunited.

72   My wife was contacted by nothing less than the classic fairies of ancient lore. Up to the point that I encountered one of them, I had questioned reports about these beings and had believed that their appearance, that of a small winged humanoid, was purely allegorical. However, one day while I was attending a training seminar at my job, I observed a small golden ball of energy approach me. As it flew by, I clearly saw a small winged human-like figure in the midst of the energy field. I learned later that my wife had sent the little being to visit me, and later still, I had the opportunity to see it, and its companions again. They were precisely as described in folk tales, and just as the tales related, traveled in a distinct troupe of roughly 4 individuals. Seeing them was not only a confirmation of yet another aspect of the Hidden World, but without a doubt one of the more beautiful things I have had the privilege of witnessing. The visitation of these beings has made me even less closed-minded than I was before.

73   In my case, I employ a simple framed image of the spirits' sigil, derived from my Oracle Wheel. This image sits on my working magickal altar. Being a sigil, it is only recognizable to me and all references to my helper's name are concealed from casual translation by an obscure magickal alphabet. Other examples of spirit-houses are items such as mirrors, statues, and so on.

74   One interesting variant on the spirit house here in the West occurs when children have a 'spirit-playmate' and report to unbelieving adults that their invisible friend has taken up residence inside a dollhouse or other toy.

75 I find this improbable, given the intense bond between a witch and their familiar.
76 It also proved quite capable of assisting me during exorcisms, literally corralling a negative being and assisting me in controlling it.
78 In particular, the being eventually displayed a talent not only as a messenger and a scout, but also showed an ability to aid me by removing obstacles in life-situations. All of these abilities were ascertained through a process of simply asking the being to act, and then observing if it was able to affect a result.
79 From the 18th Century writings of Bishop Hutchinson concerning Witchcraft.
80 While it is generally assumed that the giving of blood to a familiar is pure fantasy concocted by the Witch Hunters, it must be pointed out that there is a factual parallel with Norse Magick which does make use of blood in the creation of runic charms. Because European Lore has roots in such beliefs, I believe that this practice was fact, and not fiction.
81 While I was eating lunch with some co-workers, I noticed a bright blue-white mote of light circling the table. I knew that this was one of the fairies that visits my wife and I. Naturally, I said nothing to anyone about this, and noted with some amusement when the same being flew in front of the chest of one of my neighbors (who was eating a rather tasty salad, which the fey are known to be partial to). She didn't see the being of course, but as it flew by it must have ticked her, because she waved her hand in the air as it passed, no doubt thinking it had been an insect. I went away wondering if given the right training, if the woman didn't have a natural talent she didn't know about to perceive the Fey.
82 Some have supposed that the Celtic settlers brought the Fey with them from the Old World, but this was not the case—these beings were in residence long before they came to the region, albeit known by other names.
83 For those who are unfamiliar with this tradition, the granny witches are part of the Appalachian culture, which itself has roots in the Celtic beliefs of many of the early settlers of the region. In addition to Christianity, many families also have a long legacy of what could be termed either 'folk magic' or shamanism that has its roots both in Old Europe and the beliefs of the Native Americans. It is not a well-known tradition, and it is only recently that the practitioners of this system have begun to make themselves known to the rest of the world.
84 My first experiences with Fey folk, or 'fairies' came through my studies in the Northern Tradition. There, such beings are known of as Alfs, or elves. There are two kinds: Light and Dark Elves. Lichtalfs as the Light Elves are called, were something I had seen on many occasions in wooded areas over the years, manifesting as small points of light that flew through the air.
In Germany and Scandinavia, the custom was always to leave out offerings to these beings, usually in the form of milk, sweetened with honey. When I became acquainted with this, my wife and I made it a habit do this ourselves. In the Appalachian tradition, their equivalent, the Little Cousins, are given a similar gift, along with tobacco, and sometimes whisky. Anyone who has doubt about the reality of these beings need only leave out a similar gift and watch. If they aren't rewarded by their overt appearance flitting over the bowl, they will certainly notice the effect their presence has on household pets (which can sometimes be quite comical).

Our cat Sammy found this out for himself. On one occasion, we were watching television and glanced up to see him leaping up at a particularly brilliant point of light. Realizing that it was an Alf, my wife and I shouted at him to stop, but he was intent on catching it. But just as his paws would have connected, it vanished, and he came up with a handful of nothing for all his trouble. Undoubtedly, this was considered a great trick to play on the cat by the Alf.

85   Generally performed by the light of a full moon.

86   In some cases, the action of the mists is all that will be perceived. This is similar to what can occur in a crystal ball, and some practitioners rely solely on the direction the mists travel as their indicator of answers. For example, mists rising upwards are taken by some practitioners to indicate 'yes', while those moving downwards a 'no'.

87   Despite the hazardous nature of this experiment, I was nonetheless proud of the accomplishment. When I had the opportunity, I related the tale to a friend of mine who was a Native American involved with Apache shamanism. She listened to my account and then laughed, saying "Oh THAT! We've been doing that for years!" Although I was a little discomfited, her response confirmed what I had already suspected—that Gateways were an ancient technology shared by many cultures and peoples.

88   It is interesting to note that doors ways and gates, being liminal spaces have always had certain hazards associated with them. Many folk traditions believe that spirits inhabit thresholds and that some of them are hostile. Anna Franklin explains that the custom of carrying the bride over the threshold was originally done out of concern for the bride's well being. It is possible that these beliefs had their origins with the shamans of Pre-Christian pagan Europe who made their own journeys through the Middle World and discovered the same conditions I did.

89   Recent studies by the US Army show that blue light, rather than red is quite effective in night operations, particularly for the illumination of vehicle interiors. Blue light is also a favorite among some pilots and it has been found that this band of light also helps with maintaining alertness.

90   For those not familiar with this design, it is derived from tried and true symbolism employed since the Middle Ages by Witches for calling spirits. While there are many rather elaborate versions one can find in medieval grimoires, its most basic form is a simple energetic circle with a triangle inside of it, large enough for the average person to stand inside.

91   I know of at least one occasion where a careless approach to evocation resulted in disaster. A former student and his companions, after having severed their ties with me, attempted to evoke an Earth Elemental. While I can only speculate on what he did wrong (having as he had, evoked Elementals on prior occasions without incident while under my tutelage), I learned that while the spirits did appear, that they reportedly attacked him and sent the entire party running. To the best of my knowledge, he never attempted this operation again.

92   The location of the Triangle will change with subsequent Workings with the Elementals. It will be in the South for Fire, West for Water and East for Air as these directions correspond with the basic vibrations of these forces.

93 Unlike the Triangle of Manifestation, which will change according to the forces being evoked within it, the orientation of the Pentagram will remain towards the north from here on out.
94 Another theory is that the lifespan of a ghost may be bounded by cosmic law; that old souls must transform to a higher level of existence to make way for newer younger souls to come into existence.
95 The idea that the Egyptians believed in reincarnation, or more accurately transmigration, might surprise some readers. Although we are generally presented with the notion that the Egyptians held to the idea of death as a 'one-way' journey, this is not the case and is in fact the product of modern scholars imposing their own beliefs atop historical proof to the contrary. For example, Herodotus in is work "Histories" tells us: "They were also the first to broach the opinion, that the soul of man is immortal, and that, when the body dies, it enters into the form of an animal which is born at the moment, thence passing on from one animal into another, until it has circled through the forms of all the creatures which tenant the earth, the water, and the air, after which it enters again into a human frame, and is born anew. The whole period of the transmigration is (they say) three thousand years."
96 Mystical Judaism does however offer us an alternate explanation of the process that a soul undergoes to produce a shade that is a little simpler than the Egyptian model (albeit in my opinion, less accurate). It is believed by some Jewish sects that spirits leave this life and go to sit with God, and that after doing so for a while, return to the world and new lives. But not before an angel wipes their memories clear of what they saw and witnessed at the throne of God. The Greeks also had similar view of the same process, contending that spirits descended in the Underworld after death, and that after a certain time period, drank from the Spring of Forgetfulness before returning to the world above and another life.
97 In this same light, the ancient process of preserving the body through mummification makes perfect sense. If the body is viewed as having its own spiritual essence, then proper funerary care can be understood as being a mandatory step in maintaining the greater soul.
98 In fact the term 'shade' in this context is rather apt.
99 However, it should also be stated that some 'psychic echoes' might also be examples of 'time-slips' where the observer is actually witnessing a moment from the past.
100 A time-slip is the loose technical term for an anomalous temporal event where events such as the past and present and/or future cross paths temporarily, or where time either speeds up or pauses for the observer. One such event that occurred for me in my teens occurred when I was riding bicycle across a bridge. Without any warning, everything around me stopped—the water under the bridge, cars going by and even a jet plane in the sky. After what was for me a full 30 seconds, things resumed their normal motion. For an additional example, please read Chapter V: Past, Present and Future Lives for the tale of myself and a student when we visited Death Valley.
101 According to some experts, shadow beings are a fairly recent phenomenon, appearing in North America in the 18th century. They are not a feature of European ghost lore, and may be purely regional.

102   Which is precisely why I teach students to make a habit of completely banishing any energy forms they create. Such energy, given the right circumstances, can congeal into a thought form.
103   Hooded black figures like this one are in fact rather common manifestations. It bears mention that some paranormal researchers classify them as shadow beings and consider them to be sentient. However, while they might have some consciousness, I contend that it is rudimentary, and is, like their form, a manifestation of what they were Willed to be.
104   Although incense and salt water are certainly effective by themselves, the additional step of charging them by running the Inner Fire through each item is strongly recommended. This not only helps to increase the vibratory potency of these items, but also imbues them with the magickal Will of their user.
105   The use of sound in exorcisms is an ancient one. Many cultures have employed gongs or bells in the well-founded belief that their noise drives away negativity. Certainly the vibration created by such objects has an effect on any resident energies. For such Work, I prefer to use a bronze gong, not only for its sound quality, but also for the special energetic qualities of the metal itself, which has been revered since the time of the Egyptians as particularly well suited for cleansing a space.
106   This method is further compromised when the residents of the home are naturally receptive to occult phenomena and either possess no religious faith, or are to consumed by their fear of the being, resulting in a 'doorway' of sorts being created for it to return through.
107   I must also remind the reader that when I went through the Gateway and saw the Obsidian Plane, I also saw a bright light on the horizon. Given that this place is populated by unspeakable beings, what better guard could be set than something that would utterly consume them if they tried to escape? At the very least, its presence could be considered a grim jest by whatever forces imprisoned them in the Middle World.
108   The reader will note the distinctly martial quality of the Calls to the Quarters, and the same tone throughout the ritual. This ritual is designed for a battle—for this is exactly what formal exorcism is. The practitioner who has agreed to perform one should keep this in mind, and take all the necessary steps one would take in such a situation. Anything less than this serious frame of mind, and the operator lays themselves open to potential counter-assaults by their spectral opponent.
      Another feature worth pointing out is the directions for each element, which are different than what the reader might be used to. Unlike modern Circles, this one assigns the elements to their corresponding directions as based on ancient Greek attributions.
109   Lit.: So be it.
110   For those interested in the detailed reasons behind these associations, I strongly recommend reading both works.
111   Lit.:"Spirit". Not to be confused with the Christian term "demon".